HOW TO TURN YOUR DREAMS INTO REALITY

The Divine Self's Manifestation into the Physical World

A personal-development book by Carmina Harr

Translated from Romanian
by Gabriela Botezatu and Robert Wileman

Cover illustration created by Alina Militaru

http://alegsadesenez.com

Carmina Harr

authorHOUSE®

AuthorHouse™
1663 Liberty Drive
Bloomington, IN 47403
www.authorhouse.com
Phone: 1 (800) 839-8640

Published by AuthorHouse   01/06/2017

ISBN: 978-1-5246-5862-5 (sc)
ISBN: 978-1-5246-5861-8 (e)

Library of Congress Control Number: 2017900173

Print information available on the last page.

CONTENTS

FOREWORD

Everything goes well for me, I am very grateful for everything I have, for everything I receive and will receive. Life, thank you for the chance of being here and knowing my true self! Thank you for being so wonderful, you make me happy, you pour joy into my soul, you fill me with health and an abundance of beautiful experiences, wonderful people and superb nature! Dear Lord, I thank you for all the laws of the beautiful Universe that you have created. Thank You for a new day blessed with love, happiness, abundance, joy, peace, and fulfillment. Thank You for everything coming my way for which I am very grateful. Life, I love you! I live a great life! I am filled with blessings every day, with powerful emotions and fantastic events. My life is a Miracle and every day I live is filled with miracles.

I thank all the publishing companies that helped me fulfill part of my great dream. Without these wonderful people, this book had never come to life. It would be just a simple collection of emotions unshared with the ones that are travelling the path of finding themselves.

"Touch the untouchable star and never forget the ones who believed in you!"

I thank you and I am grateful to every person that created obstacles in my life. When life closes a door, it usually opens a gate so take notice. I thank myself for allowing me to go deep along the lowest valleys and then high up onto the highest and lightest paths. I went so deep inside myself that the light shocked me. I was a superb mermaid swimming in the depths of the ocean, going higher and higher until I reached the very surface of the ocean. Until then I didn't know there is a sun. I found the true light, not the one I knew before.

I am grateful for my divine gift that I received as a consequence of becoming aware that my life is perfect in its imperfection. I am grateful for everything I experimented up until now.

To be honest in a world where the accent is put more on what you are not, shows courage. Authenticity is a virtue.

In this book, I will answer the questions: How do I become a happy person?! Which are the steps to take and the price to pay in advance and how grateful am I to the ones who pushed me willingly or unwillingly to go up?

I thank from the bottom of my heart to those who trusted me and believed in the message in my first book. The experience of awakening is unique for each of you and it is a priceless thing that belongs only to you. Go through this experience as you like and as your soul tells you to. Real "life" begins where the comfort zone ends!

In my first book, I answered the question: "Who are you?" Healing yourself, feeling complete again, you can be what you dream to be. In this book, I wanted to exemplify the manifestations of the Real Self, what it means to live in the same house with God, how He communicates with you and how He guides you towards your Supreme Wellbeing. All the joy, peace, fulfillment and everything that means welfare come from your Real Self.

Therefore, let's begin with the first chapter of this book.

CHAPTER 1

Prosperity AND Success

"To always have success when you set it as your goal is to succeed in life, to be truly happy." Continuous experimentation of these benefactions is in fact the eternal life which Jesus was talking about when he was stating that the most important things are peace, harmony, safety, individual freedom and happiness and these are untouchable because no one can take them away from you. They come from within your own essence. When you meditate on these qualities you will immediately resonate with your divine source filling your subconscious with their powerful ideas. "But lay up for yourselves treasures in heaven, where neither moth nor rust doth corrupt, and where thieves do not break through nor steal" (Matthew 6:20).

What do you think these magic words mean? To be so intelligent that you will live a mediocre meaningless life? So I thought for a long time, but then I realized that I understood this concept totally wrong. I reeducated myself and I tried to learn from others smarter than me. I am not afraid to begin a new life, with a new way of thinking. How do I manage to think differently than the ones around me? I search for solutions. They are everywhere. You just have to pay attention to them. Pay attention to the people that succeeded in life. You don't have to copy them to be like them, just observe them. You have to do everything your way. If your style of approaching life is good or bad you will find out yourself. If your life didn't have a meaning until now, it means that it is time to admit that you have to change the values you believe in order to coordinate your life differently.

Success comes in all shapes and colors. You can be successful in your career, in your marriage, at sports or with your hobby. No matter what form of success you set as your goal, there is one thing successful people have in common: the desire and the craving for success, which forces them to never give up.

It is necessary to begin to learn to have a better relationship with money, treating them as guests, and to be disciplined. Every word has its own energy and it is very important how you speak.

Success also depends on the ability of managing your emotions efficiently, and not only on the intellectual ability of the brain. By learning to decipher the messages you receive from your heart you gain the perception you need in order to manage your emotions in an efficient way in the middle of all changes that occur in your life. The more you listen the intelligence of your heart and follow it, the more educated, balanced and coherent your emotions will become. Think with your heart.

Financial intelligence has nothing to do with native intelligence or with the one shown during school years. Believe me; I have spent many years of my life going to school in order to learn what having a rich life means. It wasn't a mistake the fact that I chose an economy college and then I continued my studies in the same field. The goal was to learn what to do with my life. At 30 I realized that the hundreds of professional books I studied didn't help me at all to have a better life. Quite the opposite, I believe they narrowed me and made me think I will never manage to get out of my condition. I wondered why everything I had learnt from books doesn't work. The answer is very simple: theory and practice are different from each other. The reality is something, what's written in books is something different. I was very disappointed when I noticed that after I gathered so many diplomas I can't use them at all. The most I can do with them is to get a job in a company and to waste valuable time there for a limited life. This isn't the life I want. The fact that I held a high position and I had a decent living didn't make me happy. I wanted something else. I wanted to travel around the world, to see places and to meet new people, and to borrow a healthy and positive life style.

I feel so rich on the inside that I cannot express the joy I feel. If I were to stay in my comfort zone with my family, the only thing I would know would be my work place with its four walls, a desk and a chair, a computer and a lot of papers. Sunday was my only free day and I was resting. Probably it was the only day of the week when I could clean the house, go shopping, cook and sleep. How the hell could you be happy with such limited life? Even if I was married, I had a job, couple of kids and many responsibilities, I was miserable. I was so busy working for others that I forgot completely about what my heart really wanted. That's why; the majority of people live for others, not for themselves. They don't even know what it means to live for your soul, and to enjoy life. For sure, they can say they are happy because they have a life partner, children and a job. But, one day, they will realize that this is an artificial happiness. It's a happiness based on sacrifices and maximum efforts in order to survive.

I am a rebel and I chose freedom. I didn't run from responsibilities. Not at all. On the contrary, I was responsible when I took the decision to be happy. I didn't know how to do that but I decided to try until I will get the wanted result.

I tried all sorts of alternatives that I thought were the best at the time. I was sure they will make me happy. But in reality I was unhappy. In my mind the question was always the same: what did I do wrong that I am so unhappy? How did I get this result when I didn't set it as my goal? Is everything so bad? I noticed that everything can be only as bad as you believe it to be. It can't be there if you don't create it. And then I wonder: "Why did I create such reality for myself? What was in my mind? And how could I do this to myself?" I knew I was guilty of taking the wrong action if I was getting the same unsatisfactory result. Where did I go wrong?

The answer finally came: I didn't do anything wrong. Each life experience I had was perfect exactly the way it came. It helped me discover myself. Helped by them, I found out who I really was, I was put face to face with what I didn't like about myself, I accepted this and I changed. I changed myself until I was satisfied. As much as I needed to.

My diplomas and my intelligence have demonstrated that I don't live the wonderful life I would like to. This doesn't mean I have made a mistake. I have followed the people of the society I live in, I have copied them and I have tried to be like them. Instead of being authentic and using my intelligence in my favor, I have preferred to walk with the others in the direction they consider to be the right one.

Travelling abroad I was lucky to meet different people. People with lots of money, who built empires and created thousands of jobs. Studying them closely I realized they didn't have so many diplomas, they didn't have money from the moment they were born, they don't eat more than a normal person and they don't wear more clothes than anyone else.

I was charmed by those people, by their simplicity and the way they lived their lives. At the first sight you don't even realize how many hundreds of thousands of Euros they have in their accounts. You think they are just like you and there are no major differences between you and them.

I have met extremely rich people that make thousands of families happy. Money can make you truly happy when you know you can support thousands of people. This is what I believe about money. I love it.

A feature of rich people is simplicity and modesty. They don't work for money, money works for them. They love money and they want it in their life.

But how did they manage to get so rich? Knowing that there is no difference between you, the one who reads these lines and them, and the ones you worship and maybe envy.

They think differently. They work for pleasure. They had a dream they believed in with their entire being. The passion they work with brought them this richness. Rich people don't wake up in the morning thinking to go to work in order to make money. They wake up impatiently and full of joy to get as fast as possible to where their soul really wants to be. They like so much what they are doing that they don't feel tired. They think how to develop their business, to make it grow so they can help tens, hundreds or even thousands of people. And in their mind they have only one goal: how to expand their business and how to make it work. They don't think how to make money so they can spend them on luxury vacations and expensive cars. They know money doesn't exist. Just papers and contacts. Just bank checks that help them transfer unreal money to a different account so they could function normally.

They didn't see in front of their eyes this real money put in a suitcase. And even if they end up having one million Euros in their account, I'm sure they didn't see it all with their eyes, they didn't sleep next to it and worship it. They were somewhere in a bank account in the form of electronic numbers and if somehow they made another major investment in the business, they moved the money into another account. They don't use this money to satisfy their whims, but their goal is to grow the business, to expand it. That makes them truly happy.

Only after years of work and sacrifices rich people get to buy their first taste of luxury and valuable things. Only after they have gathered sufficient assets, to invest into liabilities. Assets generate income; liabilities bring about expenses. When the assets' column exceeds the liabilities' column, this person makes their first major investment by acquiring a luxury car. This is just an example. They didn't buy this car from the money that could generate more income, but from that source which inevitably turns into a liability. For example: you have a business. You work three years to expand it. All the money you earned you put back into your business. At some time, your business will produce profit. This profit is divided into several categories. Some money will be reinvested into the business, another part will go towards paying taxes and some remains as dividends. The higher the value of the dividends, the better your business is valued on the stock exchange. Its shares become more valuable and chances are to attract major investors for your business. From these dividends, the owner buys an apartment or a luxury car. They can not reinvest that money back into their business. The luxury car is a liability that eats money and can be turned into an asset. The house can be both an asset and liability. It depends on how you want to use it. If you want to live in it, it is a liability. It's something that doesn't generate income, only expenses. If you rent this house, it produces income. Obviously, it becomes an asset. In other words, money works for you. Not you for it.

Rich people know the goal is to gather as many assets as possible and as few liabilities as possible. Their thinking is simple and practical.

It's very important to learn about the circulation of money, how it is made and especially how we manage it. Things we don't learn in school or in the society. University system teaches you how to work for others or how to work for money, but unfortunately it doesn't teach you what to do with the money you earn, other than spending it in order to enlarge your comfort zone. By changing your way of thinking, you will automatically change your way of life.

Don't run after money. Money should only be a means, not a goal. Your goal should be knowledge. The more you know, the higher the level you will be at. Every book you read, every lesson you learn will take you a little step above the others.

You change when you react differently to the exterior, not when the reality around you changes in order to enlarge your comfort zone.

My advice: "Turn off the TV!" A person manipulated by television has no chance to discover the genius within themselves. Look inside yourself, this is YOU! There is nothing you cannot be! You are a MICRO cosmos, HERE and NOW! It is up to you if you want to manifest your true POWER or if you want to give it to others. The choice is yours every moment. Choose wisely!

Why waste your time watching TV? If you use this time to develop the gifts you received from God, it won't take long until others will watch you on TV.

The Romanian school system promotes intense competition. I don't argue with this. Certainly it has its good side, but if we were to focus a little more on cooperation, how would it be? I'll tell you: maximum efficiency. I'm not talking about the definition of efficiency which you will find in reference books, but the real efficiency and productivity in your life.

Dear friends, there is a secret, maybe still undiscovered: all great achievements were made based on collaboration. Competitiveness means separation. Slowly, the people in Romania realized that only through "collaboration" you can get to remarkable results. Envy or fear that someone is better than you doesn't have to block you. This is why cooperation that could have led to remarkable results for all parties involved fell apart.

Every time you compete with someone, you will lose. Envy can only take you to this result.

Speaking in a simpler way, people just complain that they don't have enough money. Money is everywhere; you simply don't know how to attract it to you. It runs away from you, it avoids you because you have bad habits or beliefs that limit you greatly in this respect.

Only mismanagement and bad habits steal your money away. It's similar to a shipwreck. It's not important how quickly you remove water, if you don't fix the holes, the water will still get in anyway.

If you start your life with the belief that money is limited and you don't deserve to have more than you have now, it is obvious that the reality is exactly the one you think of at this present moment.

Be the creator of your life. You can't create anything other than what you are and you think. Learn how to think in order to bring abundance into your life, which is closely related to your fulfillment as a human being. Why do I insist so much on this chapter? Because I consider it extremely important. Whether you are male or female, you have to get a constructive financial education that will bring you profit.

From my point of view it is a very big difference between the education received at school about what it means to be a good manager and the education received from those who really created something. School teaches you to be the best manager inside a company; instead you have to learn by yourself how to be the manager of your business. They are two different things, even if apparently they seem identical.

I can give you a very concrete example. I find it very easy to get inspiration from my own life experience. You have an entrepreneur boyfriend or husband. You are very happy and delighted that you are the head of his company. You don't think for one second that this quality doesn't help you as a person to be your own boss. It doesn't mean that if you are a very good manager of a company, you know how to be a very good manager of your own business. You realize that a very important element is missing in this equation. You don't know how to build a business from scratch, but you know how to be the boss! How come? It doesn't make sense! Exactly my point. Making introspection with regards to this situation, I realized that this is the primary mistake that anyone can make. Working for someone else without thinking even for a moment of yourself. Without ever asking yourself, "What am I doing for my life? What will I do if I will stop being his company's manager? How will I manage without him?" If you never asked yourself these questions and never gave yourself a serious answer, it is time to do that now. Not tomorrow, not next month or in a year time. Now!

I will give you the answers to these questions so you don't need to experiment so much to get to the same conclusion. All I do is to shorten the years of your life you might waste without getting concrete results on the quality of your life.

First, you will feel like falling into an abyss. The wings you thought you had will be cut. But you only thought you had them, the reality has always been different; it's just you didn't want to see it.

It will be difficult to live at an inferior level from what you are used to. You will need years to gather your strength to become what you once were. But this time, you will be a different person. An authentic, rational, realistic and responsible one.

What will you do in this situation? You will try to find opportunities to get on the first place. Please, don't do the same mistake! Let's make it clear! Be the first person in your life, not in other people's life.

Do you think you'll succeed without compromise? I think I already hear many disapproving opinions. I guarantee you will be able to be what you want in life only if you don't make any compromise. Try to make some compromises to convince yourself and you will come to the same conclusion.

I know why most avoid this difficult and full of obstacles path and resort to simpler strategies to achieve their goal. Because they don't have total confidence in their forces, they don't have the courage to face the unknown; they didn't find their purpose in life, their true passion that makes them work day and night without feeling tired. This will be present, but it will be a different kind of tiredness. It will be the kind that it will charge you with energy, and it pushes you higher and higher and it is inexhaustible as it comes from within.

So, what can be done? Don't let yourself impressed by others who are very strong. Don't run away from them because you are afraid. I advise you to become friends with them in order to learn the secret that lies behind their success. Only when around you there will be very strong people, inevitably you will become the same.

What's the difference between goals and objectives? In my view, the goal is the internal motivation. The objective is the goal you want to reach. The higher your vision, the better chances your goal has to materialize. My advice: Think big! Don't limit yourself! Create something that is totally yours. Make a plan.

The majority of poor people take their ideas about money and about life from their parents. I want you to know that you have the power and the ability to have all the money you want and if you really want it. And this power doesn't depend in money. This power is not outside of you. This power is in your ideas. It has nothing to do with money. It has to do with the strength of your ideas. Money is not necessary, only the will to change some ideas is indispensable. Besides this idea, you need a business plan. To develop the idea so much, that you know exactly what it is.

Change the ideas you have with regards to money and you can get the power over money without allowing it to get power over you. We are all born smart and rich. It's just in the childhood our parents and the society we live in made us believe that we are less smart than others and they told us how to be poor instead of getting the genius within us to the light.

Most of the people don't understand what money is, what richness is, what it means to have lots of money. Money is energy and when you buy something in the return for your money you exchange energies.

There is confusion in people's mind because they always believed that poverty it's something spiritual. It's an aberration. Poverty is the most unspiritual thing in the world. A poor man cannot be divine. They can try but their faith in divinity will be superficial. The richness from within reflects the richness from outside. I said it hundreds of times. They are always interconnected. It is a great disillusion when you become aware that the poverty is a disease of your mind. Your spirit is abundant. It is joy, love and peace. Abundance has to be searched inside yourself. The sources of wealth are within you.

The relationship with money is the relationship with yourself. Does this seem strange? Maybe at the beginning it will. But if you think about this statement you will have some amazing revelations. I hope I didn't shock you. The abundance in your life, the quality of your life, your life partner and everything that enters in your life is interconnected to the relationship you have with yourself. The better you know yourself, the smoother your life. But if you are a stranger to yourself, don't be surprised that nothing works as you want. Love yourself and you will see how love turns to you. Know yourself and you will see how fulfilled your relationships with the others will be.

Because I like joking, I will make a statement: "A rich person is so preoccupied of life that doesn't have time to think of sickness, poverty, pain." They have time to think of their transformation. Why? Because they are not so preoccupied with how they will feed their children, how to have a shelter, how to pay their bills. They have plenty of time for introspection. They are interested of things that are above body and mind. It is a natural behavior; it is how it should be.

A hungry desperate person can't be interested in meditation, recollection and how they can regain their inner strength. Primary necessities take over his mind.

ANYTHING could be said in favor of poverty is that you can't have a fulfilled and successful life without being rich. No one can reach their maximum potential with regards to their talent or spiritual development without money; a person needs to use many things for spiritual fulfillment or developing a talent and they can't have them without having the money they can buy them with. A person's right to life is their right of using freely all the things they need for their mental, spiritual and physical fulfillment, in other words the right of being rich. The visible are practically inexhaustible; and the invisible resources are truly inexhaustible.

I notice many people complain they don't have any luck, that life is hard and unfair. In fact, life is fair. It gives you exactly what you ask for. If you don't ask for anything and you don't expect to receive anything good, how do you expect to be "lucky"? If you lie to yourself and you live as others dictate, how do you want to have a beautiful and fulfilled life? Why don't you start by being yourself, by listening to your heart and being honest with yourself? And then see if life is unfair?!

Admit that your wrong mentality is the real cause of your precarious financial situation. Be confident! The genius within you can reveal an idea that worth millions at any time. Some people complain they can't handle the bills. They always condemned the ones that succeeded, the ones who managed to rise above them, saying: "I know him, he is a thief, and he's always taking advantage of others." This is why they are still poor: they condemn what they want with intensity, but in a selfish, destructive way. The best way to be as far as possible from prosperity is to be envious and to criticize the one who enjoys it. Because of this, envy is the main cause of poverty in many people's case. Wish for everyone to enjoy prosperity, to have a full and happy life. When you fill someone's success upsets you, begin sending to that person thoughts of happiness and prosperity. Free your mind of all the hatred and envy thoughts and allow the God inside you to manifest and to bring joy and prosperity in your life.

 - Poverty can also be a sort of strength if you want to see it this way. It forces you to push your limits, to get out of your shell and to start thinking. You have another reason to dig deep inside yourself and see what you can do in order to have an extraordinary life. Of course, if you want this, if you want to live differently because I noticed that most people indulge in such circumstances because they consider they might stand out. Compassion and pity are enough to push them to live in the same style.

If you will read some entrepreneurship books, you will notice that very few people were born rich. Even they have the duty to themselves to explore their inner potential, and especially how to manage their wealth. Nothing stays like this, everything needs to be taken care of and administrated efficiently with the help of a bright mind. I call prosperous people "genius" because most of them were poor and they manage to make a masterpiece of their life. You don't have to envy them because they did it and you didn't. Better take them as example and see how they did it. How they managed to create a dream life without any help. The first answer that comes to my mind is: "They discovered their inner strength and they were curious to see what they can do with it." No one was born knowing everything, smart and with hero's qualities. We all have the same potential when we are born.

If you really want something, you must put all your muscles to work. Nowhere in nature can you see a "system" that gives you something that it hasn't produced yet. You can't ask an apple tree for an apple immediately after you planted it telling it that you will work for it in installments, that you will ensure its smooth growth but you want the apple now because you're hungry. Nature doesn't work this way! To eat apples from that tree, you have to take care of it and time has to take care of it. Then you can eat as many apples as your stomach can hold.

Why do some people forget about integrity when it comes to money? I asked myself this question when I saw how many people compromise for money. The first answer is: they are weak, and they have no self-confidence; second answer: poverty (the fear of not going back to where they came from).

You will become what you feel and what you think. Even if someone managed to get rich by cheating, it doesn't mean that they achieved success, for there can be no success without inner peace. What's the use of all the wealth if they can't sleep at night, suffering from guilt or being very ill?

When you choose to play at a higher level, it's normal that your need for adrenaline will overcome your need for comfort. If you haven't yet reached that level, the first step is to admit it. The honesty you show may seem the craziest thing you've heard. It will make you angry or it will give you goose bumps. It can destroy irrevocably your entire universe, or it can make it more beautiful than you have ever dreamed. Do you have the courage to enter the most dangerous caves? Do you have the courage to accept great responsibility? Do you have the courage to confront your limitations imposed by your mind or by society? Do you take the chance of being ridiculed by those around you?

You complain that you are unlucky. Whatever you do, you only get into trouble. You don't have what you need; you aren't where you want to be. The truth is that you are quite comfortable and you accept it. In reality, you are good, even too good. Put your hand on your heart and swear you are doing everything you can to get into the dark cave. Can you do it? Maybe this is the reason most of us won't live the lives we want.

Often, we lose opportunities because we have to pay bills, we have to go to work (eight hours a day is a long time!!) and we forget to appreciate the abundance around us.

Now I talk to the dreamer in action. What are the steps you need to take to fulfill your dreams? First, you need to make an authentic business plan. I will show you a model. I don't write about money because there are fabulous sums. I don't want to scare you, but on the contrary, to encourage you. You have to write the amounts required into your business plan. This means to know exactly what you want from life. I really ask you to make a real business plan, much more complex than this one. I only show you a sketch. It lacks many details that make the difference.

Business Plan

Think as a millionaire.

1. Product/ Service:
    a) What do your prospects need?
    b) How do you fulfill this need?
    c) How much does this cost?
    d) How easy can you solve it?
    e) Are there other people that do the same thing?
    f) Why is your service different?

2. Competition
    a) Do you have competition in your field?
    ....
    b) If yes, who are they?
    ....
    c) What does your competition offer?
    ....
    d) How do they offer the service?
    ....

e) Why do people buy from them?

f) How could you offer this and even more? (what they offer + additional things). Loyalty.

3. Partners

a) Who would you like to work with?

b) Why do you want to work with these people/brands?

c) What do you get from them?

d) What do you offer them in return?

e) What are the conditions to work with someone?

f) How many partners do you need?

4. Sales

a) Who is your perfect client?

b) Who are your real prospects?

c) What do these people usually buy?

d) Why do they need this thing you can cover?

e) Which are the benefits of your service?

f) What differentiate you from your competition?

5. Investments

a) What costs do I have at the beginning?

b) Why do I have these costs?

c) What can I get for free?

d) What type of investment I would like to make in the future?

6. Targets

a) What do I want from this business?

b) What are my goals for the next 3 months?

c) What do I want to achieve in a year?

d) How do I see my business in five years?

e) How much money do I want to earn?

7. Accountancy/Bureaucracy

a) Who keeps my books?

b) Who can check my accountant?

c) Who do I talk to if I have a legal problem?

d) What are my estimated monthly expenses?

e) How much do I have to earn to break even?

8. Branding/Image
a) Who are we?
> b) What do we offer?
> c) Why do we have this activity?
>> Mission:
Values:
d) Why do you need us (benefits)?
e) What do you lose if you don't come to us?

9. Marketing
> a) Where do I promote myself?
> b) Why do I promote myself there?
> c) How do I test the marketing campaigns?
> d) How do I measure my marketing campaigns?
> e) How do I promote myself using the word of mouth?

What does TURNOVER mean?
The TOTAL money you cash in.

What does profit mean?
Income—Expenses = Gross Profit
Net Profit = Gross Profit minus Tax on profit

BUSINESS PLAN SUMMARY

1. Idea:
2. Motivation:
3. Product/Service: what do you offer?
4. Sales plan: Who do you offer it to?
5. Business plan: How do you see your idea in the future? What is your vision?
6. Investment plan: How much money do you need now?
    How much money will you need later?
7. Implementation: How do you do it at the beginning?
    How do you want to do it in the future?

It is worth mentioning at this point the joke of a very good friend of mine: "If you like my business, give me a like on Facebook. And if you don't like it, ask two of your friends to give me a like ".

If plan "A" doesn't work, don't panic! The alphabet has 25 more letters. I'm on plan "Z." Persevere. Now I'm playing my last card. And how do I do this? I act big!

This is just the sketch of the business plan. It has to be more complex. The investment part is extremely important and it has to be studied in detail.

Funding sources:

1. Sell some valuable things you own.

2. Parents. The majority can't help us with money, but they can help us with their connections. If they don't have any connections, they can help you somehow, maybe they can work for you helping you arrange the space, clean it, etc.

3. Friends. You always write a document for the money you borrow. We give something in return to the ones that lend money to us. For example, for Euro 1.000 we return Euro 1.100. Each of us can be creative depending on circumstances.

4. Relatives.

5. Investors. Most of the people think this opportunity is impossible. I personally believe in this. You can't find them everywhere and easy. You won't see a big banner somewhere stating they are ready to invest in your business. It's very important to create opportunities for yourself to meet this kind of people. They won't knock you on your door asking you to do something with your life. You must already have a business plan and a dream you believe in.

If you don't believe in it, then no investor can possibly believe that business will be good. Also, no customers will trust in what you offer.

Why an investor would be willing to invest in your business? They act in this way for several reasons. Unlike you, who are at the first business, they have many other ongoing businesses. They don't have time to deal with a new business and to develop it. They know that money kept in banks or under the pillow lose its value due to inflation.

You have major advantages. Investors have an interest in your business to work out. They don't invest to lose money. Logical! They have connections. They know very well the steps you need to take to grow your business. They are skilled. Promotion and advertising are already formed and tested by the other companies they manage. For sure they tested them all before you and they know which are the most effective.

6. I personally don't recommend bank loans. I don't think it's a smart move to borrow money for 30 years and to work your whole life to return the money. It's exactly the same situation as when you buy a house by borrowing money from the bank. Only after 30 years the house is yours. It's an unfortunate choice. You get stuck and you can't develop in other areas of your life.

A great idea is when you do this the way around. You don't get mortgage for a house you will live in, but to rent it to others. The rent will pay the bank rate. Over 30 years you can have your house, and you can invest the money you earned in an activity that brings you an income. The most important is that the income to be much higher than the expenses.

The bank loan can be a good alternative for the people that want to expand their business, to develop it, but not at the beginning.

My opinion about banks, despite the fact that for a relatively short period I worked in the field, is: "Just forget about the bank, don't touch it!" Abroad, banks seem more advantageous for customers. It's good to use the bank when you have 1 million Euro in your account and you want to get from it a huge monthly interest. This is what millionaires do. They use the bank in their favor because they are smart.

7. European Funds. It's an alternative. You need to be very well informed about this. To make the first steps. To persevere and to believe that your idea is the best.

Your business will be successful only if you truly believe in it.

All people who believe with all their being in their business are successful; otherwise their distrust is transmitted to others, no matter how positively they talk about it. It is therefore very important to do what you like, just so you can easily be convincing. Why aren't all people rich? Because this sensitive part betrays them, what they energetically transmit to others. They seem credible, but in fact, they are not! People sense your uncertainty and insecurity.

If you were an employer, what would be the main criterion for selection: the man himself or his knowledge? Being a human resources inspector, the main criterion should be: the man himself (the man in his entirety). Although in practice the focus is only on knowledge. In reality, after the selection process, in a company people are chosen by instinct. If ten people are equally qualified, in the end it is chosen the person the boss wants to work with, the one the boss feels he resonates with. As an entrepreneur, I would choose those people full of enthusiasm and energy that have a passion for the job.

My business leader is in Germany. He is no 1 in the field. I'm happy I met him personally. I appreciate him and he is a role model for me. I am honored of this experience.

It is very important to have a well-defined business plan with a large vision. It is important that the leader of the business has a strong passion for what they do; that the object of the business "runs through their veins." This if you want to be millionaire.

An investor says: "There is no project you want to do that you won't succeed in doing! If you don't take your eyes off the goal!"

He is convinced that:

*   There is no project you can't do, even if you are really poor!
*   His business was such a project started in full economic crisis.
*   You can overcome an obstacle in many ways: you can avoid it, you can pass underneath it, or you can go through it! The important thing is not to stop when you encounter obstacles!
*   Set a goal and don't take your eyes off it!

In order to manage your money efficiently, you need many knowledge and an efficient behavior; that's why only 0,6 % of the people on the planet are financially free and their money work for them, and the rest are in the area of financial chaos not knowing what they spend their money on and without any savings.

How do you choose the best employees for your company if you're thinking about a business? They should be much better than you. They have to be their own bosses, even if they work for you. I call them collaborators. I hate using the word "employee." People in a company, from the janitor to the sales and marketing managers, to human resources and accounting, are their own bosses. Together they form a great team working individually for themselves to live a fulfilling and abundant life. Correct? You are business partners in a great company. Who are the winners in this equation? All of you, including the whole society. They all have a better life and they all end up living a fulfilling life.

Everyone is aware that they provide for the state for a functional society. The state administrates the profit from those who work. What does the state do with this money? It will take care of them when they retire. This money is given back little by little in the form of medical care and support. For example, when you will be old, you will have a housekeeper paid by the state to keep your house clean, you will have a nurse who will visit you weekly, you will have different facilities: swimming, karate, cycling, dance, libraries, etc. What does the state do with your money? A better world. It builds hospitals, social houses, retirement homes, and special accommodations for disabled children, parks, etc. The state offers you protection. It creates and coordinates the ones who take care of the order, like: police, army, city councils, mayors, banks, courts etc. Where does all that money come from? From businesses, from the taxes the businesspeople pay to the state. The people working in these state institutions generate value in a way that the society needs their services; but they don't generate income. In conclusion, the authorized physical person, the limited liability companies, the multinationals, the corporations are the ones that sustain the economy of a country. They pay taxes to the state. This money is used to pay the people in the state institutions mentioned above. Also it is used to pay the unemployed people and the retired ones.

The state works for you this way. If the people around you are happy, you will be too. You care about the people around you, about nature and about the standard of living in your country. You are not indifferent. You love life and everything about it.

How productive are you? Does what you are doing in this moment help you achieve what you've planned as your life goals? I remind you that it is the moment to invest time in yourself so you turn into what you want to become. Change doesn't occur by simply choosing that you want a different reality. As the entrepreneur of your life, it is mandatory to have an overview, to be aware of the pluses and minuses that you have and what consequences the decisions you make can have.

It is mandatory to have relationships if you want abundance in your life. To meet people who have done something in their lives, who live as you want to live. If you were a timid or shy person, this is the time to change this behavior that sabotages you.

The courage, the confidence and the boldness are qualities that a leader must have. You are a winner when you discover the power inside you, you love life and you stop trying to fight it considering it your greatest enemy.

After you successfully go through all the stages I talked about, money will start coming as a form of energy in your life.

Money is the result of your work with yourself. Who runs after money doesn't make it, that's why we have so many poor people struggling with difficult conditions. Money is a direct consequence of the value that you are able to create it as a person.

Once you discover what you need to do to have abundance in your life and how you do it to attract money to your account, it is time to think: how can I double my current income? How can I save half the money I make? Not under the mattress, but how can you invests it so you create an extra income?

No one can rob you of your own success and no one can give it to you! Your success depends on you. If this reality has the ability to inspire a desire in you, then it has the capacity to produce the manifestation of this desire.

The belief is the force a certain information or thought is transmitted with. It is the specific energy required for materialization. The stronger the belief the faster the information is transmitted and the faster the materialization takes place. The belief and information's transmitting force are stimulating each other and you can't have one without the other. If your belief is big, the information is transmitted with a very high speed and then the energy becomes matter. For those who have ears to hear and eyes to see I remind them the message of Jesus: "ask and you shall receive, seek and you shall find, knock and the door shall open." If your life is according to this belief, it means that you will be able to live a truly fulfilled life.

Beliefs about a particular aspect of life create your reality about that aspect. Beliefs are formed by the human mind and they exist only at the ego level. They are, most often, not yours, but taken from the collective mind. Therefore, whenever you feel that a particular belief limits your life experience, you can ask yourself: "Is this what I really feel or is just a belief that sabotages me?" Be silent, descend within your heart and stay open to receive your answer. And every time trust to walk the heart's path, even if it looks completely different from what you thought it was right. Though the heart sees the possible where the mind thinks sees the impossible.

You are Everything. You are Love. So if you are Everything, the entire Universe, why do you still struggle, why are you worried? Why don't you let everything come naturally? Why don't you let the ocean push you to the shore? Why don't you see life as heaven? Why do you lie to yourself? Why do you let your mind control you? Ask yourself, meditate, and feel.

Feel the nature, the abundance, the prosperity, the happiness, the love within you and share them with the others. Share the love, the happiness, the abundance that you are. Giving, you will receive more. Sharing with the others, you give to yourself.

Nothing you do remains unrewarded. Probably sometimes you have this feeling. It's just an illusion of your mind. The universe always takes care to compensate something done with love. From where something is taken, something else is given back. From where something is given, something else will be returned. What makes you turn a blind eye to that is fear and lack of confidence in the universal laws of life. You are blocked at the level of your mind and at what you can see with your human eyes and this is the reason you limit yourself so much. I remind you that the truth of your heart is always in what you can't see. When you will finally trust the unseen, you will get the trust Who You Really Are. The divine sparkle, the perfect manifestation of the almighty God.

The entrepreneurship is a lifestyle, the prosperity if a state of the spirit. It means you are connected to the Source. It means that you know who you really are. It means you live "Here and Now." When you are in the present, in the "Here and Now," you can see and find out things that are not connected to time and matter; you are united with everything and everyone. In the current state you have silence, peace and an indescribable joy.

A great personality, clinical psychologist accredited by the Psychologists College in Romania, psycho spiritual counselor, therapist licensed as a Bowen expert (Master Level 2) accredited by Bowen Therapy Academy of Australia, says: "My dear friends! Today I invite you to start your day with this statement: "I have always been fabulous richness." Saying this words slowly, as they are part of your inner body, as they are getting inside you and rest in every cell of your physical body, as they are present in the interior of your being, you activate the fabulous richness on all plans. You will enter on the flow of consciousness where you are richness and you have a multitude of connections, opportunities, moments, circumstances, money, happiness, joy etc. Because richness is all you have as a potential in the divine sparkle you had received since your creation. Accept that you are fabulous richness and then you will have the resources to experiment with in the material plan of your own creation. The acceptance brings the opening of the mind so needed in order to see the experiences and circumstances from the perspective of the wisdom of the Divine Ego. Become aware that you are the creators of your own reality and allow yourself to be fabulous richness, because you deserve to live smoothly, beautifully and well."

Wish as many possible things from life! When you know what you want to receive from life, act and don't stop until you get it!

Scientists launched an interesting theory which they use to demonstrate that thoughts have a fantastic power in changing the reality. One of the most renowned American scientists managed to demonstrate, after profound studies, that the human mind can modify the reality and implicitly the future. The brain is not a static organ, rigid and fix, and this is the reason our thoughts and experiences can be continuously remodeled. Thoughts become pieces of furniture and they are built consciously or subconsciously, and once applied they influence the future.

"Everything that takes place on a mental level, it will become real sooner or later. If they are negative, thoughts will attract a miserable reality with not very pleasant experiences."

The scientist researched for years how the human brain works and the ways thoughts are built. What is interesting is that certain patterns are registered with a certain periodicity in the brain, and therefore the person falls into negative thoughts.

Most people hide things they are ashamed of or things they don't want others to know about. Therefore, most of us hide their sexuality. And therefore, almost all of hide our money. I mean you don't talk openly about it. You think money is a very personal matter. And here is the problem. It's a powerful blockage. Everyone focuses its great reserves of sexual energy towards the aspiration to prosperity. Sexual excitement is a state of mind. It is a very powerful energy. Used with all the love and dedication, you can achieve plenary happiness. When you are governed by pure and innocent sexual desire, you feel that you change: your imagination improves, you become more courageous, your will becomes stronger, you show perseverance and you have a fantastic creative capacity. This very powerful energy can be redirected towards wealth and abundance.

"The one who has discovered how to give his sexual energy a valve represented by a form of creative effort is really lucky. Scientific research has revealed the following facts:

"1. The people with the greatest achievements are those who possess evolved sexual nature and have mastered the art of the transfer of sexual energy.

"2. Those who have accumulated great wealth and have acquired fame in literature, art, industry, architecture and other fields were motivated by a woman.

"The sexual energy is the creative energy of all geniuses. It had never been or will be a great leader, builder or artist which is deprived of the overwhelming power of sex."

There are large blockages at this level. Basically, true self-love can exist only when you understand sexuality at the deepest level. How do you realize that you have a blockage related to sexuality? You can't talk about it freely and without inhibitions.

Sex is connected with self-esteem. If you are good from a sexual point of view, you have a high self-esteem. This is the reason religion made sex shameful. If you don't know yourself, you can't discover the power within you.

Love gives you the power to dream of anything. And also love gives you the power to do whatever you dream of! Love brought you to the world and it helps you make this world a better place.

"...Where were we? Ah, sex. Sex for pleasure, as a habit, as a need, out of interest, occasional, as addiction, out of boredom, out of curiosity, make-up sex, angry sex, out of obligation, out of revenge, out of desperation, out of inertia. Therefore, so many ways and reasons for satisfaction and joy. The same you enjoy when you win at roulette, pass an exam, win the Lottery or on the stock exchange. The satisfaction is the maximum. Now about love: love is only one. And it makes people happy. It's the minimum it can offer. Question—what do you prefer between satisfaction and happiness? Do you know why I'm asking? In order to see what you chose."

I already know that now you perceive the huge role that love has in your life. If you have love, you also have wellbeing and success. I know you will say it's not that simple, because there are some other factors that attract wealth and success. I'm sure you can have it all if you remove the mental blocks that keep you on the same spot. Who determines what you can do and what you can't do? You're the only authority that knows best what inner resources can help you surpass any obstacle and permanently improve your personal and professional life.

From my point of view, it is very important that you take responsibility for your life and become the Creator of your life. Get rid of the patterns and thoughts in your mind that don't take you to any direction in this life and create your new patterns to help you live Heaven on Earth. Live in harmony with your Divine Self. Stop separate yourself from it viewing it as somewhere outside you. It supports you only if you know what you really want in this life. Write the script of your life and you have the chance to be a great person, a person who has something to say, and a person who brings a major change where they are.

If you believe that rich people are bad, and you don't want to be bad, you will never try to make money. Instead, if you believe that the rich people that are bad are very few and you make some inquiries and find out that according to recent statistics there are over 11 million millionaires in the world, most having businesses they worked hard for, then you try to understand what it means to be a great businessman and you realize yourself that you have great chances of making money. Depending on your beliefs, you have what you live in this very moment.

It is essential to change your old belief about life that brings you poverty with a new one: "Money helps you get happiness, long life, good mood and inner peace." Certainly, your Self lives through you when you have a state of happiness, cheerfulness and inner peace. From this point, certainly, your attention is directed to an extraordinary life, not a mediocre and meaningless one.

Your success is measured in the number of uncomfortable decisions you make.

"You've probably heard these things before. We are all created in the same way; we all have the same organs. The difference is that some are awake and very aware of our life, while others are still asleep and prefer to indulge in the situation." That's my destiny," "this is my cross," etc. This is the reason we divide into two categories: rich or poor. Precisely because of this. Wealthy people know very well what they want to do and what they are doing in life, while the poor have no idea and they don't think too much about it, they prefer to complain and to proclaim themselves victims of the society.

There have been so many stories of beggars who have become great people, public figures and people still didn't learn anything from it. They still say "it was their fate," "they were lucky." A person can build their own luck. So think again before you complain. Because you can do everything to be different! You can live a different life! You just have to know what to choose!"

What gives value to a person?

* The character
* The neuron
* Love
* The personality
* Wisdom
* Education, abilities
* Friends

* Personal development
* The way they value other people
* The capacity of inspiring others
* The respect they have for themselves and for others
* The way they treat the people around them, with the same respect no matter their social status, education, material situation
* The love and respect you treat people with
* You gain value working at your own creation
* Honesty, correctness and common sense
* Generosity
* The way you behave

I believe that the value of an individual has different perspectives depending on "who" assesses them. This "who" values differently according to their dominant values, therefore, the same individual seems valuable for some and trivial for others.

Gratitude means wealth. Complaining means poverty.

"Although social degradation increasingly attract more people into the turmoil which some call life, but there are still people who haven't given up on their backbone or life principles. The latter are not so many, their number is constantly changing, and the verb that guides their existence is "to be," not "to have."

Some people say that is wrong to be rich and it's not right to wish to be wealthy because you will lose your soul.

For as long as you live on Earth, money is important. The ones who say this are envious on the ones who have. Money exists because it is important, if it wasn't important it wouldn't be present. Man exists because it is important, otherwise they won't exist. Everything that exists is important for the creation. Stop acting like a victim. Think that if money wouldn't be important, you wouldn't be able to evolve and you couldn't have wonderful experiences. Without money will you be able to travel and see all the wonders of the world? Without money will you be able to taste all the culinary wonders? Could you help poor people survive? Could you read extraordinary books, or watch very good movies? Will you be able to get an education? NO. Stop looking at money as a diabolical object, and accept it is a valuable and loving instrument. If you love money, it will love you back and it will come to you. All that matters is not to get attached to it, to give it away, to allow the flow of the abundance to come over you and to think of money as you think of a friend. A friend who can help you evolve and live wonderful experiences and to build your ideas and creations. But this friend needs a bit of soul, needs to be shared with other people, and this will make it return to you because it feels there is no envy and hate inside you, only unconditional love and generosity. That's all.

7 qualities a person born to make something important on this planet has:

1. You don't like working for others.

   You are a natural born leader and you know it. Or you may not know it yet, but you don't feel comfortable when you are employed and work for others. You feel that you lose yourself, you are not showing all your qualities and you feel stuck in a space you don't belong to. You need flexibility and creativity to express yourself better and your vision is totally different from that of ordinary and hopeless people.

2. You never start something if you are not inspired.

   Creativity plays an important part in your development as an individual and as long as you lack inspiration, you can't carry out any project. There are days when you have so many ideas and some when your neurons apparently went on vacation.

3. Ever since you were a child you thought adults are crazy to get dressed and go to work.

   You always knew deep down that life is not made up only of work, work and work. To get dressed in a suit and to go to work is only an idea that focuses you in getting to work, and those people suddenly turn into slaves who, in the end will forget the essential.

4. When you do what you like, money is not a priority.

   This is a report which is not related to the economic principles that govern the world. Although we are often taught that everyone is rewarded based on their own value, you always felt comfortable when you were allowed to fulfill your duties with passion.

5. You are an idealist.

   Only a fool could believe in idealism today when the whole society relies on pragmatism. However, you feel different and special, and the world should develop as a good quality romance novel.

6. You can't tell how you know some things; you just "know them."

   Most of the people who lived on this planet have received information in the form of visions or revelations or telepathy. They had certain information whose origin they couldn't explain. If you go through the same feeling, then you can consider yourself lucky because you have a special mission on this planet.

7. You feel the great change is near.

   Change is the only one that doesn't change. It brings new perspectives and probably a new lifestyle. If you feel that this change is not far from today, then you can consider yourself a special person. Eventually, things must enter their normal track, for which change begins with you and it will end with the others.

If you want different results, act different than usual!

The image you have about yourself is the one that allows you or stops you to reach your goals. Think carefully of this!

Many people work for other people's dream instead of working for their own dream. Someone will be your master if you don't know which direction you want to go! Be your own master!

Follow your mission! Walk your own path even if you'll be alone.

If you want to be successful, you have to walk on new path rather than on the ones already conquered by others.

Those with high self-esteem are able to succeed and to have the relationships they want. The rich become richer and happy people become happier, while the poor become poorer and unhappy people become increasingly unhappier. Why? Question that needs an answer: "Do you know or not who you are!?"

The key to failure: try to satisfy everyone.

How would I describe a perfectionist? How do you recognize a perfectionist?
Features:

1. a pretentious thinker
2. constipated, distributive attention, goggles, for sure wearing a skirt (literally or figuratively) and they have a sense of humor with anyone else but themselves!
3. . hard to satisfy, unsatisfied with themselves, even if they had great achievements

What does success mean without happiness?

For me, success without happiness means success without results. Success with no money in the account. Success reflects the abundance. It is an illusion to believe that a poor person is successful. It doesn't work.

You definitely wonder what the secret of my success is. It is a very relevant one: always rely only on yourself. There will be turning points in life when everyone you hoped to help you will take two steps back. Probably they will say in their minds: why should they be successful with my help? Let them handle it! Your goal is to move forward with your dream. Find a solution, and if not, you invent it, but go on.

Success is a journey, not a destination. True joy comes by doing what you are meant to do and waiting for the reward patiently when its time comes. There is this misconception I hear more often from people that you shouldn't expect any reward, but to enjoy only the satisfaction of your work. It is a life principle that leads nowhere. The reward is proportional to your work. Any activity must have a result and this is the reward. If you don't receive the reward, it means that you are not doing your activity efficiently. The personal bank account reflects the best the satisfaction of your work.

To be successful, to attract abundance and to be truly happy, you have to honor yourself by trusting the message of your soul and acting according to this message.

Stop thinking of who you were yesterday. Start dreaming of who you can become tomorrow, because this is the true power within yourself! Amen!

Successful people always see the options available to them, regardless the circumstances. When you say or think that you have no choice, you automatically pace yourself in the position of a victim. You become weaker than what is happening around you and such attitude frees you from any responsibility.

You can overcome any obstacle if you understand your motivation, so that appropriate question would be: "Why do I do what I do?" "Do I really want to do this?"

The longest road is not from a corner of the world to the other. The longest road is from the thinking to experiencing it, from reason to emotion. When the two intersect, it's the end of the long path of your evolution. **

The lack of money is not the problem when you have a dream. Many people can't find financial resources because they don't believe in what they are trying to do, so is less probable to find an investor. Other people don't find an investor because they think you have to be crazy to put money on the idea they have. And probably most people don't receive money from investors because they feel that their money would be lost in a few months due to the lack of preparation of the petitioner. Money certainly comes when you know the smallest detail your dream. "The obstacles you encounter outside are the limits within yourself." See yourself as the creator of your own reality and you will see how your dream will come true.

Yes! Money brings happiness if you know what to do with it, if you have clear and precise goals. What the use of making money for those who have no idea how to use it?! If you don't know how to administrate a small amount, you definitely won't know what to do with a large amount. Attention! Money comes to those who know how to use it, to those who love money and want it. As you want to hug the man or woman of your dreams. So much you have to like it and love it!

Financial prosperity can be reached this way:

1. financial discipline
   Get rid of the producer's mentality and of the consumer's irrational behaviors.
2. goal-oriented way of thinking
   The right work for you is the one that doesn't let you sleep and makes you wake up in the morning with a smile on your face. This is what fulfills you and makes you happy. If you radiate happiness when you are working, it means you are on the right path.

Stop comparing yourself with others. The only person you are competing with is you from yesterday, the rest are not important. If you look carefully around you, you will see that many people long for what you have, and you long for what others have. The safest way to progress is comparing yourself with the one you were yesterday. Very few people do this, the majority compare themselves with the people around them and they get distracted from their own person. Each of us has a different start in life; some start with some advantages, others from zero. The tragedy is not to be born poor, but to die poor.

CHAPTER 2

HOW DO YOU TURN YOUR LIFE INTO REALITY?

"Stay as far away as possible from people who shrink your ambitions. Small people always do that. The really great ones make you feel that you too can become great."

I know it sounds like a utopian question. At first, it seems like a question that doesn't have an answer. But the surprise is big. This question has an answer too. Not only one answer, but millions of answers. Every soul responds individually and each answer is unique.

It's the question that tormented me for years. Unceasingly, I sought solutions to have a fulfilling life. And yet, I wonder: "Who the hell didn't allow me to live such a life?" It wasn't me who blocked my way. Didn't my beliefs create exactly the reality that I wanted? Didn't the people around me influence me making me think that a limited and meaningless life is a fulfilling life?

I don't believe that a classic life with marriage, some kids and a job is totally meaningless, but you can live differently. With more joy in our hearts, with more gratitude for everything that surrounds us, with more kindness in our actions. To live with God in your heart. When He is with you, your life is a blessing. Letting yourself be guided by Him is like you had already found absolute fulfillment. What greater happiness can someone have when they know they are a perfect manifestation of the Creator?

This ordinary and meaningless life can suddenly become a life blessed by God.

A spiritual author expressed in a very nice way what I want to say: "There comes a day when you give up the fight. There comes a day when you are exhausted by the fight, and you choose freedom. There comes a day when you give up all illusions. There comes a day when you embrace everything that raised you up without being interested anymore in all external aspects or circumstances. There comes a day when you want to be what you really are. That day, you meet yourself. We dream of a day when we free ourselves of all the fictions that tire us. We dream, but continue not to believe in our dreams. We dream, but we are still asleep. Dear people it's time to come to life. To Real Life. It's time to allow ourselves to live that dream. It's time to be what we dream to be. Without fear, without question, without regrets."

You need to force yourself to get out of the old patterns stuck in your mind. You need to see another reality. Different people. A different way of living. To see how people enjoy life. Yes it's true! I said it well. Don't be surprised about what I just said.

Most people don't have the slightest idea how to enjoy the present moment. How they have to think and to feel so they are truly happy. In this book, I will offer many solutions to this. So many that everyone will be able to choose what suits them best. And if you don't find in this book a solution for your heart, you are absolutely free to discover a saving solution on your own. I can only encourage you to discover yourself. It's up to you if you want to live a fulfilling and happy life.

The first thing you need to do to be on the path of your heart is to be honest. Absolute sincerity with yourself. Give yourself this chance. Stop running away from yourself. I recommend that you lock yourself in your room for one day. You'll find a way to do it. Take a day off from work, you don't waste your time in a coffee shop or gossiping with your friends about what your neighbors bought, what clothes they wear etc. Since you had the courage to make this decision, to sit with yourself in your room, I invite you to switch off the TV. I hope I didn't make you sad. The purpose of your isolation is not to punish you, but, on the opposite, to help you escape of your own prison, of your own unhappiness. Even if you are alone in the room, you will fill the room with your love. Even if you are in prison, you will instantly turn it into a temple. The moment you fill it with love, it won't be a prison anymore. Also a temple can become a prison if it's not filled with love.

For sure, you will get very bored in the early hours. You don't know what to do because I asked you not to turn on the TV. I know you will get new ideas. But please don't start cleaning. My goal wasn't to isolate you in a room so you can tidy your clothes or dust the nightstands. The goal is divine. I know you are already annoyed and you wonder: "What the hell can I do here with myself? Shall I stare at the ceiling? Shall I think of nothing? What shall I do?"

So, what can you do? Aren't you curious? Is this the first time when you have a meeting with yourself? I refuse to believe this; I would prefer to hear a lie this time.

I know you will swear and curse. I know you are almost crying. I know you prefer to go to work, even if it's Sunday. I know all this!

Do this experiment! Probably half a day passed since you stayed only with yourself, without your family and friends, without Facebook or any other activity that could distract you.

Why are you anxious? Ask yourself! Learn to communicate with yourself. This is the first step. Why aren't you happy when you don't do anything? Is it because you don't want to think about much dissatisfaction in your life? Is it because you are afraid to find out that nothing you live in the present moment is what you want? Is it so? Have I guessed the question in your mind? If so, allow me to give you my opinion. Why? Because I've already gone down this road, the road to nowhere, and it only brought me sadness and pain.

Admit it that this is not the life that you wanted for yourself, this is not the job you wanted to do, and this is not what you want from life. Be honest with yourself for once in your life! Confront your frustrations and failures. Talk to them, speak to them and negotiate with them. Always ask yourself:

"What is the life I want? What would I really like to do? What brings me happiness and joy? "I can tell you from experience, that you won't get an immediate answer to these questions. Be patient. Open your heart. Free your mind. Learn to listen to your soul. It will guide you step by step, minute by minute to everything that truly fulfills you. Trust that there is someone that holds your hand and leads you right where you want. Do you believe this? If not, it makes no sense to go on reading this book. Throw it under the bed and go on with the life you lived so far.

I'm sure there will come again the day when you will be sad and depressed. When you won't find solutions to the problems you face, God within you will take care to remind you of my book. And you will think to yourself: "Let me see what that writer wants to say in that book that annoyed me." You'll dust it and you will start with the exercise I proposed. Get isolated in a room and meet yourself.

I know that for half a day you will think of the problems you face and you will try to seek salvation from someone else. Now you hope to find salvation in my book. But I'll cut the momentum from the start and I'll tell you: "I'm not your salvation! No one can help you but yourself! The strength, the hope and the desire that you are looking for from those around you are inside yourself. "I can only give you a perspective regarding a fulfilling and happy life. I can give you my example to show you that you can also live the same if you decide at this point to make that choice. Delay no more because sooner or later you will come to the same conclusion.

Once again, try to have an honest communication with yourself. Imagine you talk to your soul. If you don't want to look crazy talking alone in the house, I advise you to use the following technique which worked fantastic for me: "writing therapy." Write what you think, all your regrets and sorrows. Write about how you feel in that moment. Don't wait until you are calm and peaceful, because it won't happen suddenly. This state is coming from within yourself; it doesn't come upon you as a reward for being sad and depressed. Write with all the anger you have at that moment, with all the frustration and upset. Don't think of what you write. Allow your hands to write themselves. You just express yourself! Put in writing all your pains and frustrations. Leave them there! They are not yours anymore. You got rid of them. If someone is interested in reading them, you can simply feel honored. It is possible that your life experience will help other people who want a truly fulfilled and happy life. They can judge you, criticize you, condemn you or they can love you and appreciate you for the courage of confronting yourself. Their opinion about how you felt doesn't matter; all that matters is how you feel after you have got out to the surface everything that doesn't allow you to be happy.

If you find it very difficult to spend a day with yourself without doing anything else, I advise you to try again some other time. Try it until you manage to set a meeting with the most important person in your life: YOU.

Here you are in front of yourself and again it is time to be honest with yourself. This time you have nowhere to run. You need your quality time spent with yourself. You sit in front of a large mirror that reflects your image as it really is, with good and bad. Do you have the courage to look at yourself in all honesty? Who are you and what message do you bring to the world? Be aware of your goodness, and also of the darkness in you. Make peace with yourself and before you start changing the world, change the world within you. You have the courage to look in the mirror and to tell yourself: 1. I love you (your name); 2. I accept you (your name); 3. I appreciate you (your name); 4. I respect you (your name). 5. I forgive you (your name). If as a child you didn't receive love, acceptance, appreciation and respect from your parents, school or the other people, because they didn't receive them either, it is time to give yourself what you haven't received from others.

"Be careful how you talk to yourself. I wrote this a thousand times, but it is extremely important! Refuse to call yourself stupid, incapable, idiot and other negative words. Choose encouraging words and talk to yourself like you talk to a good friend."

Analyze your life. Now, you are the observer of your life. Write on a big white piece of paper only two things: "What makes me happy in my current life?," "What makes me completely miserable?" On the front of the page write only what makes you happy, and on the back what makes you unhappy. Please don't write anything else on the page you're supposed to write what makes you happy, don't write what doesn't make you unhappy because I know you need a notebook for that.

What do you want to start with? Do you want to write on the page all the things that make you happy? I assume so, because you are in search for happiness.

I don't believe you wrote to many lines. That's OK. I didn't have anything to write either. I understand.

Even if you haven't found a single reason to be happy, please write in this moment what would make you happy. Put your mind to work. Use your imagination and everything else you have. It's time to bring out the best in you. Pay attention to yourself! What qualities do you have that went unnoticed until now? Are you beautiful? Are you a smart? Are you good at sex? Do you have a good soul? For sure, you will find something good in you. Search until you find something. Appreciate yourself! Praise yourself! Be proud of yourself!

Do you notice you have a good soul? That you have never hurt anyone so you don't deserve so much pain? You never cheated anyone, you never used anyone and still your life is meaningless?

The question is: "What can you do if you have a good heart? Or, better said, what did you do with this good soul of yours?" I invite you to take another blank sheet of paper and to write on the front page what pain having a good heart caused you and what made you happy.

My guess is that your kindness already made you suffer. You are my mirror, and as I said, I have been on the road on which you are now. Have you played the victim part? Have you tried so hard to make others happy and forgot about yourself? Have you sacrificed too much for those around you? Were you the person who was selling their soul to save someone from trouble? Is that you? Is this the reason that makes you believe that God was unfair to you? Is this why you are still looking for Him in the wrong place? In any other place except inside yourself?

My dear friend, all I can say at this point is: "If you persist with this attitude of saving the world around you, you will never be happy." I'm sorry I have turned your universe upside down, but this is not the solution for a fulfilling life.

You have to do the opposite. I know it's hard. It is so hard that you prefer to run again in that world of yours that doesn't satisfy you. But that's OK; you will come back to the same spot. Until when? Until you will be so fed up that you will get angry and you'll do something good with your life.

How? In theory, very simple. In practice, not so simple. You take back the power you had given to the others. More precise:

1. You forget that someone from the outside can save you. If somehow you believed in another being that performs miracles, it's time to forget about it.

2. You stop pleasing the others unless you really enjoy it. You might have really big problems.

If your mother was used to you doing her daily housekeeping, she will get angry if one day you tell her you are not in the mood to do it. If your dad was used to you pouring his wine, he will certainly get upset when you will tell him you'd rather read a book or sit in the sun.

If your partner used to leave their clothes in the washing machine waiting for you to get them out, they will be disturbed by your attitude when you'll stop doing this.

If your brother or sister used to ask for a favor, certainly, they don't want to hear from you: "No, I can't do it, even if you have a headache at that moment."

There are many examples. It's your responsibility to take into consideration everything the people around you do to you.

3. Stop waiting for confirmation from the great specialists if you are able or not to do business. You already know that you are capable and you are only looking in this moment for role models. This way, you find surprisingly that those people whom you appreciate so much began their business or activity with no money. They worked at it without thinking whether it will be a success or an achievement. Without asking others if they it right or not. They believed in it and went on.

4. Take out of your mind how you thought your life should be. This is a pattern taken from the society you live in. It's not good for you. You want to have a fulfilling life. You want to live and to enjoy life. They just want you to survive and they see happiness as pain and suffering. It's true that most people see happiness this way. It's sad. It's not normal to think that happiness comes from the fact that someone offended you or underestimated what you really are. Stop finding excuses to that person who told you off or offended because you because you upset them etc.

5. Learn to be honest with yourself every day.

6. Learn to be the first in your life.

That's one of the lessons I learned the hardest. I am 33 years old and I'm still not convinced that I am on the first place in my life in all aspects. I still have that fear that I offend someone even when I try to explain as nice as possible that I can't do what they wants and I can say what they want to hear.

7. Clean up! It doesn't matter where! Wherever you want. If you want to clean your house, do it! If you want to clean up your life, do it! Who stops you? The fear that you will lose your friends? The fear of being alone? What kind of fear blocks you from cleaning up your mind, and your life? Identify it! See which one it is! There are many. It will take a while before you realize what you fear you are confronted with.

8. Express yourself! How? My answer is always the same: "However you feel like that moment." You don't have to follow a certain behavior. Do exactly as your soul wants that moment. If your partner upset you have the courage to tell them what hurt you. If you don't have the courage to be honest with that person, then find another form of communication, through e-mail or SMS. Be brave and say what you feel and think in your favor. Don't gather all sorts of rubbish in the form of anger and sadness. What are you? A container?

Who do you want to get rid of the garbage in your soul? Your life partner? Your parents? God? Who? I'll disappoint you again and I'll tell you that YOU are the one who can do this. God is with you, works through you, but you are the one who can act. It's easy. Right?

9. Take small steps and free yourself from all fears you are confronted with. First, you need to identify your fear. Talk to it. In your mind or aloud. The way you talk is less important. Relevant is that you are not running away from that fear. Because one day it will manipulate you so much that you will have no place to run. It will catch you in the trap you built without even realizing it.

Fear is an illusion of the mind. It can become reality only if you truly believe in it. If you don't pay any attention to it, it doesn't escalate. It remains small and weak. You take back your power and channel this energy into something else. For example, you stop thinking of that fear and think of something else. You can think of a romantic night, you can think of what makes you happy. Maybe your dog. You remember how cute it is and how many moments of joy it gave you.

The great challenge before us today is to learn how to come together to form a community based not on dogma or an external authority, but on mutual equality and a deep respect for each person's experience.

A girl wrote an emotional message. I have been there, too:

"I am aware of my lack of authenticity and I take full responsibility of it. From now on, from this very moment, I'm NOT interested in it anymore and I free myself of those 'real friends' in name only, of people who know where to find me whenever they need me, whenever they feel like it because they know 'Ana is there for me!' No, starting today, Ana who is here only for who she wants to be here for, for who she feels like, wherever and whenever. I free myself from people who know how to be human beings only when they need something. And what about me, my dear? I'm some kind of statue? Some object you can use when and how you feel? No, clearly not. I am no one's rag! You can't use me and when you don't need me or you don't like me anymore you throw me in the bin!

"I have been 'human' with you all. I never said anything, not even to move two centimeters farther. I answer immediately to your fervent requests. I responded with kindness when you criticized and judged me. I compromised, but until when??? I'm no one's rag, I am not made of stone, and I understood this, but it is time for you to understand, if you … could? Unless I ask for too much!

"Don't be surprised that I won't answer to you anymore, don't be surprised that I no longer speak to you, I am no longer nice Ana you knew. Not out of malice, not out of indifference, but because I am no longer close to you. You, with your attitude, pushed me away!!! If there is still a link between us, please let keep or give me back what it's mine, my work! I don't cry, I feel free! I am not angry, but firm and determined to not step again over my decisions, whatever you do or say about ourselves or about me!

"Respect, appreciation, value for 'real people' who knew that before being respected, appreciated and valued, must respect, appreciate and cherish the people around them! Respect and my full support!

"Thank you and I wish you a beautiful life, may all you took from me be useful to you. Our paths separate here. It is time."

Ana says: "I review this message since I wrote it and each time my tears flow! I am not like that, but I did what I felt. And as I said somewhere, who wants to understand, they did understand ... who doesn't ... it's not my business."

And so it is! Your only responsibility is to put yourself first in your life. Otherwise, it's up to it the others how they interpret the message. If they recognize themselves in the message, it means the message reflects part of what they are. I just want to remind you who you really are. That's all. Nothing more. Remember, your Self always wakes you up when you forget who you really are.

Ana came to a conclusion that is worthy to remember: "I am approached by people who tell me that I am a fake and that I'm not what I seem on the internet. That I'm a fake and I only talk because I have nothing else to do. Or that this is the reality I want to live, but it's not my everyday life. Do you know what I strongly believe? That everyone is free to believe and say what they want, that everyone is responsible for what they say and live. And I might be harsh again or tough or mean (and other similar tags), but if you think it cannot be that simple, then it isn't. Whatever the world thinks they are right! I stopped (since yesterday) to say something to someone who just doesn't give up on their fixed idea. I understood that I shouldn't fight with anyone's negativity. My energy goes down the drain with such mentalities. You can't tell anything to these people them and whatever you say they believe you are a wonder, but for them everything is impossible, they can't do it, they fail. Everyone leaves them. I give up on negativity and destructive behavior. I leave the manipulation behind. They are all unhappy, unlucky. Do you know what's bad? That in some people life nothing happens and they are responsible for it. There is no "I can't," there is only "I don't want to," and if you don't want I can't interfere with anyone's decision. I can't make you happy, I can't act in someone else's benefit. Life is the way you want to live it, the way you want to believe it. There are people who don't want to change, they only want your attention, they want to complain and to manipulate (generally speaking), because if you really want to change, you do it, you don't look for excuses. Do you realize how simple it would be if all people who suffered would choose the simplest solution? Yes, they would be condemned to happiness! But no. Many have chosen the complicated way (as the majority calls it) and they moved forward with teary eyes, clenched teeth and fists. Some have endured all the pain that in order to feel fulfilled and happy, and difficulties became opportunities and their story turned into a success story!"

My opinion: "When you play different roles and you get into other people's life story, you forget who you really are." Choose to exit the games that others want you to play so you can stay connected with your divine essence. It's the only way you will stay centered in your being, and will merge with the Divine Self. True love doesn't seek to connect, to control or to enslave, but to liberate, to give strength and to leave the others free to find their own truth.

Do you think you can live detached without looking in the mirror? Without getting reflected in the world? It is possible only if you love yourself very much. That means to love every part of you without sabotaging yourself. But on the other hand, the mirror has its part. You can see in it what you still don't accept at yourself. Sit in front of yourself!

Choose to always act in your favor, to lean through an optimistic attitude towards you, in whatever situation you find yourself. Dare to defend yourself! How? Free yourself from negative people who negatively influence you and try to bring you in the middle of their drama just because they are not able to be responsible for their life. I know you can defend your divine rights. It is your birthright to really believe in yourself! Step away from people who suggest otherwise with their attitude towards you and who sabotage you and try to make you less confident.

A psychologist, psycho-spiritual counselor, Bowen Therapist Licensed Expert advises:

"Dear friends! Today I invite you to start your day with the statement: "I have always been self-valorization." Saying these words slowly as if permeates every cell of your physical body, as it would rest within your being, you will activate within yourself a state of high self-esteem. When you value yourself, you get to love yourself. When you love yourself, in fact, you declare your own value, ancestral uniqueness and divine spark. When you declare yourself valuable, you can love others around you because you see their ancestral value, divinity and uniqueness. When you value yourself, you no longer give those around you the responsibility of giving you value, because they can't enter inside your mind and soul to see what you have in there. Only you know what's inside yourself, but through facts and behaviors you sent on the outside what you have inside. So, self-knowledge leads to valorization and valorization leads to self-love. Choose to see your unique value in what you do, think and speak and you will permeate the earth with the high vibration of love. Good luck in working with yourself."

A friend of mine puts it very nicely, "In order to get to fulfill your most ardent and profound dreams, it is necessary to know yourself. And not superficially or well, but extremely well. To get inside yourself, in the deepest places, where all your fears and conditionings hide, but also where all your hopes and dreams hide."

Have this dialogue with your inner self:

— Who is your best friend? Be honest!
— Your best friend, I ask you one more time. It's YOU! Who are you? You are LIFE itself! You are the Source of Love!
— Your mind confirms you: but there are so many people who are hurt from love, betrayed, with a crashed soul, losing self-confidence and hope!

— But it's not love that betrays and hurts them, people do! Love stay with them, even if the loved one departs. And, what makes our heart beat if not love? I love to savor my early morning coffee, I love everything that surrounds me, and I love the lime tree in front of the window, the blue summer sky, the dew on the grass. I love! And the lime tree rewards my love with its scent every June, the coffee rewards my love chasing away the sleep, the clear sky and the grass give me peace. If I were not to love, what would I be? What would be the reason to live? My best friend? It's the one that gives you every day a reason to smile!

Now write on a piece of paper 10 things you like about yourself. Common!

This is the beginning that helps you become aware of your qualities and from here you can take the first steps towards your dream!

1. Perseverant!
2. Intelligent!
3. Charismatic!
4. Attractive!
5. Ingenious!
6. Honest!
7. Beautiful!
8. Disciplined!
9. Loving!
10. Strong!

Yes. You can overcome your limits, too. You can be an extraordinary person! And you can create great things with your energy! You can be what you want! You—the one who is reading these lines now. I am talking to you; I don't just throw words on a piece of paper, just because I have nothing else to do, or because I just fancy writing. I write because I want every soul that reads this book to make profound changes in their consciousness. It's a support that it will help you become what you want. Be an example to the others. It matters enormously for those who seek to change their life from an ordinary and meaningless one to an extraordinary and meaningful one. I'll explain with real examples everything that happens to your life in order to help you understand that you can also do this inner work with yourself, until you have the life that you desire.

I want you to believe that your whole life is supported by the Divine Spirit. That every step you take is a step that Divinity takes through you. That everything you live is perfect just as it is. That you should never worry because your life is in God's hands.

You are the most wonderful, most special, most beautiful creature God ever created. For who could reject such greatness? Not even God could find fault to such a being.

The first and the most important step in having a fulfilling life is to be aware of your value. You must confirm to yourself with every occasion that you are strong, honest and integer with yourself. Just because you fell many times or because others, stronger than you, pushed you into the bus, it doesn't mean you are a person without personality. On the opposite, you become aware that you are not afraid anymore of anything and anyone. You pushed your limits; you got out of the shell of your limited life. Thanks to all those who pushed you so many times into the abyss, you notice you became what you are now. So you have to thank them. Forgiveness becomes a way of living. It's a quality you develop. You changed and nothing seems difficult to you when you encounter another challenge. You love challenges so much you can't live without them. Life challenges you not to fight with it, but to love it so much that you will make a masterpiece out of it. Be the architect of your life and give your best so you can have the life you want.

There are many ways people come to have a fulfilling life. I noticed that sometimes this statement is not very well understood. I will explain in my book why this confusion is created.

Entrepreneurship is a subject that has always fascinated me. So much so that in the present moment I continue to improve myself in this area. This was why I specialized in various fields of business. Not accidentally I studied accounting, trade and human resources as subjects in college.

I still support the idea that entrepreneurship is a characteristic of those who are really creative. They act and create the reality that they want. They don't expect the world around them to change, they don't expect the state to take good decisions for them, and they don't expect anything from the others. They are the ones who have taken responsibility of their life. They stopped blaming the people from the outside. They are aware of the inner strength they possess.

When they don't know their true value, people make compromises to get attention, appreciation or love from the others. Because they compromise with themselves, they won't be satisfied, no matter how much they will get from others.

True fulfillment comes when a person is himself and the feedbacks they receive from others are a direct consequence of their true value.

We all want a different life, but few of us do something about it. If you remain in your comfort zone without making changes in your life, it is impossible to create a different reality. Change starts with yourself. The questions you have to answer are: "How do you manage to change something? What do you need to do to become what you want? What are the concrete action steps that need to be done to have the life you desire?"

As I said before, the most important thing is to know what you want from life. Once you set your goals start acting. Do you want to become a leader in your field? Then you must get in contact with such people. Do you want to have an open mind? Do you want to see if you are still driven by beliefs that limit you? Every life experience shapes you. I'll tell you something new about yourself. You are in constant transformation and development.

Whatever the present moment, if you are not satisfied with your life now, you will never be. The dissatisfaction is not related to what happens in your life, it's just a habit that doesn't allow you to enjoy what you have and it doesn't matter how much you have, you will always feel something is missing. Your chances of success in anything you do can always be measured by how much you believe in yourself.

Good observation! In the first book I wrote, I told you how important it is to set your dreams. Without them, your life is meaningless and has no direction. Perhaps you've been thinking for about a year what you want to do with your life and certainly you think how to make you dreams come true.

Even if you have no idea, don't panic. There are solutions but they need to be found. How? I asked myself the same question. First, look for people who inspire you. People who have done something with their life. Watch them to see how they think and what they do to fulfill the dreams they believe in with all their being. If you can't find such people around you, don't be sad. They are somewhere, but you have to look for them. Where? Exactly where you don't expect it.

I found such people and they motivate me enormously. They all have similar stories. The majority of them will tell you how they started the business that now is very successful, how they evolved professionally to get where they wanted, how much effort and energy they put into it.

I discovered with amazement that you don't need money to fulfill your dream. Yes, you understood correctly. You really don't need money. Money doesn't exist. Money is just the end result of the work you put every day into your dream.

They believed in their dream so much that it didn't matter how many difficulties and obstacles were in their way. In their mind and soul there is one goal: I must succeed, there is no "I can't," only "I don't want to." Anything is possible if you truly believe it.

In the new energy, everything works in reverse from what you were used to. If you keep going in your old style, you'll see that the longer and harder you work, the less you will have. Money will flee from you because you don't want to understand that it comes to you only when you do what you really like. It's impossible not to like something you could do easily. You need to get out of your head that you have to work for money. Think! What would you like to do all the time without expecting money in return? What activity or service can you offer the world without asking anything in return? What can you do with love for the world?

Once you have decided what you really want with all your heart, act. How? Good question! First, you have to work with yourself at few important aspects. Eliminate the barriers that stop you from acting. These are:

1. Delay. You're not disciplined in what you want to achieve. You fail to give up everything that seems urgent in your life in favor of what is truly important to you.
2. Lack of self-confidence and in the activity you want to do.
3. You don't have the courage to do anything with your life. So learn to be brave. Handle every situation. Put your mind to it and think about what you have to do in a completely new situation. Search, ask, and insist! Some people might not pay any attention to you. Ignore

them. You must be persistent and convince them that you are the best and you really want to do what you set your mind to do.

4. You enjoy your comfort zone. It's not a good solution to stay in bed, without thinking for one second in your life what you have to do to be happy. You are young, you have the whole world at your feet, don't stop at such young age. Be active according to your age. Don't stop at a boring job, with money enough only to survive from day to day, with a life that brings you no joy.

5. Inaction. Act! Have the courage to explore the world. Who should you be afraid of if you are always with God? Believe me, nothing bad can happen. Always, without exception, you have the divine protection. The main condition is to listen to the voice of your heart. It whispers softly all you need to do.

6. If you do not have enough confidence in your strength, try to do something in addition to the job you have in this moment. Working on your dream day by day, certainly in one year time it will evolve and I am sure money will come too. What greater joy then what you do fills your soul with happiness?! To see firsthand how your work changes the life of tens, hundreds or thousands of people.

7. Don't you ever be afraid of anything. All the fears you feel are illusory. They don't really exist at the level of your True Self. The source of all fears is living separated from your ego. You are one with God, one with the Divine Spirit, which has no beginning and no end. It has no shape, because it is infinite and immeasurable. It's just there, beyond all forms and in all forms. Just because you can't see it, it doesn't mean it doesn't exist.

The key is to make the first step…today. No matter what your project is, start TODAY!

Start cleaning a draw of your desk… today.

Start setting a goal… today.

Start listening to motivational audio materials… today.

Start reading good books that help you progress… today.

Start saving and investing for your prosperity… today.

Write a letter you supposed to write long time ago… today.

…Or whatever you want to do, start TODAY!

"What did you do today for your dream? Your financial freedom won't be handed to you. Your six-pack doesn't come if you only turn on the other side instead of going to the gym. Your soul mate won't be knocking on your door asking you to move in with you. So? What did you do today that matters for your strategy for having a better life? Today you put a brick at the base of your new lifestyle?"

Now that you understood that you can fulfill your dream without money, you can get back to work. Make a strategy, a plan of action. Inform yourself in the smallest detail what steps you need to follow to achieve your dream. It might take a year for your dream to take shape. Be patient and trust that all will be well. Work for your dream without stressing yourself about the lack of money.

Surely, money will come exactly when you need it. You will probably ask me: how will money come if until now they hadn't?

Simple. In the new energy, money comes. You need to get used to the idea. It comes exactly when you need it. Until now money didn't come to you because you didn't know what to do with it. Now you know! Certainly, this statement really angered you and you will say: do you mean I didn't need money? I have always been looking for money, I always wanted more money. Really? I don't think so. Then why do you stay in a job that limits you? Why don't you do what you really like? Why don't you change your thinking and your attitude? Why don't you read some books about how money works? Why don't you do all these things? Or, if you do this, why don't you put them into practice?

Be sure money will come when you do what you like. Only at this point money will start coming to you. Otherwise, you block it. Sabotaging yourself, you sabotage your money and it will go further and further away from you.

I know you are still confused and you will ask me: where will the money come from? From Heaven? Do I find it in the street? Will I win the lottery?

Dear friend, I confess that this is how I thought. I doubted the divine force that is in my heart. I didn't trust that the God in me will do everything for me. I hadn't stepped aside to allow Him to work through me.

That's all I can say: money will come. Your soul will create some opportunities. Maybe you will borrow money from someone. Maybe someone will help you for free. Maybe someone expects money from you when you will have it. If I met such people, for sure you will meet them too.

I'll give you an example from my life: I wrote my first book. Then I wondered what to do with it. The answer came through a video on the Internet. There I discovered the one who brought a high energy value to my book, the person who corrected the book. I call her doctor in letters.

I put down in my diary her internet page. I hesitated to contact her because I knew I didn't have enough money to pay for the work she performs. I sat and I wondered. When will I have money unless I do something to generate money? The answer was never. At that moment, I decided to contact her. I ask, I talk, and I act. It's as simple as that. I gave her the book to correct it without thinking what I'll do next. If I took the time to think for longer, probably my dream would take shape and wouldn't be fulfilled.

It was close to the winter holidays. I decided to have Christmas at my sister in Ireland. At the time, I was in England. I had no money, but an opportunity appeared. I washed cars. I bought ferry tickets and went to Ireland. I had many surprises. I received money from my parents and my brother. Of course, I received lots of presents from my sister, too. She cleaned her closet and gave me lots of very nice clothes. I was very happy. I couldn't believe how beautifully the Universe worked for me. Just because I came out of my comfort zone I received money and everything I needed at the time. I paid my friend and I continued on the path to fulfill my dream. I read my book again and I felt the need to make major changes to it. At one point, I felt that a big change had occurred. My current book was no longer the same one as the one I had given her to proofread. To be sure I didn't have grammatical errors I gave it once again to be checked. With what money? I never thought for a second. I knew that somehow money will come. My friend finished proofreading the book and gave it back to me. She said that her passport had expired and I didn't have to send her any money right away because she couldn't withdraw it from the bank. I could not believe how beautifully the Universe was working for me and how much patience it had. I still had no money.

Then the situation in England became more difficult for me. I felt that my place was not there and I didn't manage to make the money I wanted. Why? Because I was doing something I didn't like. So I decided to go back home to Romania. The old problem occurred again. Where could I get money for my plane ticket and my trip? A new opportunity was created to work hard for money getting out of my comfort zone where I was completely blocked.

Arriving in Bucharest, I met for the first time with my dear friend. Finally, the moment had come to meet her in the flesh. I used quite a lot the communication via e-mail. At that time, I gave her the money for the work she had done for me.

Meanwhile, I gave my book to a publishing house. That time, I didn't thought about where I would get the money to publish the book. I was sure it would come exactly when I needed it. Until then, I could work with love for my dream. And this time I also found an absolutely extraordinary parson. His kindness can be felt from thousands of kilometers away.

Then I thought about how to sort out the book's cover. Where will I get the money to pay for a genuine and wonderful drawing? I got in touch with the artist who drew the cover of my book. She is a genius in the art of drawing. She gave me the cover of "Your Inner God" as a present. Things were working in a simpler way than I could have ever imagined. You can find wonderful people with big hearts everywhere. You just have to find them and to have the courage to approach them.

Then I thought. What do I do with my book after I publish it? Who do I sell to? Or how do I sell it? No one would know it if I weren't to advertise it. It may be the best book, but if it isn't where it should be you won't have the expected results.

To find answers to these questions I got in touch with a businessman who knew exactly how money are made, how you have to promote your product and the steps you have to take in order to see your dream fulfilled.

I found a fantastic man. He offered me the answers to my questions with all his heart. He told me exactly what to do so I can reach my goal. I never imagined that I would find so many wonderful people who will help me to fulfill my dream. For free. Nobody asked me for money or for something else. It can be done, my dear friend. You only have to want it.

I'm not selling you bedtime stories; I tell you exactly what you can do. You don't have to take me as example; there are thousands of other examples around you. Search and you will find! Ask and you will receive the answer.

Love life and the people around you and life will love you just as you deserve. The universe is at your feet. It serves you in the best way possible. But it is waiting for your orders. It will give you everything you need only if you tell it what you want. Believe that the God inside you will take you exactly where you deserve. You're never alone. Your steps, your heart directs you towards the supreme wellbeing. Don't look back at what you have left behind. Move forward. With full trust in life. Life loves you and it wants what's best for you. Nobody wants to hurt you. Nobody wants you to suffer or to be poor. Just the fear of yourself can manipulate you so much that you think you don't deserve to have a different life. Only the reality around you can convince you that you can't live a different life. Courage! The change of your life begins with you. It doesn't matter if those around you are not like you. It doesn't matter if no one trusts you. It doesn't matter that your life has no meaning in this moment. You can always change the reality you live in. The quality of your life it's only up to you. It's up to you what thoughts you want to have in your mind and what you want to do from this moment on.

The secret is universally valid for everyone: Act! Without action, nothing happens; nothing falls from heaven, a plane maybe, but nothing more. When you know what you want to do with your life, start taking the steps you need and you will see how the Universe brings all the tools you need to achieve your dreams. Life loves you, it is at your disposal, but you have to do something about it. If you don't know how to act, learn from those who had already done something beautiful with their life. Pay attention to them; watch them step by step to learn how to think in order to believe what your soul wants.

If you have a dream, find a way to fulfill it. If you don't have a dream, it's just an excuse. Without goals, dreams, faith, light and mission, you have nothing to think about. It is logical that when you rise above your condition and you think of high scale, you also attract opportunities that help you reach a different situation than that of the victim!

The universe reflects in you, and you are the universe itself, but not a miniature one as you may believe. So stop waiting. Accept today your unlimited power. Learn from every experience and notice how your attitude creates everything that happens around you. And most important, understand that being part of the whole, you have a greater power than you have ever imagined on what Whole means. Be as you would like the others to be and "miraculously" their attitudes, thoughts and behavior will be different and nice.

A special woman, a psychologist, a Bowen expert therapist, says:

"Dear creator friends! Today I invite you to start your day with the statement: "I have always been fulfilled." Saying these words slowly as they would rest within your body, as they would be part of your being, you will activate within yourself the state of fulfillment, the state in which you will work to fulfill your life and the activities around you. When you live this state of fulfillment, you know exactly what, when and how you should do all the activities in your reality in order to bring the inner joy which is the natural state of the Divine Self. Inside, you have all the resources to live the fulfillment in everything you do. Be aware that you are fulfillment and you will accept the fulfillment in everything and everyone. Success in your work with yourself."

"You have a purpose. You are part of the creation, and nothing here is useless. Including you. Even the most insignificant blade of grass has a very definite purpose. It exist, therefore it's impossible to be useless. And if the blade of grass has a purpose, you definitely have one. And your purpose is to live happy and fulfilled and to share this to all those around it."

An encouraging message from a beautiful soul. The creator of the cover for the book "Your Inner God":

"Hello!

Today is a special day for me, although I don't celebrate anything in particular. Maybe just a decision I took more than five months ago, the decision to start a business, a decision taken with the hope that it will help me to keep doing what I love to do, to draw, to enjoy art, to explore new ways to do that.

As time passed, I came to appreciate enormously that I discovered my talent and my passion for drawing since I was small and I got to work at it long enough to turn it into a skill.

I have come to appreciate that because many of the wonderful moments in my life were related to drawing. It's about those feelings of contentment, fulfillment, joy, curiosity, enthusiasm that bring with them the energy to get things moving.

Then there are those shorter or longer moments when time seems to stop, when things and life begin to be meaningful, the movements are much easier and more pleasant, the words like "work" or "should" no longer find their place, although a large amount of energy is consumed.

It's that lovely fatigue at the end of the day that I knew it came because my hands created something beautiful.

It's a pleasure to put my head down on the pillow and to wake up impatiently the next day to start over.

In addition to that, I can mention all the connection I have created with people I share my passion with, the moments spent together and the things we do together.

If you have at least one thing that you do with pleasure, joy and dedication, I'm sure you had this kind of moments and you know what I'm talking about.

Going back to the reason I write all these things, I was fortunate enough to find a way to continue to do what brings me joy and I was even luckier, I think, that I chose to take this step and to attend this business course that ultimately led to the birth of my site.

The course lasted three months, during which I had great experiences, I met people as crazy as me (in a good way, of course), I learnt many things, I experienced and I enjoyed the journey and the transformations it has brought into my life."

This beautiful creature chose to express herself through her talent. She decided to create a new reality. One in which she could do what her heart feels with passion. What are the steps she took?

1. She discovered her genius.
2. She decided to attend the business course so she can learn from others what to do to make her dream come true.

3. She turned her passion into art. It's not enough to have a talent in the art of drawing if you don't create a small business out of it. Besides the fact that you're a pretty creative person—which might mean for others that you have your head in the clouds—you must also be a small entrepreneur. Your imaginary and creative world must intersect with the real one.

4. Thanks to her perseverance and her strong inner desire, she did everything in her power to see her dream come true. She was the one who took this decision; those around her only supported it. Nothing else.

5. She didn't forget to thank herself for the decision she took, for the effort she put into it. It wasn't luck that she worked on becoming what she is in the present moment.

There is room for everyone, even if they share the same passions. People are different; everyone is unique in their way. This is the divine intelligence and no one can be compared to anyone. Don't compare yourself to someone else. How can you compare yourself? You are you, the other is someone else. Because you are not the same you can't compare to each other. Perhaps you were told, you are taught to constantly compare yourself with others. Directly, indirectly, consciously, unconsciously you live comparing. And this leads you to disregard yourself and your own value. There will always be someone more beautiful than you, taller, healthier, and more different than you and you will burden yourself with all the shortcomings which you discover in you if you keep comparing yourself with someone else.

There are many people. At one point, the comparison with all the others will destroy you. And when you think that at birth you had a beautiful soul; your being wanted nothing more but to flourish, to become a golden rose, and you didn't allow it. Let go to the burdens you carry always comparing yourself with others, forget about them, regain your innocence, and regain your childhood. Reborn again and look through the eyes of your soul at God's creation.

It is very important to know how to choose the people in your life. You will live in a similar way to those around you. You can do great things with your life if you really want this. The inner motivation must be extremely powerful. Even if you don't have examples around you, no one stops to look for them. Look until you find what you want. I found when I searched for it and for sure you will find too. That means that you always want to get out of your comfort zone. Challenges and changes are your best friends. Your life is full of action and can't afford to be lazy if you want to fulfill all your dreams.

Life changes occur only when you do something about it. Nothing comes by itself. Try until you succeed. Do you find it difficult? If yes, I'll give you bad news. Only the winners succeed in creating a truly fulfilled life. If you wish to follow their footsteps, keep up with them. Stop complaining or pity yourself. You don't have time for that. Time is very precious to waste it this way.

Another clear indication that any dream can become a reality is confirmed by another beautiful soul. Her life experience and her example is a motivational engine. She created a special program for you to help you change your life step by step.

She says: "In the last two weeks, I had a wonderful experience which taught me that we should never lose hope. Never give up on our dreams. And always be prepared to receive what we want. Nothing happens without a reason and everything happens at the right time.

But what do we do until that moment comes? What do we do until our dream comes true? LIVE every moment!!!! We live life to the maximum with what we have in it at the time. We don't wait until we get what we want to be happy. We are happy and grateful for every moment we have.

And when we least expect it, our dream will appear before us, apparently by accident, but certainly at the right moment. And when this happens, we will immediately know that this is what we wanted and what we were waiting for so long.

Maybe you don't understand me, maybe you are wondering what I am talking about here. It's OK. When the right time comes, you will surely understand. All I can tell you now is never lose hope in your dreams. Always have it clear in your mind what your dreams look like, what you really want (in every area of your life: social, personal, professional, etc.). And fully live every moment, every experience, enjoy everything life brings you. Without asking yourself, "when will I get what I want?"

Enjoy life as it is, do what you feel when you feel, without asking yourself too many questions. And believe that you will get everything you want when you are ready to receive it. Every moment I am grateful for everything I live. And it seems that life rewards me for the courage of living authentically, to be myself and do what I feel, in agreement with who I really am.

It's so simple, still so very few are doing it! Why?

Why is it so difficult to be authentic and to live our way?

I encourage you with all my being to follow your heart and to begin to live authentically. Do what you feel, be yourself. And life will reward you infinitely more than you could hope. Believe me!!! I live it every moment! You can do it too! Dare to be YOURSELF!

A fulfilled person is the one who lives according to their own values.

Hugs from the sunny Egypt."

"The things you wish for and you don't have yet are OUTSIDE your current comfort zone."

Comfort zone

Strong points:

• Safety
• Familiarity
• Relaxation

Weak points:

• You don't learn new things
• You don't develop yourself

- You risk to become the prey of your own behavioral patterns
- Routine

Outside your comfort zone you can get:

- Change
- Diversity
- Novelty
- Adrenaline

To succeed, you have to be more rigorous, more organized, make clearly the difference between mediocrity and excellence. You must learn to get out of your comfort zone whenever you need in order to regain your enthusiasm for moving forward! How much? As much as you want. The greater your dream, the comfort zone becomes non-existent. This applies until you get as high as you want. Looking from the top, you can you set a new comfort zone depending on your new expectations. Until when? Until you'll want more from this wonderful life! Take advantage of it and don't hesitate. Be determined!

I like the change, and the others have nothing to do it and they have to accept this side of me. Life means evolution. I change my activity, my job, my residence, I specialize in something, and then I find that studying another area it would be more useful.

I am brave. I have a strong character. I don't stumble in details, I prefer to go straight to the target. I have specific goals and don't move further away from them. When I start something I finish it. I like to take a walk and to see foreign countries, and if I like what I find, I might move there, of course I don't know for how long. Curiosity pushes me to find out everything that moves. I am always active and open to new experiences.

I am very correct, I can't stand injustice and I keep my verticality, even when there is pressure on me. I don't know what compromise is. I am a rational person. I don't give in to impulses. Intuition helps me a lot, and I count on it when I'm in contact with other people.

I'm good of making jokes and bring people out of their numbness. I enjoy what I have, yet I always seem to want something else.

I love everything new and travelling is for me the best solution to recharge my batteries. If there are limits imposed to me or I feel I can't stay blocked in a particular place or job that doesn't satisfy me, I turn 180 degrees without blinking, because I am flexible and I adapt easily anywhere.

Now, few opinions with regards to the attitude a winner feels when they are for a long time outside their comfort zone:

◊ "Every foot in the back became a step forward! This is the reason I appreciate the ones who always had obstacles in front of them! The cozy comfort is not a trampoline, neither it motivates sufficiently (we are quiet OK this way!), but we have to be honest and to admit that "self-infliction" sound a bit masochistic and very few of us have the courage to do this consciously. I would say there are very few of us in this category, but if we at least try to understand the meaning of the losses and to use the best of the situation, we are already winners. Anyway, the soup doesn't stay warm for long. At some point it goes off and we will have to make another one!"

◊ "I, for one, since I was a little girl, I knew pain, I had to manage and go through many situations that frankly I didn't deserve, but today I can say smiling that they brought me down this road! Every time when things get clear and I reach my goal, I need to move on and find something more intriguing! I simply cannot sit doing nothing! I can't settle for less! And the best engine sometimes to rise above is pain. Often, I found myself alone provoking painful situations that motivate me, and wake my ambition and fighting spirit up! Perhaps, at some point, I will get tired, but I'm young and I want the best from life. I want when I'm 60 to be able to say with a smile: "Yes, I really loved my life!"

◊ "The conclusion I reached after learning the life stories of those who have managed to overcome their condition: they all have a common start, a great pain caused by certain shortcomings and inconvenience that motivates them to do something with their life, to become successful."

◊ "Another good motivation is when you have no choice or when you set a goal and decide what your priorities in life are. You follow them more, since you make sacrifices for it. You don't need to get a full body tattoo so you won't have any chance to get hired. But make sure that you won't get back to the classic solution: employed by someone."

◊ "You're absolutely right and I know it from direct experience. I spent years in a warm, comfortable and underpaid job simply because of the comfort and safety of tomorrow. I was afraid to let it go although the income was barely enough for me to pay the rent and to live mediocre. I wasn't on vacation for years, I never got a car, I wasn't married, I never dreamed of having my own place. Until one day when I was laid off and I had no income.

That moment was the one that mattered most, perhaps out of desperation, but also motivated by the lack of income, I went alone to Cyprus. I gave up everything: friends, family, girlfriend and I set a new target: I will not return home until I have enough money to buy my own apartment. I was away for three years, but I reached my goal! This was the step that changed my life and the moment from which everything started to flow in the right direction. Now, after ten years, I have my own apartment, I am married, I have a son, I have a car and a happy life. I often wonder: if I didn't receive that kick, where would I be today? Probably I would be starving and employed in a public service, in a warm, comfortable and underpaid job."

◊ "I'm 18 and I wanted to run a marathon by the age of 20! I have to train hard, but I thought it was the challenge of my life. What would life be without challenges?"

◊   "I said it, when you no longer stand the situation you are in, you will "wake up" from that uninterrupted sleep when you haven't done anything but finding excuses and feeling guilty etc. And you get up, you quit weeping and you act (even if you don't know what to do). Only at 25 years I really saw myself in the mirror. Only after ten years when I struggled and I turned my life into the heaviest burden that I carried with me everywhere. Only then I saw myself beautiful because I really am beautiful. Only then I smiled to myself and I said: "My dear, it's time to be the happiest being on earth! What fault, what pain, what punishment? Nothing else matters! Be YOURSELF!" The idea is simple: change comes only when you are willing to give up on everything you know or think you know about yourself and start living knowing you deserve the best and the most beautiful things in this world! When you will take this step, you will be supported and have everything to gain, you will see how miracles happen and they happen to you!"

◊   "I was determined to change my life and to give up everything: friends, love, comfort, parental home, money, job, laziness, and excuses, everything that could keep me back. Only then, when the pain was unbearable, when I got angry on the whole situation and everything seemed so pathetic that there was no other alternative but to succeed in getting where I wanted. No excuses that I can't do it, I don't know, it's too hard. They don't exist any longer. Even today when I have the tendency to delay something, I motivate myself thinking (or even writing) what I could lose if I don't act immediately."

◊   In my case, it took two years to realize that I have to take the bull by the horns and not let others do this thing for me. In the present case, I gave up the job that brought me that monthly material comfort, which didn't allow me allow me to achieve my personal goals. So I took the risk to not have a secure monthly income and to start on my path and I wanted very much to succeed.

The fact that I have to pay my monthly rent and I have expenses gave me ambition to do what I want. Basically, I gave up that minimum level of comfort hoping for that maximum level of "comfort" given by fulfilling my dream.

I am in my last week at my workplace, I launched my own blog and although I didn't start writing articles yet, and I only had couple of discussion with potential clients, I already have my first orders in. orders I got in only after I quit my current job.

Now it's up to every person how they react when they are in difficulty, if they do everything in their power to get out of the situation or they stay there and accept to be cut into pieces.

There are many people who succeeded and, as you were saying, they gave up that little comfort in order to fulfill their dreams."

Dismiss your boss! Because you're better, smarter, more educated, more prepared, more experienced and sexier! Or because you deserve a better leader or a better businessman or a better life! Do you know your limits?

The winners have the great ability to turn pain into success. They don't see the pain as something negative, but on the contrary, it motivates them not to give up their great dreams. Pain, in another form, is nothing but love in disguise. From the greatest love, some experiences inflict pain so you can discover the genius within you, the power that lies hidden deep within your being.

If you want to defeat your fear, don't stay home and think of it. Go outside and act.

Many people will tell you to get rid of your fear; I say: "Accept it, be aware of its cause, and transform your fear, because the energy given to that fear up until now can be directed to a higher level of awareness where harmony manifests in its entire splendor. Whether you like it or not, you attract what you are."

Excuses are nothing else but lies induced by your fear.

What are the methods you will use to change the "landscape"? How will you prepare the ground for your massive success? What do you think? Can you have good results if you don't make a plan? No! Without a plan, you are without direction! You need to know what the steps are and especially where you want to get! If you don't make a plan for yourself, then others will do.

Wake up! Get rid of the big illusions that comprise your life. I always hear the idea that it's enough to have a desire and without stressing yourself out solutions come from Heaven. Or I heard the expression promoted by many people: "Wish for something, but feel no need." If you want to do something fabulous with your life remember for the rest of your life what I tell you now: "Desire without constant and permanent action is void."

What is the difference between two people with the same intellectual level, the same level of culture, intelligence, and beauty? The attitude! One evening, I was watching a show whose main characters were two pretty, interesting and clever girls, but who were also very poor. Their goal was to collect a sum of money to start a business, so they took it step by step. What "struck" me was their attitude that reflected in everything they did. One of them was pessimism in person and the other one was optimism personified. Then I realized how much your attitude can influence your life. The optimist was seeing herself doing something and trusted that she could get where she aimed and she succeeded; the other one only saw the half-empty glass and she was stopping herself from achieving her goals. Attitude makes the difference between a full life and one filled with frustration. Of course, a touch of realism doesn't hurt, but if we don't also see the ray of sunshine, we can't move forward in the dark. Be a winner! The conclusion: "If a person changes their attitude to what happens to them, then, with time, the nature of things that happens to them will change. Human perception to the reality of their life is what actually leads their destiny."

A winner is charismatic. It's a defining quality. Attitude and charisma are essential elements that guarantee your success in all areas of your life. A charismatic person counts on their extraordinary personal value, their sacred exemplary character, and enjoys great prestige. They are endowed, talented, and gifted.

One day, a man came to Buddha to tell him about the many years he devoted to meditation. He said: "I have meditated for 20 years and today I can levitate across the river." Buddha laughed and said, "You've wasted your time. For five bucks, you could cross the river by ferry."

Yes, massive action = massive success. Take a step forward and life will take trying to catch you up. Play "hard." It matters: 1.where you want to go; 2. why; 3. how; 4. what attitude you have.

Pain taught me why I was so afraid of death: because I never really lived. With cowardice, you can die little by little each day. A brave man dies only once; they look death straight in the eye and say: "I am ready. I did everything in my power. If the time has come, so be it."

Yesterday I heard a story told by Thay. A Zen master and his student lived in a temple. But they were so busy they didn't have time to go out for a picnic on the green grass. They thought of it several times but failed to do it. One day, going to a conference in a big city, the Master saw a funeral procession: "What is happening here?" he asked his disciple. And he answered: "Here is a picnic Master." Their only picnic when they die.

This story makes me say: "Yes, Leo, put up for grabs the money for your vacations, change the landscape, give up "pieces "of your comfort, but not the few well programmed "lazy days," when you set as goal just simply to learn how to sit doing nothing. Yes. That's hard too! To sit all day and enjoy you exist. To keep your thoughts in check, not to let them wander in the past or in the future; to plan. And to bring them into the present moment, to be one with the space, the time, and the body where you are. To feel like you've come back home, to your essence."

Someone said that the meeting between two personalities is like the contact of two chemical substances: if there is a reaction, they both are transformed. The existential alchemy is the one which gives meaning and ascendancy between two people. Surround yourself with people who make you smarter, not by comparison, but thanks to them.

A psychologist explained very beautifully and very simple what kind of behavior you must have to succeed to fulfill your dream. "What is the attitude that can help you fulfill your dream?

1. You will trust yourself once you take the first steps of action. You can also sit and imagine that you're confident and strong, but the results will be seen later and only when you'll start acting. So the solution is to do what scares you. Forget about others people's voices, they are scared and project their infirmities on you. You can do it! Don't try to climb one hundred stairs from day one, but one step can do wonders. As hard as the climbing is, remember why you want that dream. What is the purpose behind it? What inspires you?

2. No matter how hard it is, don't give up! If that is your goal and that is what you want, go ahead. You can make things easier if your mind is oriented towards the solutions and gains and you act now. People who have succeeded are those who persevered even when everything seemed useless.

"If man can devise a mechanism to fly at 12,000 meters above the mountains, then he can also find a way of thinking to lift him over a greater difficulty than a mountain."

3. The material gain won't come immediately, and, moreover, you will often have to take money out of your pocket for your passion. I know that no matter how fond you are of your dream, you also need money to come out of it, and for that you can search for a way to monetize your dream faster or to use your skills to earn money from elsewhere in order to support that dream. The question that you can ask now is HOW? Well, use your mind. Think. Calm, relaxed, oriented towards finding

solutions. How can I...? Search for solutions. Who thinks, finds solutions (if they agitate, they will find stress hormones).

And the first money time you make money out of your passion, dance, sing, shout. It might be a lot. Or it might be 3 dollars. The amount doesn't matter; it matters to see the results and to be grateful for it.

4. When you encounter an obstacle, use perseverance and thinking. Think about solutions and move on. Slow or fast, run or crawl, but don't stop there! Each obstacle hides in it a key that will help open other doors to your accomplishment. Look at the people who succeeded. Do you think they didn't encounter any obstacles? The bigger the success, the more obstacles they had. But they didn't stop.

Many people ask me why it has to be so hard and have so many difficulties. I believe that the so many obstacles are there to push you further; and they also contain the solution; and if things were much easier, life would have no criteria by which to choose the winners.

5. I know it's uncomfortable sometimes. You have to change many things, but start with small steps. Keep a dose of comfort, but educate yourself in increasing your skills. Think of your dream. What you do today determines what happens in the future. No matter how seemingly insignificant it might look, the choices of today build your path for tomorrow. Is it a path in agreement with your dream?

The difference between a hard way chosen by you and an easy one chosen by others or imposed by the rules of the society is that yours has a heart. It has life, joy and the seed of an achievement that will be useful to the others.

As much as you love the people in your life, you know better what you want and what makes you happy, and their fears don't help you too much. Instead, fulfilling your dream, you can show them your courage and you will be an example and they will dare to walk confidently on the path that has a heart.

Life is easy. Or it is hard. And there are also middle ways. But it depends on you how you look at it and how you persevere in fulfilling your dream. We all have the potential to reach the top of a mountain and shout I DID IT! The difference will be given by those who didn't stop when they encounter the first problems and continued to climb. Through the dark, fog and clouds. I wish you to have a heartfelt path which will enlighten your life and the life of others."

You can't let yourself carried away, you have to know the way! Take the best path! Take your dream as far away from where you started put it to germinate so tomorrow will find it in "green coating." Go with your dream near impossible. And once you're there ... go back to the sleep where you took your dream from and sleep having good thoughts! Rest your dream! To make it big, to grow its wings, to teach it to fly and then make your only permanent reality out of it!

Don't let anyone tell you can't do something. You have a dream, you have to protect it. People who are not able to do anything on their own will tell you that you're not capable. You want something, you get it. Period. Do you understand?

Your vision will become clear only when you look inside your soul. Who looks on the outside is dreaming of false illusions with their eyes open. Who looks inside, into their heart, wakes up. Being aware of who you really are, you can begin to bring into manifestation, into your reality, your dreams, not the ones of the others.

Your daily statement: "I give up on all fear and doubt. My life is so simple and easy." You have to get rid for good of the belief that there is a God whose desire is that you will be poor or whose purposes are served by keeping you in poverty. You must know what you want and to be clear. "Anything you want when you pray, believe that you have already received it and you will have it," said Jesus.

To live waiting for suitable occasions, without doing anything, it's like sitting in front of a closed door waiting for it to open itself. Until your dreams reach a physical manifestation you have to take advantage of every opportunity that comes your way. You feel the right opportunity that helps you to find something new about yourself and helps you get rid of some wounds that sabotage you. Every step you make it will help you for sure to make a step towards your dream.

To fulfill your dream, you need to take three steps:

1. Awareness. You know who you really are. You become what you want to be.
2. Action. Your Self will guide you your steps towards the fulfillment of your dream. Allow your mind to express through you.
3. Materialization. Your dream appears in your reality according to your actions.

A psychologist, psycho-spiritual counselor, Bowen expert licensed therapist says:

"Dear friends! Today I invite you to start your day with the statement: "I have always been Divine passion." Saying these words slowly as they would rest within your body, as they were part of your being, you will activate the state involvement. When you are passion, you always keep that activity on the first place of your consciousness, that situation that you manifest here and now. Passion is what keeps you awake today. It is the one that involves giving here and now and releases you from the past. When you are passion, you want to do something and only that thing. When you are just there, brilliant solutions emerge, and maximum efficiency in the minimum amount of time. Good luck in everything you do and be aware that you are the creators of your own reality."

Creativity comes from inner peace. Only at that moment the genius in you expresses in the most beautiful way. Life can be lived in a beautiful manner, it can be enjoyed as a journey, not as a desperate race to the final destination. The creator of the cover for "Your Inner God" explains on her blog alegsadesenez.com, what this means.

Creativity exercise:
"I was talking to a friend about mistakes. The idea of «making mistakes» feels heavy I the air when brought into a discussion, especially when you talk about a professional area as drawing is for

me and my friend. I think you know that sensation in your stomach when someone tells you did something wrong. Sometimes you get nauseas, you shake and you can't focus.

Maybe I am more emotional, but I felt these sensations several times during school, especially during college. That restricted my creativity and prevented me from trying new things, new techniques, ideas that I had, but I wasn't sure I can carry them out.

A mistake can be a scary thing and yet I realized that I can't learn anything new if I am not willing to accept that I can make mistakes. Hesitating, making sure I don't hurt my ego too much, for few months, maybe a year, I make a point in trying something new, a new technique, a new position, a new idea.

I am often surprised by what I can do and the beautiful results I've had. And there are many drawings that went wrong, but I learnt more than I expected. Returning to this seemingly childish exercise, I invite you to make mistakes. It's about allowing yourself be surprised by the results, not knowing whether they will be good or bad. I was asked at one point where do I get the ideas for my drawings, where do I get my inspiration from.

The truth is that ideas are the last thing that I miss. Ideas fly in my mind worse than birds in the sky. The question is not where you take them, but how to catch them, how to bring them to reality. First, I made it into a habit to write my ideas, no matter how quirky they might be, even if I don't have the necessary materials and the knowledge.

If I were a bit tidier, this habit would prove more useful, but even with my untidiness, the exercise proves to be as useful as possible. ART IS CREATIVITY SUPPORTED BY A GOOD TECHNIQUE.

In my last article I talked about technique. Today I balance it writing about creativity.

How do you get creativity?!

Practicing, the same you get any other skill.

We all have ideas. Just we don't have the habit to write them down on something. Maybe we think we will remember them; or they are not important enough; or they occur in a much too vague manner.

Ideas are like birds. They won't stay forever perched on your fence. They will fly away because they are born to fly free until they meet someone quite anxious to bring them to reality.

If you fear that you are not a creative person, my advice is get a notebook in order to write down all your good and not so good ideas. No one will stick their nose into your notebook, so don't worry, they are safe.

I tend to think that more than a natural feature, creativity is rather a muse if we mystifying things a little. It has to feel at home when is visiting us, to feel they receive our full attention so they begin to come more often, they become more talkative and they are coming with more pleasure to share ideas.

Let's play a bit now.

When I heard of this exercise, I wasn't convinced that it will work. It's something like finding known shapes in the clouds. But today I grabbed a pencil and a sheet of paper and I tried it.

The idea is simple: first, doodle on your paper as you like. I haven't drawn many lines because I was afraid I would tangle.

The idea is to learn to see what many others cannot see.

There is no question of realism, nor of the creation of an artwork.

Creativity is important, creativity only.

You also need to admit it is possible for you to make mistakes.

To be completely honest, it's hard to start a drawing with the thought that you have no idea what will come out in the end.

Being creative is a bit connected to this unknown ending. That's why I referred to creativity as a gift from a muse, something outside me or you. It's connected to the need to let yourself be surprised by the result and master your fear of making mistakes.

It is something that I, personally, remember every time I draw: TO MAKE A MISTAKE IS NOT A BAD THING. Moreover: TO MAKE AN ERROR IS ABSOLUTELY NECESSARY TO THE TECHNIQUE, BUT ESPECIALLY TO THE CREATIVITY WE TALK ABOUT TODAY.

It's an ordinary thing and very well known. Still, I feel the need to remind it to myself often.

Many people punish mistakes, but you be aware that you need them."

It's not enough to know it, we must apply it. It's not enough to want, you have to do. Action means to live fully. Inactivity is basically a challenge to life. Inactivity is to stay in your comfort zone, years and years, because you are afraid to be alive and to take the chances of expressing what you really are. Self-expression means to act.

"Sometimes, even creativity has its limits, depending on the individual... It can't give you ideas forever if you don't apply them. No it is not stupid either! At one point, it gets bored to provide you all good ideas that will be applied to others." Even if people laugh at you, take yourself seriously. The crowds laugh and ridicule what they don't understand and what's above them. What's the use of being immortal if the person can't use properly half an hour of their time?

Believe in your dream. Feel it! It's here already. Be sure of this.

Everything is much simpler than you think. Stop analyzing so much every situation or you will create problems that didn't even exist. Assess the situation and act. You can't change the things that you refuse to confront. Progress involves risk. To score a goal, you first have to let go of the ball.

I'll give you a few examples. It's morning. You wake up. You go to the bathroom. You take the toothbrush. You put on some toothpaste. Then you brush your teeth. If you think of all these steps, I think everything will become very complicated.

Another example: you want to take a shower. You get your clothes ready. You go in the bathroom. Get undressed. You switch on the water. You wash your head. You rinse. Then you wash your body. You get out of the shower. You get dressed. Then you dry your hair. You apply some face cream. Believe me, if you sit and think ahead to all the steps you need to take, I think you won't wash so often because everything would seem very complicated. Do you think when you do all these steps of action when brushing your teeth or taking a shower or when you dress? I don't think so. Act without using your mind, act instinctively. I know it sounds all too simple, but this how it is!

Today I have the life I dreamt of yesterday. It wasn't a small dream nor too big, but it was my dream. You have to learn to enjoy your successes before chasing new goals related to your much grander dreams. You are satisfied with your life in the present moment and this is the most important thing that can happen. You live now, you enjoy life now, you are now working for your dream, and you are acting now with small steps. Now is the only moment that matters.

A few very simple techniques that can help you fulfill your wishes:

1. You write your wishes on a piece of paper.
2. You put statements on the wishes (using the present tense).
   For example: "I am in the right job," "I am rich, successful and prosperous," "I am healthy," "My life is simple and easy," etc.
3. Pay attention to your wishes for a period of time so new neuronal patterns are created.
4. Detaching. When you detach, you have full faith that the Universe works for you, you are convinced that your wish or dream will be fulfilled. Doubt and distrust shouldn't exist when you think with your whole being that anything is possible.

It's up to you how vigorously you vibrate. You are capable of amazing achievements. Be aware of that, be grateful for the amazing power that lies dormant in you and use it.

Failure occurs only when you give up on your dreams. Until then, you are called "the victor" of your doubts, of your fears etc. You're a winner as long as you had the great courage to push aside mediocre opportunities and even good ones for an extraordinary opportunity. It doesn't matter what others think. It doesn't matter they can't think like you or don't have broader visions on their life. You are a winner if you had the courage to leave the restricted life that you have for the desire to exploit life of its full capacity.

Often people tend to be too realistic or too serious. Dreamers are too few, but those who dream the most are those who succeed in life at one point. Most people who are used to discourage those around them, those who call themselves "realists," they are not necessarily aware that they steal energy from those they discourage. Why do they do this? They discourage the others because they don't others to be better than them in any way, so they don't do what they are not able to do or simply to prove to us that something is possible when they think the other way around. They project on those in front of them their limited infirmities and mental patterns. And that obviously comes from their lack of self-confidence. They think that if they and their friends have failed, the others can't succeed either. If you are around such "realists" who claim they are down to earth, it would be advisable to get away from them and to regain your inner strength in order to fulfill your dream big.

The key question in this chapter is: "Do you live your dream?" What does a dream really mean? Because I noticed that this notion is not fully understood. For example: "My dream is to stay all day to watch movies, series, to be lazy." "My dream is to travel, to see as many places that you're your breath away." "My dream is to be with that man or with the woman of my dreams." But my question is: "What is your personal contribution on this earth? And do you do for that today? How do you we change people's lives where you live? What's your passion? What are you extremely good at?

Almost always the first steps are uncertain. Perhaps you don't remember, but surely you saw at the other little children when you grew up that the first steps were uncertain. You fell often. You probably got hurt and you'd been through many other adventures, but you have stood up again. So you learnt to walk. You manage to get where you are now. A grown person entirely responsible for your life. As you learn to walk, you will also learn to do anything else.

Try several times. Go walk a little, you might wobble, you might fall. Stand up. Try again with small steps, but more secure. This is the secret: stand up! As long as you do it, you will not give up and you will be picking up speed and confidence. This how you will achieve Success!

It doesn't matter how many people with "No" in their arms you meet. What's important is to reach your goal quickly. When you have deadline in your mind and it expired long time ago, you lose your patience. In conclusion, you don't get any response from those with whom you come in contact with, be sure someone will have to answer. You are not talking alone. Certainly, the question in your mind is: "Am I invisible?" If so, you have to somehow make yourself visible! How? You try all your options. It's true that when your mind is agitated, things don't come together. But even if you wait for the "salvation" still nothing comes out. I think I tried almost all options. However, I want to believe that there are still options I can test. I'm still testing them, I'll let you know which ones worked at the end of my adventure. It is important not to give up when you are at your hardest. Only then, you realize that you only have to do one more step to reach success. When no one believes in you, it's time to believe in yourself 100%. This is the last option and the safest.

Eventually, I don't think it's about serious or not so serious people, but it is simply the level of vibration and the level of consciousness of which you got to.

"When you feel that everything is going against you, think the plane flying against the wind, not with it."

Question: "I'm 38 years old and I have a well-paid job, but I'm tired not to have time for myself. I want to start my own business, but I am afraid of failure. I think every day and I don't know what to do, to take the risk or not?" What do you think?

The answers are: Sofia: "A bird in the hand is worth two in the bush." Ovidiu: "No I wouldn't give the bird in the hand, but I think that with good time management, you get time for yourself; I think we allocate time for ourselves and it depends on us how much we allocate. The business idea sounds good, but it is for those who like to risk in my opinion."

Bogdan: "To make the dough for bread. But you also have to put in nuts. You make your bread "job" branded, so you are not fired; I think this is the problem."
Dorina: "If you want to give up the time and money you have now, it's OK. You will berry yourself in taxes."

Monica: "I was in that exact situation, I was 36 years old, and I risked. It is extremely difficult on your own, but I have no regrets. I'm pro for your own business. In fact, after I was a corporatist, it was the only logical step for me. The alternative was to continue to be a guest in my own home, but with a good and secure wage, but I couldn't stand to live in a cage."

Bogdan: "The European Union declared war today; Angela Merkel ordered it today, on the national day of Germany."

Adrian: "I would prefer to start building a business while still keeping the current job and to make the transition smoother, not so sudden; it's a risk, however I think everyone should have several "arms" to support themselves, I mean more options, more opportunities at hand in case an "arm" weakens or disappears.

It's like baby's grasping instinct, the more things you start, the less you suffer when a link disappears or weakens, using the principle: "if something doesn't work, something else will."

Monica: "Plus it's good to consider one thing: in our country, if you become unemployed at around 40, you're done because recruiters won't even look at you, you are a fossil. That's unfortunately the mentality of many in the field of human resources. But if you have your own business, you work for yourself and no one can belittle you because you exceeded the «fatal» age of 35. On the contrary."

Me: "Monica, I got you perfectly. I am a human resources specialist and I gave up to this profession because the Romanian mentality is not the right one."

Laura: "Let's do what we feel and what brings us joy; I think this is how all energies of the universe support us."

Ciprian: "Don't take the chance."

Me: "If they managed to have a well-paid job, they will certainly succeed in business. Everyone is afraid to get out of their comfort zone and take risks. I recommend entrepreneurship courses that explain step by step how to start a business avoiding mistakes that can lead to failure. Is one to be employed and another to be an entrepreneur."

Ciprian: "If you have entrepreneurial skills, that's OK!"

Me: "If you don't have entrepreneurial skills, you form them, you change your way of thinking; this is the difficult part."

Alexandru: "I think having more details about the situation would be useful in this case. There is the possibility that the lady in question is under the influence of the trend of opening a personal business as a substitute for an unfulfilled professional life. The only detail we have here is "a very well paid job," combined with an imbalanced personal life. From my point of view, the imbalance is the cause, not the result. The external imbalance manifests as a result of an internal imbalance. I don't think giving up the job and starting a personal business would lead to solving the time allotted for her. At first glance, I'd be tempted to say: "You have so many positive examples that it can be done, so do it!" Let us not forget, however, that happiness, balance and peace come from within, for timeless and intangible reasons. As advice from a personal perspective: "developing your self-confidence, identifying the real cause of the imbalance (might be a cause provoked by thinking you are a "victim"), treating the actual cause, coaching (focusing on career)."

Monica: "The biggest difference when you get be independent is that you are the one seeking and eventually finding work, you don't have the boss coming to give you" tasks ", and you might have or might not have money. But if you want take a short trip to the mountain, you don't ask for permission! But you also have the reverse—when you feel like giving up, but you remember the freedom you have and you don't do it."

Tiberius: "If we think better, there is no perfect answer for this question. Failure is caused by something, we have to deal with the cause of the failure, and why this feeling exists, and then we deal with the others."

Violeta: "I was in a similar situation. But sometimes you have to be careful what you wish for, because I was "helped" to decide, I was made redundant. And I'm trying for more than a year to do something. I went in one direction, but it didn't work. Now I'm trying something else. It's hard, but freedom is very sweet, although money is very few. So be patient, be prepared for failure, to not abandon the idea to have your own business. You will always ask yourself how it would be if... You need to have some financial resources, not only investment ones. And if it really won't work, you get employed again, although I don't think you will ever want to do it again."

Adrian: "To take the chance of having success? This is the real fear, is even bigger than the fear of failure. If a friend were to ask you what you just asked, what would you honestly answer? Well, this is your answer, too."

Oana: "I say think ten times, not once. If you feel strong and you know you can fight regardless of the circumstances, then it's worth it, but don't be undecided and insecure because then you will miss any chance of growing on your own. It's great to be your own boss, but also much harder, it's much more stressful than being an employee. The important thing is to wish it from all your heart and, at one point, you will really enjoy your free-lancer status. See first if it's what you really want, so you don't regret it later."

Laura: "No risk, no chance!!"

Enache: "I think you're afraid of losing control! Sometimes you just have to jump in the water! You are not ready, that's why you're asking questions! When you'll be ready, you'll do it! If you are there, it doesn't mean you are strong, but just that you had an easy road!"

Viorica: "Is this a joke?"

Me: It's not a joke. "Life is better than a movie!"

I found that most people remain at the dream stage because they don't treat their dreams seriously.

You want your life to be simple, safe and quiet, and therefore the problems are taboo. You want certainty, not doubts, you want results, not experiences, without realizing that certainties are born from doubts and results from experiences.

When you realize that you don't have anything in your life, and I am talking about family, children or anything else, all you can do is to have the courage to risk your life in order to become a great man. You cannot allow mediocrity to put its print on your life. You can't allow people living without meaning in this life to dictate your life because they don't know a different life. Simply detach yourself from all those who pull you to become mediocre. Believe in yourself; believe you will succeed in everything you do, even if no one around you supports you.

There are situations in life that end up because your consciousness grew. When you raise up in vibration through your life experiences, the only people who stand by you are the ones who are on the same frequency with you.

For me, life itself is the way to fulfillment or to happiness. In my mind it has was been the desire to reach balance. Stable, unstable, or whatever. The idea was to accept what happens with serenity and to use every experience as a springboard. And everything happens naturally. You can't impose a scheme, certain steps; it is absurd because everyone has their own unique way to understand, to experience, to be. And when you read a book, if what it's written in there doesn't go through you, and you don't filter the information; if you don't absorb what you need as an individual; then it's just a useless reading stored in a folder in your short or long term memory. If it's not coming from you, then it's artificial and unnecessary. What comes within you, you see around you every second. If you accept and learn, it's enough. About "bad," I learnt that there is no such thing, just situations that you accept more difficult because of your pride. Give up your pride, give up all evil. I know it's easy to say and hard to do. I like to encourage people, I say "try, I know you can," but from experience I know that not everyone can, which is good, they are also part of this world and it will always be a stable, unstable, or indifferent equilibrium. I love life! Peace to you all!

Perhaps you are always animated of the rush of doing things. Just knowing is not enough, you must put into practice. You don't have to limit yourself of knowing. It is necessary to achieve.

"Take time for yourself and for your dreams. Set long term goals. Now, if you've set an ambitious goal, fragment it into mini objectives so you avoid feeling overwhelmed or crushed by the importance of the task and abandoning everything.

Remember that a mayonnaise is cut if you mix from the beginning the egg yolk with all the oil, however, if you pour the oil gradually you have every chance to succeed. That's because it's easier to solve a problem in stages, starting from simple things and going on with the more complex ones. Each performs, acts as an impulse to go on and reach the final result.

It's time to give priorities priority! It is your time!!

What did you answer when you were a child to the following question: "What do you want to be when you grow up?" Personally, I don't remember to have been asked. But I know that I was writing full diaries since I was little, without being aware that this ability is a passion. I was writing for myself. And my diaries were the most precious things. I am still the same in this regard.

Have you ever asked yourself what kind of people will you be once you reach your goals? I did!

Spread the word! It is time to share with others what you do and how this can help them or someone they know. You plant the seeds of possibilities. You never know when someone might be interested or you meet someone who might be interested. Share your divinely inspired gifts.

If you want to achieve something in life, you must believe that you will do it, you have to believe in yourself and in your potential.

If you don't believe in yourself, the only reason is that you convinced yourself of this. Thinking certain thoughts and accepting them as true, beliefs are formed. You were born believing in yourself, and if today you don't do it anymore, this basically means that throughout life you got to accept about yourself thoughts that others have inoculated into your mind and you considered them true. The only way you kept your lack of self-confidence was through your own thoughts, through your inner dialogue. Every person's inner dialogue is a clear indication of his belief in himself.

Someone says, "I have failed in more than 1.000 attempts in my career. I had lost more than a 100 matches. 20 times I was sure I will win, but I failed. I failed again and again. But this time I succeeded."

CHAPTER 3

HOW DO YOU TAKE CONSCIOUS DECISIONS?

"Everything is energy and this all it is. Just tune your frequencies to reality you want, and it will inevitably reach you. There can't be another way. This is not philosophy. This is physics."

"Good intentions are never enough. They are necessary but not sufficient. It is not enough to realize what you have to do if you don't get to do what you know is right to do. Your spiritual journey doesn't mean only to figure out who you really are, but it means to live at that. And this is true in thought, word and act. It doesn't mean you become ignorant to what is outside of you, but to change what you can change for the better. If you understand that you're more than this body and this life, this doesn't mean that you have to ignore the help that you can give someone or the good that you can do where you are. The true self-consciousness means freedom. But freedom is not the one that hurts the one next to you. So, detachment from the physical world doesn't mean ignoring the physical world. Being aware of this you get acquainted with responsibility, which is a wonderful thing, because true self-knowledge can never exist without responsibility."

The decisions you take, not the circumstances, mould your destiny.

You are now at this point in your life because of the decisions you have taken over time. You chose who to marry, what profession to have, you chose to be employed or self-employed, whether you have children or not, you chose your friends, your car, your wardrobe and so on. You choose what and how to think, you choose what kind of behavior you have, and you choose how to react to everything that happens to you.

You choose to see yourself as a helpless victim; you choose whether to let the past define you, if you want to stay in that point or if you want more for yourself. You choose every day to live exactly as you do—from the smallest to the biggest decisions—whether you allow yourself to be aware of it or not.

When will you learn to make conscious decisions? It is quite difficult to manage to take a conscious decision, because, until now, your mind has been set differently. I came home to Romania for couple of days. I made this conscious choice because I realized that the experience in England had sabotaged me a lot. It caused more sadness and suffering than happiness.

Yesterday, incidentally, I got a job offer which looked very interesting at first glance. In Greece, Santorini island. At sea, in the sun, a dream place.

Only today I had the clarity on the situation from yesterday. When you make a choice out of desperation, the experience is difficult. I realized that I wanted to take this decision to prove to my friend that I can handle it. Again I was forgetting about myself, again I wasn't first in my life. Again I forget what I wrote in my first book. Only when you take balanced decisions, without relating yourself to others, it is a good life experience. Someone tells me: "It's so good you became aware of this!" It's an elegant expression. But in fact, he wanted to tell me: "Thanks God you woke up!" My answer is the same every time: "Better later than never."

Otherwise, you're running around in a maze with no escape, without realizing why your life is so hard, why you suffer so much and why you fail to enjoy life. The answer is always simple, it's just you don't take it into consideration. Firstly, because you are set to believe that life is very hard. Secondly, you don't really believe in the existence of God. You still don't let yourself in his arms. You are still stubborn and go down this hard and painful road.

Now it's more difficult for me than it once was. Before, it was much simpler. I could easily blame the God from outside of me, life, the government, the weather. Anyone was guilty for my uninspired choices, but me. Now it's pretty hard to learn to be responsible for my life if all my life I was irresponsible.

Sometimes it's annoying to be aware that you are the Creator of your life. You are responsible 100% for your life. Surely, you ask yourself: "How the hell do I manage to make such bad choices?" When, in fact, I want a different reality? Is it something stuck in my mind that unconsciously leads me to this path? I must discover what is blocking me. I should know myself better. I must have a serious discussion with myself.

When the internal transformation had already occurred, you know what to do to create the reality that you want, only one thing remains standing as a pillar. ACTION. It's time to act according to your new vision about life.

I'll tell you a secret. The hardest part is to manage to climb the mountain. Once on top, no one will be able to take you down. That means you have a fantastic inner strength, and you feel it both literally and figuratively, how you can move mountains with the power of your mind. If you get tired on this road, stop and rest. Ask yourself honestly: 'Why do you continue to go on it? Ah, I got it: otherwise it's no way you could get to the top of the pyramid. You need all these life experiences to discover your inner strength that lies hidden inside you.

You can make conscious choices when you're connected with your inner source. If you are disconnected from the source, certainly your choice will be an unconscious one that leads to a painful life experience.

From a human point of view, a bad experience can be a divine message from the God inside you. When we look everything through the eyes of the soul, nothing is as tragic as it seems. I can give you an example. You go to work in a hurry, with the speed of light. At one point, you remember that you forgot to send in your petrol bills that your company will reimburse you for next week. An interior monologue occurs between the inner voice and your mind. The inner voice tells you to go back to the post office; the voice of your mind tells you to keep going because it is possible that on your way to work you will find another post office. What will you choose? Certainty or uncertainty? Let's say you absolutely trust your inner voice and you go back. You put the petrol bills in the mailbox and when the moment you start the car engine, one of the tires bursts. What are you doing? You get angry because you can't go to work? Or are you happy you escaped a great danger? You are aware that if you were on the highway at high speed, your car would crash. So, I ask you again! Are you happy you are alive because you listened to the inner voice or you curse and swear because you can't go to work today, which is why you won't get paid and the car fixing will cost a lot? How do you see this experience? As a joy that you are alive? Or as bad luck that caused you also big expenses? You can deduce from this example that a negative experience can be a great blessing. You are happy because you have chosen life and you can continue to enjoy it. Therefore, I always support the idea that God is not guilty for the tragedies and misfortunes in your life. You create them. I know you disagree with me on this and that is why I want to explain to you why it is time to change your vision on the bad things in your life. God always wants to communicate with you. But, most times, you don't allow it. You are very disobedient. You don't really believe in what you can't see, but only in what you already know. If your mind manipulates you in a way that makes you live in your own hell, that doesn't mean God doesn't love you.

Quite the opposite. He doesn't interfere in your life, because you are the master of it. He is convinced that this painful experience will wake you up to find out who you really are and to realize that you're not a petty and insignificant person. You are the miracle the Creator expresses trough and you have absolute freedom. If you are separated from the Source, automatically your life is out of love, abundance and happiness.

Be careful how you choose your words today! Verbal communication with people around us is important, and words have more power than we can imagine. A few words can completely change a person's life! And don't forget, smile!

How to make your choices? It is very important to address to people who resonate with your inner truth. If you address to anyone at random, they are likely to cut your wings so you can't fly as high. There are still people who are used to label those around them without knowing you and without knowing much about the subject in discussion. If the other people's opinion still affects you, it means that you didn't make the right choice. Your only concern is to change so much that you are not affected by the others' opinion. Everyone is free to talk and think what they want. Reproaches or criticism on you most often have nothing to do with you, but with their projections on you. Knowing all these, it is much easier to understand what happens to your life. You don't take all the frustration and lack of fulfillment of others upon you. Everyone is responsible to reach an inner balance that gives them a state of peace, tranquility and love.

Choose continuously your own freedom of expression, understanding that everyone is here for his own thoughts, words, choices and actions, with the freedom to keep in your life those people with whom you can grow harmoniously with and to quit those who seek to impede you, humiliate you, manipulate you, lie to you or use you.

Mind is a set of invisible forces, which are the thoughts, and thoughts influence our biology, and physical functionality. For this reason, if you have thoughts that are not in harmony with life and the cells in the body, if you have unbalanced thoughts, you destroy yourself unconsciously! These invisible thoughts modify the biology of your body. If something is wrong with you, in 90% of cases, this has nothing to do with the physical body, but only with your thoughts, with the way they "lead" your body and the damage they do. Your thoughts do this!

For a more accurate understanding of the phenomena that occur in your mind, you can think of the mind as a garden. You're the gardener. Don't say now that you don't like gardening because I will deduce that you identify yourself with your ego that has revulsion to such activities. Yes, even the gardener can be connected with the Divine Self. We are all human angels who just play some roles. Imagine that you are a great gardener who plants seeds of thoughts throughout the day. The big Garden is your own subconscious. What you now plant in your subconscious you will later harvest as effects on your body and destiny. Therefore, you have to clean up your garden, to remove all the weeds from it and to start planting a new crop with thoughts of peace, joy, goodwill and prosperity. Meditate on these qualities in silence and full of aspiration; accept them naturally in the conscious mind, the deliberating one. Continue to plant with perseverance these wonderful seeds form of thoughts until you reap a rich harvest and you are happy with the results of your work. Your subconscious is like a soil that nourishes any seeds you put in whether they are good or bad. Every thought is a cause and every action is an effect. Therefore, it is essential to guide your thoughts so as to create only beneficial effects.

You will always find beauty in your mind because only it can make the difference between beautiful and ugly. A statement is a mental thought spoken aloud. A statement opens a gate. It is the starting point on the path of change. Choose consciously the words you use, saying only positive statements.

Whatever you give yourself, no matter how you perceive yourself and how you feel about yourself; the Universe makes sure it gives you the feedback that will reflect exactly your beliefs. This awareness provides a great opportunity to know that it's up to you what you want to get out of your life, being able at any time to readjust your emotions, beliefs and values until what it is offered to you will feel like it completes you exactly in agreement to who you chose to be.

If a person is horrible to you, but, nevertheless, you manage to feel inside yourself you a blissful state of calm, it means that things are good for you. But if you feel uncomfortable, it's better to take a note of this so you can work on it afterwards, because clearly there is a wound there, a limiting belief, an anchor or it's missing something.

The courage to be yourself means self-esteem. The courage to be yourself means the opening to your Divine Self, seeing life as an opportunity and not as a long and difficult chore. Depending on the choices you make, you can be reborn in a new painful destiny or in a positive one.

At one time, this transformation occurs and you become a new person. The new person is divinely guided. That means that their life is no longer driven by their ego. They have the responsibility to make conscious choices, not to live like the wind. It has already been created the fusion between man and God. Divinity works through the person, but the person must act somehow. Everyone is unique and is a unique expression of God. Together, we are ONE.

You are the Creator of your life. You are a perfect manifestation of God. It depends on you what you choose in life and how you want to live. Nobody can act in your place, even if you are divinely guided. I will repeat this over and over until you get bored and you will be convinced deep inside of this truth. Certainly, after you finish reading this book you will have in mind one belief: "I am the Creator of my life and it's up to me how I want to live this life!"

Every time I have a deep revelation, I tend to exemplify what I say. This way, I make sure I understand what I became aware of also outside my mind.

A few days ago, I came in contact with a person who gave me the opportunity to go to Hannover, Germany.

As you already know, I made a business plan for my club and I thought to act somehow. As nothing is accidental, this club that I wanted to work in was a lot like the one I wanted to create.

I made a business plan, but I realized that it's not enough. I don't have the knowledge to create this large project. I never worked in a club and I have no idea what this business practically means. I talked to the person administering the club so I can work there for a few months to gain experience. I was really happy. I said to myself: "How beautifully the Universe works in my favor, how easy and simple this opportunity appeared in my life. Incredible!"

For few days I was super excited. At one point, I realize again that I tend to choose at random. I said to myself: "Carmina, what about conscious choices?" Wow! I took a step back, and then I looked at the situation as a mere observer. I realized that I was making an unconscious choice without knowing exactly who the people I come in contact with are. The fact that I sent all the real information about me and I have not received information about the people outside that job, made me consciously choose not to leave the country.

If I was getting answers to my questions and my conditions, then I could have had the security that everything is okay. From my point of view, all that glitters is not gold.

The quality of your life depends on the choices you make. God is not guilty if you walk into a hopeless situation. It is your responsibility to listen to your inner voice about the opportunities that arise in your life. You tend to be very happy when something appears in your life, but I recommend you take a few steps back and analyze if that the choice is based on desperation, ambition or balance and sheer joy.

Have you ever tried to make conscious choices through meditation? The sensation is divine! The meeting with yourself in such an environment lifts you up both literally and figuratively. Your soul can be exactly where you want it to be in this moment. You return from this short journey with great joy and satisfaction. You've already taken the first steps towards what you really want.

Believe and feel with all your heart that everything you want you already have in your life. Don't separate from yourself because you will feel something is missing. Shortcomings and infirmities are just illusions. They are real only if you believe they are real. But why wouldn't you believe that you already have everything, you are perfect, complete and divine? Feel it with all your heart.

When you are depressed or have strong emotions that come from the mind, your energy is drained out. You're not connected to your divine essence. The energy leakage leads to a lack of abundance in all aspects. We are masters at this. Only the conscious choice can take you in the center of your being when you realize that you are outside of it.

A trivial example of this: you walk down the street, it rains torrentially and a high-speed car passes you by and sprays from head to toe. It happened to me one morning when I was going to work. I was very well dressed. Just had a new office suit. At the time, I had to choose: I got angry and lose energy? Or I accept the situation easily? Slowly you begin to be aware of yourself and how you can keep your energy intact. Is it worth wasting your energy? If you can afford this luxury, don't be surprised why you have so many shortcomings in your life. It's your unconscious choice. I'm just asking you to be aware of how you waste your essence.

You need to be careful how you manage your energies, in what area and activity you use them. If you waste your energies in anger, in an excess of sensuality, in selfish activities, they will feed the Inferno. Because it is ignorant people who, through their ignorance, feed the Inferno. They are extraordinarily trained in all the sciences, but they never heard of being responsible when they use in their energies.

Do you know how the energy is stolen? Do you know how to protect yourself? Very simple and at the same time very complicated. When you get angry, you give in your energy, when you get upset, others have stolen from you energy because they are disconnected from the source. You lose energy by stress, impatience, agitation, induced dark thoughts. You don't need special protection shields, because you have in your personal archive all the tools you need. If you identify the person who steals your energy and you can control not getting on the same frequency with them, you win. You win yourself and this is the most important. You must be careful how you react to the outside world.

To do something great requires determination on your part. Discipline. And lots of action. The truth is that most of us want safety. We want comfort. We want to be well, so to speak. And this thing is kind of in contradictions with those who have wider visions on life, with those who already have a dream they are willing to make an effort for. The world needs determined people, people who threw out the window everything that limited them in order to get what they wanted. If you want sit peacefully your whole life, you can retire already. If you are content to be known only by your neighbors and coworkers, then you have no reason to do something great with your life. What do you choose? Safety, warmth and a comfortable living space that you already have? Or action, adventure and a fairy tale life? In both cases, you can work as much. In the first case, you earn just enough to survive, and in the second case, you live like the real god you are.

Divine dignity brings confidence in everything is outside of us, because we attract into our reality people, situations, moments, experiences worthy of a divine being. Dignity is the spiritual quality of humans rising towards the Man-God. When you have this condition as a natural way of living, it is a sign that you are united permanently with your divine side and you accept the divinity. Thus, you don't need to use people to fulfill your needs, but you are the solution to all your needs. Be divine dignity and life will be beautiful and creative!

You have two main choices for your life: 1. You use your divine intelligence to understand yourself, to acknowledge the reality beyond the illusions and to live in the highest way you can possibly imagine; 2. You settle for a false sense of self-fulfillment which is well below your true potential, creating thus a limited reality, choosing to invest your energies on defending this reality that you created.

You choose where to use your energy: in a feverish passion or in fears and doubts.

One thing is certain: "The universal laws don't respect that you are "x" on the social ladder or "y" poor and unfortunate. The universe gives you everything you expect to receive. It gives you exactly what you think and feel. Focus on the bright side of life, and see the good side of every situation and thing. You will get more and more and more!

If your statement is that you are a good person, you love what you do, but your belief is that money is not good, inevitably you create a blockage between you and abundance. If you live in an environment where people around you are poor and only think about shortcomings, automatically you are what you think. So attention to your beliefs that unconsciously coordinate your life. There are so fine aspects that you are not even aware of them if you don't try to be your own observer. Observe what you say. What you say is what you will express and create. Try to pay attention to everything you say and think! To hear yourself thinking, to hear yourself talking! Thinking and speaking at the present tense you activate energy HERE and NOW.

It's better to avoid the word "hope!" This means that you accept success, but also failure. Try, if possible, to be very careful when you choose your words. By choosing and using words with high vibration such as extraordinary, fabulous, magnificent, brilliant, perfect, super, awesome, beautiful, harmonious, calm, quiet, peace, well, your life takes faster the direction you order to it.

If you say: "I don't want to be poor," well, that "I don't want" will bring you exactly what you don't want. The energy you consume when you think you don't want to be poor grows until the subconscious mind has nothing to do than to give you what you don't want.

When you step into your life, do you emit joy and celebration? That is the attitude which makes money and everything else you want come to you. Money loves to play its part in the celebration. It is energy.

The first step toward change is to repeat continuously to yourself: "I love to live, I adore living, and I choose to live. It's a magnetism that is happening."

If you become emotions it means that you are not present in your body, but in your mind. If you're frustrated, you live in anger or you daydream, you are not present in your essence; you are in your mind. For this reason, your mind can't receive what you want. It means you're not available to receive. "Here" and "now" is the only place where you can receive from your essence. The mind doesn't know what it means "now." Your mind knows the past, speculates the future, but doesn't know "now."

It is not surprising that in the category of conscious choices fall also the most important aspects of your life. It's time to choose how you want your life to be. There are some questions that you have to answer honestly:

1. How do I want to be?
2. How do I want my lover to be?
3. How do I want my friends to be?

If you are in business, it is very important to know:

1. How do you your business partners to be (or the co-workers if you are employed)?
2. How do you want your customers to be?
3. How do you want the team that will work to be?

These are not simple questions that you just read then overlook them. You need to give yourself time and answer them. As you already know, first of all, you have to change yourself if you want such a reality. Surely you've heard this phrase often: "Be the change you desire in the world."

To know how you want to become, you first have to know what you want from life. This is the main purpose of this book: "To determine you to enter inside you to discover yourself." Once you have determined what the criterion that satisfies you are, you will know from the start how to choose the people in your life. When you know what you want, your life will settle on your heart's liking.

Often, it is time to clean up your life totally if you realize you are not living the life you desire. Nicely and elegantly, you free yourself from those people who don't make you happy and don't correspond to your inner value.

I assume you have already become that person who doesn't need confirmation from others that you're okay, beautiful, smart and wonderful. You already know this about yourself, so you can afford to clean up your life. Certainly, it will appear in your life exactly what you want when you freed yourself of the old entourage.

Most of us live with many illusions. I can be an example in this regard. I thought that if leave the place I don't like, I'll be very happy. This is the greatest illusion that someone could have.

Right in this moment I was thinking: "How happy I would be if I were on a beach in Ibiza instead of staying alone in the house staring at the walls." I have not turned on the TV in last five years. Sometimes I turn it on a music channel while cleaning or cooking.

I wandered far and wide to reach the same conclusion: I realized that there is no reason to lie to myself anymore; it's time to make a major change. I realized that where ever I go, if I'm not happy with myself and with what I do, I don't get anywhere.

The most important lesson for me was to realize that if I continue to go in a direction I don't like, I will simply accumulate frustrations again which at some point will need to be resolved again. I realized that I lied to myself enough, and now it's time to do what I really want. I know there will be changes that will not be easy to do, but the most important thing is to walk on the path I want to walk and leave the rest aside.

When was the last time you asked yourself what do you really want to do?

Where do you think you'll get if you keep lying to yourself and ignoring the path you want to walk on just because you are afraid?

You may feel that it is time to talk to someone or even better to give yourself the gift of having quiet moments with yourself, when you could look slowly at everything in this present moment, to talk to the God within you, to contemplate a meditation or even to write about yourself if it seems easier to you. To write down and acknowledge your fears, to allow yourself to simply be free.

Allow yourself be Nothing to you reunite with the Whole that you are. To allow yourself to feel every emotion that goes through you without judging it and without resisting to it, to let it be free. Allow yourself to be free and confident in the Divine will! To go through life free but still connected with the energy of life from within yourself, with what you really are. The whole universe is inside you. Everything starts from your soul, from within you. Be careful what you feel and follow your soul feelings with great confidence and courage.

Don't forget that the God inside you always speaks to you. It will send you a story, someone who will give you the divine message. If you read this book at this time it means that the God within you guided you to it because He knows you'll find answers to your questions. The divine guidance is permanent, even if you stay alone isolated in the house or maybe you are now on a deserted island. It doesn't matter where you are and what you are doing at this time. He constantly talks to you. Even a thought that comes to your mind is a message from the God within you. It's up to you whether or not you give importance to that thought. Every moment of the day you can choose what you do, what you think, what you eat and where you want to walk.

Be here "now" and observe in how many ways God talks to you. Be present in your life every second.

Give yourself the attention you need! Enjoy your spare time! Read a book, go to a movie, and give yourself more attention today. Remember that you are important, first of all, for you. And don't forget to smile!

Whoever studies the living standards of people who currently live on Earth in any place or in a so-called civilized country, or elsewhere, they will discover that all human beings, men and women face the same problems created by how wrong they conduct their own lives.

You will discover that many human beings live in disorder, slaves to their own uncontrolled desires and unrestrained emotions, slaves to their passions and weaknesses that raise a tyrant selfishness that tortures them and those around them. Often, some people fail under the weight of malice and hateful animosity towards other people, generating a poison that becomes the foundation for many diseases—malignant and incurable—in their material bodies.

What is life? What are we as phenomena of life? What are we as human beings who live in the material world with billions of other life phenomena?

All of these conditions of life should be studied seriously by each individual and not only by the seeker of the Truth, so that everyone could get out of confusion and become the master of their body, the master of their own life.

After someone studies their own life, desires, emotions, feelings and weaknesses, they have to approach bravely introspection, going boldly into the subconscious of their personality.

Many systems of self-development have been given to the human beings by great teachers. All these systems intend to get people out of their confusion, of their illusions, and to help them free their personality of ignorance and to go towards Self-achievement.

You always have the power to choose. You can decide whether to be friendly or hostile. Always choose a cordial, cheerful, cooperative behavior and the world will respond in the same way. This is the best way to develop a harmonious personality. Always think that something wonderful will happen soon in your life.

The negative opinion of others towards you can't affect you in any way. Only your beliefs can confirm that they are right in what they say about you. Therefore, you can firmly reject their statements that are not beneficial to you. Again, you have the power to choose how you react.

You are master of your destiny. Always remember that you have the power to choose. Therefore, choose life! Choose love! Choose health! Choose happiness!

Health is a natural state of our being. When you know this and say it with confidence, from the heart, not only mentally, that "Health is the natural state of my being and I believe in my health!," then it will be exactly like this. In fact, it's not your body that stops the healing, but you and your beliefs in disease and disharmony.

It's amazing when you get to have so profound awareness. Your simple thought can create your own reality. Your belief about one thing or situation creates the reality you live in the present moment. Medicine as a science of sickness has contributed to the spread of diseases. Religion, studying the sin led to its promotion. The economy, as a study of poverty, will fill the world with poverty and lack of fulfillment.

Lately, I follow individuals who have reached a "phenomenon" in a short time. For example: a singer. I was wondering why some are known only in Romania and others are known worldwide. The answer is quite simple: that soul dreamed and believed with all their being that will become a public person. It's not related to their talent. Maybe some sing better than others, but the big difference between them the vision on their life. They allowed themselves to dream and believe that it is possible to get on the greatest stages in the world. Maybe they didn't tell this to everyone, but certainly they wanted this deep inside.

What stops you to have total confidence in you that you will be able to be known worldwide? Maybe the people around you who live a limited life? Your work, your children, the house? Routine? Does your family believe that it is impossible what you want? Do the people you interact with every day? Your friends you want to work with, but who don't want to get involved in your project? If you don't like something, change that thing. If you can't change it, it's in your power to change how you think about that thing.

I'll give you a tip: just when you see that everyone gives up on you, it's time to have the most confidence that you will achieve what you want. You gave them a chance and they didn't take it. It was their choice. Your choice is to go forward. It's time when you discover that the power is within you and all everything depends on your will and faith. Outsiders don't support you. You need to find your inner strength in order to move mountains. Don't you think? I do.

Probably many of us thought that something good will happen in our lives, but it didn't. Why? Because our faith was not pure. Surely you have some programs in your subconscious sabotaging you and you don't realize at the moment. Something like: it can't be done, I don't believe it, it's impossible, don't you see the economic situation in the country?, others tried this and failed etc. Be careful what pattern limits you and doesn't allow you to believe that what you want is as accomplished. Pure faith, genuine faith, from the depth of your being, is the key to your success. When you learn to go to the others to ask them what you need, an entire Universe is given to you.

My dear, you are surrounded by indescribable beauty that you refuse to see. You are loved and appreciated and you ignore these FACTS. You are guided and you are looking for faults thinking you don't deserve it, you are a being of light and you refuse to admit it. Yes, you're awesome and I speak from the heart. Everything you see it is so because you choose to see it this way. You see flowers—it means you are like flowers, you see dirt—it means you are dirt too, you see smiles—it means you are smiles, and you see anger—it means you are anger too. Decide what you want to see, choose what you want to live and allow the God inside you to show you what to do. He is here for you now and forever.

Your everyday acceptance! You can notice/observe every day that there is something more to accept at yourself, something that bothers you/you don't accept from others, something that happens in your life in the present moment. Therefore, remind yourself to accept everything exactly as it is given to you in the present moment, as if you chose it this way, even if you prefer something else and then act if there is something you can change, or let go, or make new choices. This way, you no longer oppose to life, you flow with the life, you are not at war with life, with others, and in fact, with yourself. Your life changes miraculously through total acceptance. You choose and believe what you want!

Every day I see people who can only see their faults and they have no love for themselves. These people are those who say they are angry at others, at Life, at God and everything that surrounds them and they don't realize that, in fact, they are angry at themselves. They lack self-love completely. They are the kind of people who will always blame everyone and everything for their unhappiness and they will always seek causes in others for their unhappiness.

These people are angry with themselves, they are dissatisfied, they are unhappy and therefore they can't see around them anything but gray and black. Before they heal inside, everything outside will be bleak for them. Unfortunately, the people around you are your mirror that reflects your darkness that has to be accepted, loved, integrated and turned into light. Nobody can do that for you.

If you destroy the harmony between you and the universe, you will get sickness, unhappiness, sorrows and sufferings. Gloomy thoughts, distrust, worries, hatred and fear, together with their relatives: anxiety, bitterness, impatience, greed, lack of courtesy, the habit of judging and condemning others, they all attack the body at the cellular level, leading to pain, unhappiness and depression. In such circumstances it is impossible to have a healthy body. With your thoughts, desires and your habits you induce physical health or sickness to your body. You are solely responsible for your health, for your happiness or misery. God doesn't send you illness, accidents or pain; you create them with your destructive thoughts. In other words, you reap what you have sown in the past.

I hear from many people passionate about personal development the statement: "I want to understand who I am." The mystery is not to understand yourself with your mind, the secret is to choose who you want to become. And you can become anyone you want. Focus on who you really want to become, not on what you are now. Everything in this life depends on the choices you make. And, believe me, you choose every second.

If something outside of you makes you restless, it means that you choose to be agitated. What you experience has the value and the meaning that you give it. This is the reality. I know you wanted to hear something else from me. But unfortunately, I can't lie so you consolidate even stronger this illusion. Do you get angry if someone yells at you or talks to you badly? Do you lose your temper and say that person upset you? Wrong! You chose to lose your temper. You might as well choose to be calm. It's an unnecessary waste of energy. You can use this energy that you gave away being angry into a different direction. You can use it for your passion or you can choose to give joy to those around you. To lose your patience is only your decision. No one else can decide for you. Everyone is free to challenge you if that's what they want. But you are not obliged to respond in the same way. Be more intelligent than the person that challenges you and think only of your own inner peace. Choose peace, joy and love instead of conflict, anger and hatred. It's in your power to make clever choices.

In the two months since I returned to my parents' house, I had four opportunities to escape to the real world. The first opportunity was in Greece, the second in Germany, the third in England and the latter in Ireland.

This is how you realize that every moment in life is a choice. Depending on the choice I consciously make, I create the reality I live in. The first three opportunities I felt being inappropriate for me for several reasons. The first opportunity I felt inadequate because work was very hard for me. Money was very little too. The second opportunity didn't give me the feeling that I won't be in any danger because the activity was quite controversial. The third opportunity was with my ex-boyfriend in England with whom in this moment I don't feel like having a relationship because I admitted to myself that I don't really love him. And I found out that it makes no sense to make the slightest compromise, even if might mean to hurt the other person. The fourth opportunity came from my sister. She became pregnant. Although she is the first month of pregnancy, she already feels tired and she can't continue her demanding work. She needs my help. And I choose to support her. She is cleaning many houses and the effort is simply too big for her. She wants to give me some the houses and to work less because as the pregnancy advances the effort must decrease. It's a new challenge for me. But I already I feel I am in my comfort zone and I feel the need to quickly make a change. What will this experience bring? What else should I find out about myself? I'll see.

Probably you wonder why I chose to travel abroad. First, because I want to meet different people, a different culture, a different way of living. I love Romania very much because it gave me the opportunity to find myself again and helped me learn to choose what it's really worth it. I had learnt countless lessons and I am profoundly grateful for it. But, still, I choose to live in a different country. Where I feel that the mentality resonates with me 100%. I admit I don't have the patience to wait for things to happen the way I want and the way they should be in a normal and logical way.

In Romania there are many controversial subjects, when in fact everything could be clear and concise. These topics will be conversation subject for a long time. But one thing is worthy to remember: "As long as the change will depend on someone whether is the state or someone else, nothing extraordinary will be achieved in the education system, the medical one or the financial one which are part of a national system that functions for years and has one goal: enslavement of the population. In what form? Subtle and elegant. Intelligent children go to university, get good grades, get a degree, take a job, get married, borrow money from banks, work to exhaustion to pay their loans, and then go to the doctors to treat various diseases. And people believe in all these! The only solution remains self-education. The Internet is accessible to all, you have access to any information, you just need to have the desire to get rid of a mediocre life you might have and you can't expect anyone else to come up with the magic solution! The change must happen in every individual. The real change starts from here. If you expect salvation from the state or from others, you can wait quietly for another hundred years. We are so smart and hardworking, that we forget the essence of life. We forget why we work and what our direction in life is. This is pretty much our problem, Romanians': "We follow the others to tax them when they are wrong, because we are perfectionists instead of thinking like a great team for a very good and civilized living. The difference is clearly done by the people who live in this country. For this reason, I preferred not to comment too much on this quite controversial subject.

What is important is that we live well as it is, in a spotless country. I am convinced that there are geniuses in Romania and I am sure that there will be more and more every year. I'm one of them and I know other geniuses too. A little confidence in themselves and in their own strength would change the situation radically. It's not hard, you just need to have courage to get out of a system that you feel it limits you and to create the reality that you desire. Create your own reality, don't expect miracles from others. Others don't have the interest that you do well. Believe me they have more important worries than this: "Dream vacations, and to live their own heaven through you." You are kind and do charity for others. Your gesture is nice. I really appreciate it. But my questions are simple: "Who stops you to make a different choice? Who doesn't let you change? Who makes you unhappy? Who doesn't offer you the life that you desire? "I let you meditate deeply on these questions. This book will help you to answer to all your existential questions and it will help you answer to questions that you didn't even dare to think. Think, dear soul, this is why you have a mind! Speak, that's why you have a mouth! Act, dear soul, that's why you have a body with two arms and two legs! You have on hand all the tools you need. Who do you want to use them instead of you? I just wonder. I wonder what holds you back. I'm curious why you play the victim part when you could very well make the choice to be happy. I'm just curious. I try to put myself in everyone's shoes so I can understand it. It's not too easy because each person is unique, has their own thinking, a way of being and seeing things. I don't judge anyone, I just express my opinion. I am free and I can even speak what I want, when I want and with whom I want. Nobody stops me. It is free. It costs me nothing. I am very amazed when I find Romanians who have a say in the world, leading large organizations. Everywhere there is a genius who invents or researches something. True role models.

"In Romania there isn't a job crisis, there is crisis of people. Romania is in a crisis of authenticity. The void within appears as a crisis." The opinion of a Romanian successful entrepreneur.

The crisis never existed, it has been invented by weak people. It's an excuse used by people who like to play the victim part. Everything you believe is possible; if you believe there is a crisis, that's right, if you think you can be anything, that's right! Anything is possible, just as you think.

What do you think is the main source of problems in your life? The lack of faith. You don't believe enough that everything is possible. You say you are optimistic, but you don't even know which your passion is, you don't even made a single step to achieve it in the physical reality. Optimist means perseverance. And this perseverance is the equivalent of notable results. To claim that you are optimistic without basis behind this statement means that it is just a lie you deceive yourself with every day. When you're optimistic, it means you think you can achieve your goal. You can't be optimistic if you have no purpose in life. It's an illusion to think that's enough to be optimistic hoping that a miracle will fall from the sky. Think hard about it!

Wake up and realize that no one has anything with you except yourself! Realize that you don't like yourself anymore; you don't like what you are, how you are and "adjust" yourself to the new beliefs.

Why do people cancel everything you've done well when you do something wrong for the first time? This is for you to figure out that their opinion doesn't matter!

The opinion of a Romanian who visited the capital of Ireland.

"In Dublin, I have the feeling that I went back in time, to my childhood, with my grandmother in the countryside... Everything is very green; people are calm, relaxed and friendly. Dublin gives me such an unnatural feeling of peace. I feel that something's wrong with the peace around us, it is like the calm before the storm; here, in Romania, it is a belief: after a period of peace, something bad happens. For us, inner peace doesn't last long and it costs a lot.

I understand from the Romanians here that this peace is normal, that it lasts and that life in Ireland is slower than at home in Romania. Irish sing damn good. Last night I was in at least ten pubs and everywhere they sing live. People sing and dance. People are dressed very normal, not fancy. Girls drink a lot, and sometimes collapse, but no one's bothered, it's really funny to see this. You don't see arrogance and no one cares what you're doing, no one analyses you from head to toe. We have the impression that the best parties take place on the Romanian seaside resorts. It's a lie! I say you should visit Ireland to see how people who don't know each other, sing, dance, drink and enjoy themselves together!

What is the most attractive quality in a person? From my point of view, fairness in everything and everywhere is the answer to this question. That would translate like this: Stop lying to yourself and inevitably you will also be genuine with the others."

A teacher from Sweden first came to visit the Romanian coast in 1985 with her family when she was just 13. She returned in 2011 and since then she has returned 15 times. She grew up in northern Sweden, went to university, lived in several places in Norway, France, Reunion Island, England, and Denmark, after which she returned to her native country and teaches at the International School in Helsingborg, in southern Sweden. Her purpose and her blog's purpose is to spread the beauty and the meaning of Romania to the world through the eyes of a Swede.

Her opinion about Romania is: "Romanians don't have a well-built self-esteem or confidence, too many still look down. When I came for the second time in Romania, I was amazed of the potential I found here. Why don't they show all these? Romanians have a lot to offer at different levels, even if they don't know it. I met a lot of hospitality here, I am moved by the nature and the landscape of the country, the food, the Romanian villages with their life and authenticity, the life in the cities across the country, I could continue for hours to remind you the beauty you have here. But I think things are moving in the right direction."

"There is so much beauty in Romania; it's hard to overlook it. You have a true spiritual traditional treasure, the spirituality of the Romanian village, all your traditional culture is impressive and should be promoted, shown to the world. Personally, I'm in love with the authenticity of Romanian village life, and the traditional Romanian blouse "ia." I brought some from Romania and I go out wearing them here in Sweden. I want to tell you that every time I do so I am asked about them on the street. They have a real impact. The entire cultural heritage you have is completely undiscovered outside Romania and there is so much potential here."

Over the years, life has taught me that you can start from scratch any time, even if you need to do this several times. The question is: "Do you have this strength? Where does this strength come from? From Heaven? From Earth? From a Spirit or unknown God? No. It comes from the inner strength that needs to be discovered inside you, waiting for you to wake up to life. The chapter of your life called "survival" ended, time has come to live life like a teenager again, as if it's the first time you experience something. No one can ever take away your inner strength, because it's really just yours. Everything else that seems yours goes as it came!

You're human! You live every day and you make a lot of choices that impact your life. Some are less important and will influence you in the next few minutes, hours, days or months, while others will completely change the meaning of your life. The quality of your choices is the one that put in balance if you will struggle with frustrations or you will live an extraordinary life, like the life of your dreams. With options, you can afford to make selections, to choose and then decide between the possible ways forward.

You choose whether to go forward or stand still, to be happy or sad, loving or hateful, satisfied or dissatisfied, to be good or to be the best. Your present is based on the choices you made yesterday and the three days ago, three months ago or even many years ago. It is true that you don't gain ten kilos because you ate more once, neither your relationship end overnight because you had an argument.

You are where you are because of some subconscious choices, absolutely inappropriate you take every day and which get to form your reality. Your life is not a game of chance and you are very unlucky, and you can't blame your parents, your boss, your lover or your spouse. The disadvantage is that you are solely responsible for your life. The advantage is that you—and only you—have the power to change your life and you can do it anytime you want.

If you want to achieve all your goals and create the life you want, you have to make choices that lead you to action. When you make a choice, you would like to know:

— whether it will push you towards a happy future or it will keep you locked in the past;
— whether you will have a better life on long term or it's just a short time pleasure;
— whether you do what you want or you do it just to satisfy others.

When you have decided, you made a decision, you have chosen, tell yourself: "This is the best decision I make at this time. I am pleased with what I can do now." Live your life without regrets. Enjoy yourself and make the right choices for you! Remember: the main reason that most people don't get what they want is because they don't know what they want.

You live in a universe governed by your own conscience, by your own thoughts, and the experiences you attract are the result of how you think.

There are people who come into your life and through them you access your wellbeing, harmony and inner peace. There are other people who come into your life and bring with them agitation, emotional whirlpool and a state of uncertainty and disorder. The first are those who show us which is your naturalness, while others often have the potential to draw you away from yourself and interacting with them often leaves deep scars in your psychic and soul. Choose the people around you depending on the state you visit around them and so you will find yourself, the real you.

Who wants can be a genius. It is a conscious choice. I chose to be a genius in manifestation. And so it is! Choose to be a genius! For your heart and soul. Why is conscious choice so important? When you make a choice, you actually change your future. Remember! It's very important.

It is the action that (if you are truly aware of it) helps you realize that choosing something you actually open a new line of potentialities that changes your entire future according to the vibration you have triggered at the moment of your decision. Behind a choice there is an intention, a strong inner motivation, and emotions. Be where you want to be, who you want to be with, when you want to be and do exactly what you want to do! Choose and act. That's all you have to do.

"Take care of yourself, be happy and at peace with yourself and your decisions, get out of situations that make you unhappy, dare to dream and to wish! Why? Because you deserve it, regardless of what you did in the past, what decisions you took, stop punishing yourself, forgive yourself and move on. Love yourself, respect yourself and then those around you will do it. I believe in you! I think you can be as you wish! I think only you can make something unique! Get up, shake yourself and go on your way!"

You are totally responsible for your life. You are fully responsible for your fate. Your destiny is in your hands. It is time to realize and admit that pain, disease and poverty are not accidents, but the fruits of your inner discord. You and only you can find the solution.

How others feel is not your responsibility. Your responsibility is not to betray yourself. Each of us should learn to manage their own emotions and to choose how they respond to life challenges.

Your emotions depend on you: how much you are aware of them and you want to keep them under control. Emotional intelligence and emotional self-control are the pillars that determine what your life looks like. They are an indicator that shows you how easily you overcome problems and how much you manage to enjoy life.

If you're a driver, it's even easier. You associate your inner state with the indicators, the road signs. "Stop" means stop getting angry because it takes you nowhere. "Give way" means to allow the person full of anger to manifest as they want. Let them have this portion of negative feelings. Give them the way in your favor! The indicator "Mandatory to the right or left" means stop going forward like a lemming when you see that a relationship, or a job doesn't work the way you want it. It is mandatory to take it to the left or the right, but not straight. The "One way" indicator means not to enter any combination that has the risk you will face a problem. Don't cheat, don't lie. Otherwise, you will meet the "problem" created by you consciously or unconsciously.

The sign: "Bumps in the road ahead" means to pay attention to yourself, precisely at that point that hurts you and consumes all your energy. If you don't stand up to the situation that upset you for so long, there is a risk to wake up with "boulders on your shoulders." And then see how you stand up! Be preventive!

The sign: "Priority road." That means that when your road is full of obstacles, you keep going on your way! Trust yourself that you are on the right road. Anyone has the priority to be a movie star, to be a famous writer, or a phenomenal musician or any other skill or talent which you are gifted with. Bring that ability that looks insignificant at first glance to an art level. Give it credit, power and energy to grow! Once it becomes great, it will certainly be seen by others, who are part of "Doubting Thomas" crowd, i.e. they don't believe it until they see it. But you, being smart, you believe in it before it appears visible to others. Your dream is part of you, you know that it is more real than the reality around you and it will come to light when you are ready for success.

Dream what you want to dream, go where you want to go, be what you want to be. Because you have only one life and one chance to do all the things you want to do.

CHAPTER 4

HOW DO YOU KNOW WHEN PEOPLE ARE EMPTY INSIDE?

"There are only two kinds of people in this world: those who try to fill the inner emptiness and those very rare and special people who try to see their emptiness."

Simple definition of an empty person: "You pretend that you are who you aren't, because you're afraid that you'll be rejected. The fear of being rejected becomes the fear of not being good enough. Finally, it turns you into someone you're not. You punish yourself whenever you are not in accordance with the rules corresponding to your belief system; you reward yourself when you are "a good boy" or "a good girl." You try to hide and pretend to be what you are: a husband or a wife who is trying hard to look the ideal partner. You hide behind the material aspects by which you identify yourself: a nice mortgaged house or apartment, an expensive car that you may not be able to afford, but you need it to identify yourself in society, expensive vacations. All these are normal and perfect if you don't define yourself through things and the image that you tried to create about yourself.

In our society, feeling "empty" or "meaningless" is very common and most of us have experienced it at some point in life, more or less prominent, more or less conscious.

The feeling of emptiness is a somewhat a confusing feeling, hard to explain in words and each feels it in a different way. You may feel it like a lack of energy to go further, because the meaning of everything that happens is elusive. Another person may feel an acute shortage of something, a something unclear that they can't really identify. Thus we continue to live our lives on autopilot, by virtue of inertia, because we "must."

The sensation of emptiness that you feel has the root in the center of your being, deep inside yourself, an area that when you don't connect with it and you don't feed it, you feel that something is missing. If you usually lives on the periphery of your being, on the surface, "the emptiness" grows bigger and bigger. Thus, you try to fill it with aspects related to this surface area. Some try to fill it with material possessions, houses, cars, shopping, others believe that if they change the place and they go somewhere far away, the feeling will disappear, others try to fill it with rational knowledge that only feeds their mind and there are cases when we believe that others and friendships with others can fill this gap. You do all these and eventually you realize that the feeling of "emptiness" doesn't go away. It might be tempered for the moment, but it doesn't truly disappear. Why? Because it's a feeling that acts strongly in the very Center of your being. You feel unfulfilled in your life, though you may already have your dream life partner, a couple of kids and the job you always longed for. Emptiness is really a cry from your soul that is trying to be heard through the layers you buried it under, because its nature is to express itself in your life and you may have forgotten about its existence.

That feeling of deep emptiness inside yourself seeks fulfillment in things that don't complete you: food, TV, alcohol, drugs, cigarettes, meaningless relationships etc. You are doing this to keep alive the emptiness inside. I don't know how your life would be without it.

The biggest obstacle in the way of change is that you can't see the problem. You think you have one set of problems: you don't have enough money, you don't have enough will, you have bad luck, and you can't make the right decisions etc. when in reality we have a totally different problem. It's exactly as when you go to the doctor. You have to solve the problem from the root and to discover the real cause. Otherwise, it's just a bandage and the emptiness in your soul is not filled. The deep wound in your subconscious is not treated. In a world of superficial solutions, psychology that doesn't take into account the human spirit, drugs on top of drugs, the true solution becomes almost impossible to find. The whole idea of the current psychology, of education, is that if a person doesn't have a strong ego they will not be able to fight in life where there is so much competition that if you're a humble person, everyone will sidestep you; you will always stay in the background.

Disconnected from the depths of humans, society will never fill this gap. Society and its artificial institutions will make it bigger, turning it into an abyss. And you, disconnected from your divine essence, will feel more acutely this chasm, this lack of "something" that you try to fill continuously without any success or, with results that don't last, with "something else" an outside "someone." You will have a permanent feeling of "hunger" and these are the premises of a consumer society that wants to feed both your hunger and your illusion that it can truly "satisfy" you. If you feel that the emptiness is deep within your being, if you understand this and you start listening and "feeding" your soul, then the hunger will disappear and the illusions created by society will become unnecessary because they will have no effect on you. You will not look desperately outside yourself for what should be discovered in the depths of your being.

How many times did it happen to waste your life running to collect or to get goods that are much less important than life itself! Have you ever thought of this? If you knew how to give priority to Life, if you were preoccupied in keeping it and protecting it, preserving its integrity and purity, your possibilities of getting what you want would increase significantly. Because such bright illuminated intense Life is the one that can give you everything. You think everything in life is allowed. Well, no! After years and years of continuous work to satisfy your ambitions, one day you will feel so exhausted, so blasé that when you put in balance what you got and what you lost, you will realize you lost almost everything to gain so very little. How many people don't say: "I have a life! I want to live a full life, to get everything, I want: money, pleasure, knowledge, glory..."

And then they pull hard, they work hard and when they don't have resources anymore, they are forced to stop all activities. We rush more and more. But where to? A life like this makes no sense, because if you lose your Life, you lose everything.

And where are you running to? What victory do you want to obtain? Dear soul, life is happening right here, right now. Stop in your rush to nothing. Think for a moment about your soul's desire. Why run towards the future? Indeed, you can be anything you want, but why do you want to live the illusion of the future when you can experience the certainty of the present? Why do you want to leave your life and live another life? Do you think it is better "out there" than "here"?

Someone says: "You are fools! I'm a fool. We are all fools. We all dream to have a great career and to be in my place. You think it's the best you can do in life, to be a director, to lead hundreds of people, to have your own office, it's the first place in the race of life. You are fools because you don't understand that you are running the wrong race. I'm the greatest fool because it took me years to realize that. I started from the bottom, I worked really hard, 12-14 hours per day, I went through many companies, I have made many compromises to reach this position and now, at 45, I could say I was wrong. If all these years I were to invest at least 10% of the work and stress in a personal business, I would be a millionaire now. I didn't do it and I ended up getting divorced with a child who grew up without me and an ulcer. You can't be free as long as you are an employee." Smile and live! All the beauty of the Universe lies in your heart! Allow yourself to discover the hidden treasure and dispense it back to the world with all its wealth! You will be surprised to see how much love is hidden inside you!

Priests or spiritual elders of all religions who listened to thousands of people who came to them to tell them their problems can say with certainty that they found out that people are unhappier than they realized. This feeling you get when you feel a deep void in your heart, when you feel powerless and hopeless.

How many times have you been staring at the ceiling with tears in your eyes, wondering: "What the hell can you do to be happy?" knowing that you tried all possible and impossible options. What is to be done just to feel true happiness? You feel deserted, sad, only you with you, away from the world. Where does this come from? Out of frustration? Of lack of fulfillment? How many versions have you to try until you succeed to have the life you've always wanted? It's like the lottery: "You play a lifetime for a winning ticket that changes your life." You try; you persevere until your life will be exactly as you dream. I know that when you're tired and sad, you feel it's no use to go on this road which you have no idea where it leads at this time because you feel that it's not in the direction of your heart. What else could be done?

What then? Continue your journey with the most important person in your life: YOU. Together uphill and downhill, together for coffee and a dinner, together for a ride. You with you through this world that is really charming! It is so beautiful that I feel the blessings of life every second. And yet, why do you feel unhappy sometimes knowing that you are everything in this life? Is it because it is difficult to get out of the pattern of the society? Is it because people have chosen a different life, one based on programming? Is it because it is too beautiful to live among people like you? Yes, I am happy because around me, at this moment, I have people who live free and happy. They show me by their example how simple and beautiful life is.

What is the gift behind this state? You discover how much love is inside you when everything goes wrong in your life. Therefore, in a genuine process of transformation, when we are willing to make a leap of consciousness, we must be very careful at that negative inner counter suggestions which likely to arise every moment. It's all about consistency.

Since I came to Romania, I keep thinking where my place is, where I could live the way my heart wants. From experience, I found that I felt good in all other European countries. The people are fantastic and the vibration level is very high. Of all the countries known to me until now, Germany is the country that best resonates with my soul.

Someone once asked me how I figure out what is the vibration level of a country? There can be several answers:—the degree of civilization and development of the country is very high;—nature is the main priority of the people of that country;—people living in full harmony with themselves; they are satisfied with themselves, even if they don't have exclusivist jobs or other material things to make them happy;—they put emphasis on interior and not so much on the exterior;—they live each moment as if it were the last.

How do you know if you are in the right place or not?

You feel a chronic fatigue every time you get into contact with people who display a false happiness. They absorb you like sponges and you are drained.

I found this very often, but I never thought that this phenomenon is real. It seems it is. When you're in the wrong places with the wrong people, you feel that feeling in your whole being. How? First, your mood changes. If you had inner happiness before, you notice that after coming in contact with them, you feel sadness and fatigue. You feel that you're not where you should be.

You meet people at every step. With some you resonate immediately, you feel that you have known them for a lifetime. Others, however, arouse in you emotions or feelings of fear, reaction, and frustration. With the latter, the first impulse is to ignore them or to react. But they are the ones that appear in your life for you to evolve. They reflect exactly those issues that you don't accept of yourself. Even if you turn your back and leave, the issue is still there. It will be another person who will show you that side where you have to work with yourself. The faster you choose to look at you and confront the side that you don't like, the sooner you free yourself. You just need a little courage and time with yourself.

What are the characteristics of empty persons?

- They do everything possible to seem what they are not.
- They highlight intentionally exaggerated happiness.
- They desperately want to show those in contact with how happy they are in that moment and how fulfilled their life is. They always tend to demonstrate it to outsiders.

- They make great sacrifices. Some of them think that money will make them happy and they will manage to climb high in the social hierarchy.

Others believe that if they look very good on the outside, the world will appreciate and love them more than before. I want to give a good example in this respect: The body image & the slimming diet. Empty persons react in the following way in order to have the body that they are constantly dreaming of:

— They punish themselves.
— They believe that the only way to lose weight is starving themselves.
— They are convinced that they will have a much higher self-esteem if they look perfect.
— They believe that they will be loved more by the others.
— They think they will attract an interesting life partner.

If you want to lose weight while maintaining good health, there are some things that you don't have to do: for instance, you should never get angry with your body for any reason. Anger is in itself a statement that tells your body that you hate it (whole or parts of it). Your cells are very aware of every thought that you have. Therefore, it is best to think of your body as a sacred temple that hosts your spirit.

We often gain weight because of the fears we repressed and they've now come to the surface to be healed. We react by building a defense. We also try to settle ourselves, to raise our mass resistance against high frequencies in the body.

You look younger. As you clarify the emotional problems and free the limits of your belief and get rid of the heavy luggage of the past, you are lighter. Your frequency is higher. You love more yourself and life. You begin to look like the perfect person you really are.

If you look around, you can make a quick selection of optimistic people and the pessimistic ones, even if you don't know them. Their vibrations allow you to do it. Around optimists you feel good. They are simply contagious. Their positive energy (high vibration) "touches" you, too. The same happens after talking to a pessimist. You suddenly wake up unwell and your world seems gray or worse, black.

Give up on building every day high and thick walls of fear, possession, shame, distrust and so on. Don't make a mountain out of a mole hill there is nothing more effective than Love. Learn to be happy enjoying what your life gives day by day, being grateful and fascinated by all Creation, inspiring the beauty from everywhere. Admire, love, take delight in the others presence as you admire and love a butterfly. Allow all that you love to fly free. That's love, when you enjoy others and whatever comes your way without putting on their back the heavy stone of possession. Transform the walls around your ego in caresses of the soul.

A complete person has the following attitude:—they know that the most important thing is to accept yourself exactly as you are;—they cease to sabotage themselves;—they love their body; they respect it and doesn't intend to punish it in any way;—they trust that they won't gain weight, no matter how much they're eating;—they are present when they enjoy food; they love food; they introduce it inside their body with pleasure and great joy;—they are convinced that they are perfect exactly as they are and nothing should be changed.

It is a great joy to help people eliminate the overweight-related programs. People are overweight for different reasons. One of them is that someone reflects this that they should be overweight because the rest of the family is obese. Another reason is that, being overweight, they feel safe and protected by their fat. The person may have what it is called the gene of obesity, an interesting belief system. They believe that being overweight means to be strong and safe. However, everyone is different and they might have other beliefs. Make sure you have removed the "I am a victim" program.

The "I am overweight" program should be replaced with "I am slim" or "I am healthy" programs. You will find that these beliefs on being overweight are usually carried at least at the genetic level.

Hidden beliefs may be "I am strong when I am overweight," "You have to gain weight to be intuitive" and "I'm heavy." Make sure you test these programs historically. Don't be surprised if the Basic Beliefs have nothing to do with being overweight.

From experience I can talk about this very interesting topic for people. When I was 18, I was about 65 kg. I was on a permanent diet. I noticed that as I aged, my weight was decreasing. After 30 years, I had 57 kg, then 55 kg. I was eating anything at any time. In recent years I settled at this weight.

I came to the conclusion that if I starve to lose weight the issue that made me plump will still be there. If the cause is not detected, you immediately put back those kilos that you have struggled to take off. It often happens to put back more weight than you had before. Why? Because you punish your body. You don't love it. Working only on the physical side you only fix the effect. Working on the inside you fix the cause for good (depends from case to case). My method was: self-love and the renunciation of all fears and obstacles that prevented me to look the way I wanted. Day by day I was healing a wound; I loved myself a bit more than yesterday. The result was influenced by my psyche and very little by food, nutrition or exercising. Indeed, I ate my meat very rare. I listen to my body and give it exactly what it asks. The communication with it is very tight.

I found step by step the barriers they had in mind. Do you realize that behind all lamentation is actually a shame of being beautiful and to show myself to the world as I know I am inside? You have many monsters to defeat to embrace that fear and to love it, so it doesn't lead you anymore. It's a very long process of self-discovery and slowly you will manage to fall in love with yourself every day! Every day you will discover something beautiful, something you didn't know about yourself. To appreciate and like yourself exactly as you are! Speak nicely about yourself and say something that will caress you heart every day. There are magical and unique moments when you discover the joy that the woman you kept locked in a castle so many years came to the surface as a princess. Not as the ordinary and faded woman that you thought you were.

Being overweight means more than what you eat and what you drink. You are the child of the parents who abused you (physical in some case, emotionally in others), and the layers of fat are in fact layers of protection—an emotional protection.

All the emotions that you repress: envy, hatred, frustration, lack of fulfillment, emotional blackmail form these protection layers in the form of fat.

When you feel bored, you can satisfy your mind hunger flipping through a magazine, talking on the phone, turning on the TV, surfing the web, going shopping, transferring that feeling of lack of fulfillment and the need for "more for the body," this satisfying the shortage through the ingestion of a bigger quantity of food.

The moment you accept yourself as you are, you become beautiful. When your own body will make you happy, it will delight others too. Many men will love you simply because you are in love with you. Now you're angry with your own body. This idea, however, rejects the others, it doesn't help them falling in love with you; it keeps them away. Even if they wanted to come closer, the moment they will feel the vibration, they will step back. Seeking other people occurs only because you don't love yourself. Otherwise, people will come to you by themselves. If you love yourself, others will love you too.

"The man had the age of the woman he feels, the woman the ones she shows." What do you think about this proverb?

A nutritionist advises us: "My dear ladies, if you love your partner, if you love your children and if you love yourself, stop cooking, and preparing for hours the menu for the next day, wasting so much time for nothing, to be fair! The food prepared for you might be tasty, no doubt, but for having good health and to prevent diseases, it's time to learn to eat differently, to consciously choose the food for good vitality. Learn to prepare meals on the spot, when everything is fresh and as lively as possible. You'll save time that you lose now processing the food, you will eat less and you will be healthier!

Today we don't cook anything, nor tomorrow, today do we eat live food, raw and full of enzymes and nutrients!"

There are several categories of people. Some of them realize that it makes no sense to do everything possible to seem happy in front of the others and they begin to work with themselves. Others continue the same lifestyle because this is how they charge with energy. An energy that is there just for the moment, which depends only on the people outside. They feel that when they are no longer in contact with the world, they are worthless.

Recently, I met a very good friend from my town. We haven't seen each other for a year since I was away in England. Meeting her was a true blessing and joy. Initially, we met in order to have coffee together in a beautiful place in my city and I discovered we could talk for hours. Time passed so quickly, I didn't even realize.

She is a strong and independent woman. She is that woman who has done everything possible to create the life she wants without the support of a man. Working in a government institution eight hours a day. She runs a small business that she manages herself. She is part of a women association which she supports in her spare time. Helped by the bank she bought a studio and a very nice car. She is bright and she looks like a model. I would say that at first glance she is the perfect woman. But is it really so?

After that long talk with her I felt very exhausted. The next day, I felt very tired and had to recharge my batteries. I didn't know why I feel so exhausted because it was a meeting with a person who gave me so much pleasure.

I talked too much because I wanted to share with her the joy in my soul. I exaggerated when I wanted in a few hours to help her discover herself. I wanted to show her the light inside and what a remarkable person she is, releasing the image that she has created around her by the ego. My hidden intention to change her exhausted me. I forgot that she is perfect exactly as she is! You are divine! It is clear that my mind wanted to look very interesting. So what should I do in this situation? First, to remain a simple observer. To speak only if I'm asked to. And the tiredness doesn't appear anymore.

Every time you say "I'm not trying to convince you of something," but you say with a superior tone, then somewhere within you there is certainly the intention or the desire to convince the one next to you that you are right or you simply feel that your truth is the valid one. That shows your inner need for confirmation or appreciation from outside. Your ego needs to be approved. Then you have the great opportunity to take two steps back and observe where this need comes from. Instead of maintaining the idea that you are not trying to convince anybody of anything, ask yourself honestly: "Is it really so? Am I really free to give ideas/beliefs/appreciations to other people? Am I really not trying to convince the other of anything and am I really don't consider myself superior to the other?"

In my vision:

1. If you prove that you are a woman holding a lot of responsibilities and worries, it doesn't make you strong, but on the contrary, all these things make you increasingly weaker. The real power is the interior. The self-confidence gives you wings, it doesn't cut them.

2. Authenticity means to be exactly how you feel every second of the day.

3. You are on the first place in your life. You don't make sacrifices for others. You cherish yourself very much. When you discover who you really are, your life changes 180 degrees. Keep in your life only the things that make you truly happy.

4. You become aware of the fact that the passion of your mind is not the same with the passion of your soul. You realize that the more you work for the passion of the mind, the more exhausted and miserable you are.

5. You discard those activities that eat your time. It can be used for your own person. If you have a job or an activity just to have a confirmation from the outside that everything is okay with

you or if you always seek appreciations from those around you—that means that you still want to be a savior for others, forgetting that everyone came for themselves in this life experience.

6. When you begin to be very careful at the relationship with yourself, you realize how much you matter to you, not for others. How much you love yourself if you won't have by your side those people that confirm to you that you are a special person

7. When you decide to be the most important person in your life, you become the observer of your life. You see the relationship with your spouse. What don't you like to that person? Or what attracts you to them? Always, without exception, people around show you knew things about yourself.

How to take better care of yourself:

1. If you feel it's wrong, don't do it just for rational reasons.
2. Say exactly "what you wanted to say."
3. Don't do something just to please others.
4. Trust your instincts and intuition.
5. Don't talk bad about yourself.
6. Never give up on your dreams.
7. Have the courage to say NO.
8. Have the courage to say YES.
9. Be gentle with yourself, you've been through a lot.
10. Accept what you can't control and let them be.
11. Stay away from drama and negativity.
12. LOVE!

Look around you wherever you are and you'll notice that most people live in the outside world. Only the truly enlightened ones are focused on the formidable discovery of the subtle and spiritual world inside them. Always remember that inner your world which consists of thoughts, feelings you feel in your being, which create the outside world. As a result, the one and only true creative power is the world within you and any phenomenon that you face on the outside is actually created by you unconsciously inside your inner universe.

The infinite treasures of the world are right here, close to you, waiting for you to open your soul to contemplate them. There is inside the human being a real "gold mine," a priceless treasure where you can extract everything you need to live a beautiful and happy life. Unfortunately, many people are still deeply asleep, having no idea about this treasure of infinite intelligence that dwells inside them.

Whatever your thoughts, opinions, theories of the world, dogmas and prejudices that we accept as truth over time, you are doing so that they get in your mind as behavior patterns. As a result, you live some experiences that are clear and objective manifestation of these beliefs. What you express inside yourself, you will live in the phenomenal world around you. The one who can sincerely thank God for the things they have only in their imagination is the one with true faith. That one will be rich. They will be the reason of the creation of everything they want.

The mystery of the world is: "What is up it is also down; what is inside, it's also outside." Everything you think is true, sooner or later, will become possible. Think and talk about all that you have asked for as you had already received them.

From my point of view, empty people are half dead. They survive, they don't live. The person who believes that life is only the process of birth, youth, maturity, old age, followed by death, is truly worthy of profound compassion. Such a person doesn't know who they really are, and the spiritual dimension of life doesn't exist for them.

His theory raises frustrations, stagnation, cynicism and a sense of despair that leads to neurosis and all sorts of other mental aberrations. What people call death it's only a passage to a new life in another Life dimension. You are and you will continue to be young if you feel young. What a person thinks deep in their heart is what they become.

Some feel old at 30, others feel young at 80. Regardless your age, you can tell that you really old when you lost the joy of living when you stop dreaming, when you think you've got nothing else to discover. As long as you are always open to new ideas, as long as you allow the divine light and inspiration from you to get your whole being, you will remain forever young and full of life. Watch that every day you learn or do something new. This is the secret of eternal youth. This secret you can find it in love, happiness and inner calm.

Don't allow statistics, newspapers, television news to hypnotize you and "to make you old." God is Life itself. Learn to live fully with all our being and all your spirit.

It is not by chance that you were born on this earth, in this country, in this city and so on. You have a purpose; you came here for a purpose that will show only at the moment when you choose to discover your talent, that field you are good at. That is your role. Life is not about the strain, is not about fighting, it is not about working hard, life is about retrieving your own Self, about your role here, what you can offer to the world. When you take responsibility for you own purpose and you choose non-attachment, when you do what depends on you, in a natural and easy way, when you do everything with love and passion, all energies align and on your path appears exactly what you need in order to fulfill your purpose. Life is about love.

Stop watching the others people's desires, trust their inner power, allow the people in your life to live their experiences, let them find themselves, help them to become aware of the divine within them, and that they are able to face any challenge at any moment.

Often, we tend to become saviors of others, compromising ourselves and "stepping on our soul," and so we also tense the other, and ourselves. Our true Self will choose the path of peace and transparency, it will choose to be free and to give freedom.

Choose to be yourself, honest, open-hearted and connected to the Source. Choose to allow yourself to express yourself and you'll see how others will be born again like Phoenix. Just be!

You get to know yourself the best when you are in a difficult situation. By what you do, not by what you say, and so you know the others. I noticed big differences between what a person says and what they do.

When you understand that all voices of those around you are actually your voice, you no longer live at a personal level but at the level of being. No one comes to tell you something, accusing you of anything, challenge you if they don't express your own doubts. When there is interaction between two people, in fact, the conscience speaks with consciousness itself. If we were to listen to each other more often, we will realize what is happening inside us. When doubt disappears, chaos disappears too, because there is no more drama. If something is happening in your life now and you label it as "bad" you already created a relationship with this and the movie begins to untwine exactly around this relationship. The happy ending comes when you give up on labels, watching the as a spectator.

Your value is in what you are, not in what you possess.

A spiritual master answers very simply at the question in this chapter. "People always create big problems out of nothing. All problems are imaginary—you create them because without problems you feel empty inside. Without problems, there is nothing to do, you have nothing to fight for, and you have no place to go. People go from one guru to another, from one master to another, from one psychologist to another, from one group therapy to another because if they don't go, they feel empty and suddenly they feel that life has no meaning. They create problems to be able to feel that life is a great work because they have to work hard, to struggle.

The Ego can exist only when it struggles, only when it fights. And the bigger the problem, the bigger the challenge, the greater the Ego.

Don't create unnecessary trouble. You are a problem creator—it's enough to understand this and suddenly the problems disappear. You are built perfectly; you were born perfect; perfection is your innermost nature. You just have to live. Make up your mind and live it! If you are not tired yet of the game, go ahead, but don't ask why. You know. The reason is simple. The Ego can't exist in the desert; it needs something to fight with. The Ego exists only in conflict—Ego is not an entity is tension.

If you understand this, understanding itself makes the big problem become small again, and then they disappear. Suddenly, it's desert. That means lighting—depth understanding of the fact that there are no problems. And then, without any problem to solve, what are you doing? You immediately begin to LIVE.

Start living this moment and you'll see that as you live longer, the problems become fewer. Because now the emptiness inside you flourishes and lives. When you don't live, the same energy becomes barren. The same energy that would become a flower is blocked. And stopped from flourishing, it becomes a thorn in the heart. It is the same energy.

If people were to dance a little more, sing little more, be a little bit crazier, their energy would flow more and, little by little, their problems would disappear. That is why I insist so much on dancing ... allow your entire energy become dance and then, suddenly, you'll see that you have no head—blocked energy in the head moves in all directions, creating models, images, beautiful motions. And when you dance, there comes a moment when your body is no longer a rigid thing, it becomes flexible, flowing. When you dance, there comes a moment when the border of your being is not so clear anymore; you melt and you merge with the cosmos.

Live, dance, eat, sleep, do things as completely as possible. And remember: whenever you find yourself creating a problem, get out of it immediately!"

The people that who are empty inside act like this:

— There are people who, feeling constantly unfulfilled, always complain of anything, and on the other side we have the happy people who always see the half full side of the glass and are constantly looking for increasingly interesting things in their life. Positive thinking is an essential condition in the economy of a happy life. Focus on the positive aspects of your life, not on the negative ones.

— People who fail to mind their own business feel, most likely, "miserable." They look for the mistakes of others just to feel, somehow, better. These people don't know how to spice up their life with exciting activities and then they waste their time "interested" in what happens to others.

— Many people tend to hold tight to their beliefs, because they want to be right all the time. Many don't give up what they think even when strong reasons are presented to them; in front of such people it is better not to talk about subjects that you know they don't want to think about because those discussions will be a waste of energy. To not accept other perspectives betrays a strong ego, infatuation. It is better to keep our opinions to ourselves, knowing how to listen to the arguments of others. Finally, both parties can agree that they can have the same opinion.

— They are attached to their opinions and when they believe something, it's almost impossible to change their opinion.

Every time you look outside exclusively, fear comes to you.

Whenever you look inside yourself, you remind yourself that you have no reason to fear. There's nowhere to hurry. There's nothing you have to prove to the world. Looking inside, you find peace, tranquility and clarity, understanding the essence of everything that comes your way. Whenever you are afraid, remember to go inside. Breathe consciously. Think and let go of resistance. You will feel like love and peace will spread in your heart.

Have the courage to look in the face, through the eyes of the heart, through the eyes of this moment, all your experience both inside and outside yourself and see how you feel the gifts that rise from your heart. Embraces wholeheartedly everything as it is and feels how the pure joy comes on you and caresses your beautiful face. You will see how, step by step, a lot of awareness, a deep understanding and higher perspectives will make their way to your heart. Give yourself permission to open yourself and to get this opportunity in your life, the opportunity to connect with something more than what you can see, that something that is in your soul, allow yourself to connect to that something that includes everything that exists and turns every moment into a huge blessing.

Examples of people who tell me they don't know why they live and are unhappy I met everywhere. If you are a person who doesn't know the purpose of their existence and doesn't want to learn, be kind and gentle with yourself and ask yourself as honestly as you can you be: "Why do you choose this?" Why do you choose to live in ignorance when you have so many sources of information and so many people waiting to support you? There were others who have walked this meaningless path. Are you that person who has no purpose, who doesn't know why they live but claim they are fulfilled? It is impossible to reach fulfillment without connecting with the God inside you. Outside fulfillment like: family, money, a good job is an illusion.

These things don't complete you as a human being. This is not the ultimate goal for which you have chosen to live in this life. The reason is much deeper and the answer lies deep in your heart. So deep that you don't want to live without your illusions. Aren't you curious to know who you are? Who are the members of your family? Who are your children? Why do you experience this life experience? I challenge you to ask yourself these questions. You'll be surprised by the answers you will get. I talked about this in detail in my first book.

I noticed that people who look outwards, not inwards, are intensely interested in the following areas:

1. How can human nature work for their benefit? They are not interested in creating a collaborative partnership with others in their favor. They tend to fool others in an elegant and subtle way.
2. How can they "control" the actions and attitudes of others? They look for very subtle forms of manipulation to achieve their goals. Such people have no long-term visions. They don't want to create a strong and secure relationship with others.
3. They use different techniques for making friends and maintaining friendships. They try at all costs to keep contact with the others because they have a direct or indirect interest. They make a phone call or they just spend time together because they need each other.
4. How effective are the addressing techniques to help them succeed? Their main goal is improving their technique of making friends. They want at all costs to keep their friends because otherwise they feel worthless. They need constant confirmation from others that they are brilliant, extraordinary and they did something with their life.
5. How can they successfully "maneuver" people? What much power do they have in this moment to have the world at their feet? They think that when they are on a very high position, people will do their best to be at their side, because they need something. They are always waiting for praises and thanks.

How do empty people love are? Dramatic! I want to give you a real example in this regard. People who have not found the resistance pillar inside and are unable to manage difficult situations in their life. They condition others to do what they want because otherwise they can't find their meaning in life. People who didn't understand that they have come to this physical reality to experience and evolve. They want to be blocked in one experience because they don't wish to understand the purpose of life. I saw a conclusive question on Facebook. Question that is seeking answers on the outside when in fact all the answers are inside the person being faced with the situation.

"What shall I do about my marriage? I have a child with my husband. Now I have a relationship with someone else, my husband knows about my relationship, but he say that he will commit suicide if I leave him and tells me I cannot leave the child without a father. What shall I do?"

Mirela: "Who can possibly answer to this question?"

Anca: "Difficult."

Coca: "I don't like these situations, I never thought of something like this, so I can't answer."

Alina: "Question is: how did you get in this situation and what did you learn from it? About getting out of this, I don't know what to say. I abstain."

Mirela: "I actually had been there (except for the suicide part). I think it varies from case to case, the stories are alike, but what each feels will remain a secret. I did exactly what I felt, although I was judged and I still am, but if we don't take the decisions with our heart and we let the mind take it before the heart, we will suffer the most. Everyone who goes through this should speak to themselves, to observe closely how they feel, and to not regret their decisions."

Loredana: "God forbid."

Gabriela: "That it got to this 'point' of relationship is very obvious that something determined her to take a different path than her husband, and, on the other hand, suicide is only an attempt to hang on to a relationship that he is aware that it shouldn't continue, but he is stubborn and says "what's mine is mine," maximum emotional blackmail! Weighing the alternatives and choosing the best solution for the future will certainly light her up and will give her another perspective."

Ion: "Give the child to your husband and continue your affair, they don't deserve a mother like you!"

Monica: "Parallel relationships create confusion. I will think what I can do with my marriage if I had another relationship."

Ama: "She needs to ask the help of a good therapist. Maybe this way the husband will understand that this type of attachment made the wife choose something else. And until he'll get over this stage, no other relationship will be successful. They could both have the chance to start over again, complete and wiser. Suicide is the gesture of extreme weakness."

Giuliana: "They both should go to therapy, but especially the husband who hangs on the relationship that hurts him."

Eugen: "It's so simple: clean up your life! How? That depends on what everyone really wants. Clear and simple things are the ones that give light to your life. For now, the person lives in the cellar. I would stay with the child and nothing else."

Elena: "I'll answer. That happened to me too and I agreed to keep the relationship for the child's sake, but things don't change, they might even get worse. Then the father went through a cardiac arrest and I was by his side, but things don't change if the relationship is no longer alive. There's nothing to hope. So after he returned, I took the child and started my life from scratch. He didn't commit suicide, but after a while, he apologized, accepting that he lost me. So we stayed friends and it was the best decision at the time. Thank you!"

Tibi: "It's an extremely difficult situation, the child is in the middle and what happens is that he will suffer! So careful what you want to do! Do not play with his feelings! I'd like to give you a clear answer to guide you, but I don't want to! I'm truly sorry."

Elena: "It was a very toxic relationship and now the child is a teenager, he is 15 years old, and I have never forbidden him to see his father and I never spoke badly about him in the child's presence, on the contrary, I was the one urging the child to talk to his father. What was up to me is that I did everything possible not to involve the child and I communicated with him always reminding him that if Mom and Dad don't get along anymore, that will not change the love they have for him. I feel at peace with myself with the decision taken at that time and now, though his father died in recent years, I can say that they were the best years of friendship we have."

Antoaneta: "He probably knows about the relationship. Have you thought if the other is right for you? I hope you'll make a wise decision."

Gabriela: "Every situation is special and it's usually risky to have an opinion without having all the problem's data, if the advice is taken into account you might become the moral author of a thing you didn't want; and even when you know exactly the situation, you cannot feel what the two involved people feel because you haven't lived their lives. In my opinion, this is a situation of coaching/mediation which solves by asking questions and a lot of empathy, so each of them to understand their position; the point is how did they get here? What does each of them want? And how will the child be affected? (Because the child and their lives are their responsibility, the threat of suicide is the attempt to throw the responsibility upon the shoulders of the other)."

Elena: "I don't know if it was the question for me or not, but when I took the decision, there was no other alternative, I didn't live for another person. I hated men, until I started walking on the road of personal development and to understand how things and situations work in this journey of our life. So I began to understand how the couple relationship work and that not all men are the same, as us women are not the same. I am still single, it's my choice, and I'm sure I will meet the right person at the right time; you don't have to look around; the right person will come when you are ready.

From what I know, it is wrong to jump immediately into another relationship until you are healed from the old relationship. Because another person, when they come into your life, you should know how to be happy with yourself, to have time to know yourself, to know what you want from a relationship, to know that you are ready to offer and only then you can think of another man. And then, we humans are masters at "critics," we experience it daily. For free.

Because of "critics" we don't evolve. We don't reach our goals fearing the criticism of others. I think it will be good for each of us, before criticizing others, to get a little in their shoes and ask yourself, "Why did they do it like this?"

I apologize that I dragged it on. I believe that whatever you do in life, you will still be criticized, this gives me the courage once again to go on in reaching my goals, to cover my ears and to do what I think is best for me and my family. In the end, everybody goes homes, and I'm still thinking about what others will say. That's life! Thank you and if I offended somebody with my experience, I apologize. I wish you inner peace and enthusiasm."

Marina: "No one is responsible for the decisions of others and decisions can't be taken for other people's life, but humanly, you land a hand to the fallen one, even more if it is your husband. You have certain responsibilities and you're not wrong if you sacrifice yourself a little. You think that the one who wants to quit his life does it because he feels he lost his life support. You made him depend on you foe several years, then you accuse him that he can't handle it alone, that's cowardice!"

Elena: "And one final comment. We, humans, expect a Savior, one person to lift us up, to love us, but most importantly, is to save ourselves, to stand up for yourself, because each of us is extraordinary, with huge potential, and we have inside everything we thinks we will find outside. Until we find love within us and we understand that we all depend on what happens around us, we will wait that something from the outside will come to make us happy. When we accept ourselves with good and bad and we love ourselves as we are, we will change the external expectations and we will be happy. Thank you and please forgive me."

What is to be done in such situations? How can we avoid a dramatic situation? Simple! Be honest with yourself, look to connect with the God inside, radiate love and peace where you step foot. Hatred, jealousy and judgment are tools that take you away from God so much that you don't even know anymore how it is to live with Him.

Be responsible for your life and seek the best solutions for living a happy and fulfilled life. Be responsible for your behavior and stop grumble like a helpless little child who got lost on the road of life. Be mature and take the best decisions for you, even if you know that this could bring pain into other's life of. Only those who are far from themselves will suffer, those who are far from God and have no plan to really know themselves.

Empty people always tend to unconsciously use emotional blackmail in all forms. Some are using children, others get married because they can't stand being alone, others are moving from one relationship to another believing that someone will fill that emptiness. No matter what form of emotional blackmail they use, they will never be happy unless they have the courage to be totally honest with themselves. This sincerity may harm them, but the wound will be irreparable if they continue this game that leads nowhere. You don't have to die physically to discover what a wonderful creature you are, how valuable you are on this earth and how happy you can be if you trust yourself.

If you have reached the stage where you declare to yourself, "Damn the opinions of others! I'm tired of thinking about what people say. I'm tired of criticism, I'm tired of falsehood, and I'm tired of traitors and people eager to see only what they want to see. I don't want to satisfy anyone anymore, I just want to live my own way, beautifully. I am perfect exactly as I am. I am an exceptional human being, a person who can make mistakes, but who has the power to start a new life. I'm sick to satisfy others, I'm sick to live my life according to the script they wrote." Congratulations! This book is for you.

When people tell you that "you've changed," it's a very good sign. Don't worry. It just means you stopped to go on living your life in their way. You live in your unique style and that means you fully recovered yourself. It's clear that you no longer resonate with the old circle of friends because your inside, your perceptions on life has changed tremendously. You evolve and this is the best thing that can happen to you. You cannot be the same person with the same way of thinking as ten years ago. That would mean that you certainly have stagnated and, therefore, your life is full of discontent. Change means change in the true sense of the word; otherwise it wouldn't be called this way.

It's okay to let some people go out of your life. Not all people you meet in life should remain near you, as you will not remain in the lives of all the people you meet. Let go those who want to go and make room for those who want to enter. It's the law of void, the law of compensation: get rid of the clothes that don't fit you anymore, let them go, and make room so you can refill your wardrobe. "The most important thing is to be ready at any moment to sacrifice what you are for what you could become."

What causes people to change? It depends on the vision each has on life. In my case, I felt I wasn't part of a pattern dictated by others. I love changes. They became a lifestyle. Looking at it from another point of view, the main reason why the majority decides the change is "drama." They get tired of a life of deprivation on all levels.

Empty people have no dreams. They cut off the wings of those who want to fly towards what really fulfills them.

Someone says: "I am a student, I am 18 and I want to study music, which I am mad about. But my parents don't want to hear it because I won't make money from music, they say. Their dream is to see me becoming doctor, but I hate blood and this profession. I am at the edge of the abyss because it's almost the end of high school. What shall I do?"

I warn you! Probably the first who will stand in your way of becoming a great man may be your family, followed by friends whom you think are the best, then the society you live in. A person who is focused only on the outside has no chance to discover the genius from inside or to even have the curiosity to find out who they really are. Don't identify yourself with these people; go on your way because you will certainly succeed.

Can you believe that? It is said that the family always supports you. False. It supports you if you please them. If you do something different, they are against you. Just to see how much emotional blackmail is there. That happens in most families. Children need a dream, a story to build their beautiful world on. They still have the power to believe that "Once upon a time ..." can begin now.

Obviously, you must follow your intuition (inner voice). Unfortunately, sometimes parents should be ignored. Some of them are very good of cutting of the wings of a child. They have a great talent in this respect. They can easily turn a great kid into a mediocre kid. Simply they don't allow him to fly. They want you to stay within the limits of the society. This is the naked truth. For this reason, there are so many people with bad performance in what they do because they work out of obligation, with no pleasure or interest. It's good to go on your way from the start. Otherwise, you will start from scratch again at 30-40 years, if you dare! They are many extremely frustrated people because they have a profession that doesn't tell them anything.

At the end of the day, you chose this wonderful family. You knew they were going to help you to discover yourself. They have supported you in their own way with their minds. You must thank them for that. You have nothing more to ask from them. It is important to not think to return to the flock, you go ahead with your unique way of being. You're perfect the way you are now. You don't need to change to make them happy. To make yourself happy, that's important. They call it selfishness, but in fact, it's called self-love. How much love and compassion should you have for them? I'm just asking. I believe with certainty that true love for them is if you detach totally. Be only with yourself. That's love!

The truth is that in this experience you have the chance to completely forget about yourself, so hard you could get involved in this game: mother, father and child. You feel like all pull you to return to the flock. How the hell can you become a great man if you don't get out of the flock?

Some parents don't even know 10% of their child's potential. They will be shocked if you fulfill your dreams. It is vital to detach yourself from them and to impose respect when they are talking to you. They don't know how you the way you know yourself because you accepted them as they are without trying to change them somehow. You have changed and this is revolution.

Don't try to please everyone. You have to please yourself.

Of course you always tried to please them all. You tried to satisfy your family, friends, coworkers, but you were never fully satisfied with yourself. You were too busy to please them. Dear parent, don't burden your child with fulfilling your dreams, for he is a different person who will have his own dreams.

How can the parents who think they have rebellious children be happy? From my point of view, rebellious children are real Masters for their parents. Parents have a lot to learn from them. I know it sounds paradoxical what I just said, but children become rebellious because they come in inappropriate families. They aren't understood and this is what triggers the "conflict." The Masters come to experience "strong feelings," they don't come here for a monotonous life. I am sorry for these parents, but their children know what they're doing. These children, parents should treat as grown-ups, responsible, to respect them and to not control them. To trust that they can be the best version of themselves. To support them at all times and never be on other people's side (no matter what they do!). This is how the child regains confidence in their parents. Otherwise, they will be considered traitors and they will always be in conflict. Love your child unconditionally and you will see the change! If the parents were to know who they live with, they would bow in front of the child's Divinity. And their relationship would be great!

How much do children from dysfunctional families suffer? There are many things to say and many factors to consider ... positive and negative. The child will be marked anyway. If a parent is missing, the child won't experience the normality of a family life, which later puts its mark on how the person sees and addresses situations as a teenager and later as an adult. No matter what, the child is a victim. You cannot give advice, you cannot judge. There are so many situations that the only suggestion that comes to mind is caution. No wonder it is said that before getting married, you should live some time with the partner and the decision to have a child is a very serious and responsible one. Even so, no one can foresee the future and nobody can ensure the happiness and the solidity of your relationship. Choose being aware of the love for yourself, not because you fear you'll be alone. Two parents can live separately and the child doesn't feel pain. I'm talking about two parents who made conscious choices. That where the child is not used as a tool of revenge or reconciliation. Only two frustrated parents use their child to resolve inner conflicts. My advice: don't get into relationships and don't take important decisions if you are frustrated!

According to current research in neuroscience, various mental programs are implemented to children during 0-7 years of age (some authors even refer to the embryonic period); according to cultural and social beliefs they belong to, including those belonging to the family where they grow. What do you understand from this statement? You are the Creator of your life and there isn't a God up there who dictates your fate without you being able to do something about it. These programs are recorded in the subconscious of children and, in most cases, will be automatically untwined over their lifetime; they become the foundation on which they are built as individuals. What do you understand from here? You can change your life anytime if you make this choice consciously. Automatically after seven years of age, the personality and life experiences of the individual are based on what they believed out of what the adults around them said, on what they accepted as truth about themselves during childhood. The language the parents and teachers use when addressing to them will become their unconscious inner language.

Only when you go outside your comfort zone you can tell how empty people live. There are so disconnected from the inner Source, that it is impossible for them to realize this. They are so far from the divine essence, as is the distance from Earth to Heaven.

They live in the spirit of the flock, they have no idea what a life in harmony means and how it is to really live. They have never known this magical feeling and, therefore, they don't know what to look for. They think they live a normal life, they are part of the crowd and the others are freaks. They have no idea what it means to have a financial education and how much their lives would change if they had some notions on this. They are called robots of society created to support others to have a truly fulfilled life. The sad part is that these people who have this lifestyle don't even want a different life; they don't even want to hear the word "self-education." They simply find it more convenient to live with the patterns taken from their family and society than to start working with themselves. They don't have time for themselves because they are much too busy working for others, do excessive shopping to cover the emptiness from the inside, to buy very expensive things just to feel that they have value, to go on holidays to impress the others how happy they are in this life.

These people could not stay alone with themselves even for half an hour. It is too hard for them to reserve this precious time to get introspective, wondering: "Is this the life I want to live it?" Ignorance costs a lot. Ultimately, it is their choice to live in their own Hell. They don't know the concept of inner paradise and they don't even want to know anything about it. Indifference, ignorance is the strength of people disconnected from the source. Everything else matter to them but their own person.

The way people treat other people is a reflection of their own opinion about themselves. If you don't love for yourself, then you cannot give love to the other. You can say that you love, you can even believe this, but that doesn't mean it's the truth. You can believe that everything ends, that your life is empty without someone, it's an illusion! It's just your ego screaming and feeling the need to possess, to have, to feel loved and raised on a pedestal.

Someone says: "I got to have everything I wanted after many years of work and although I am only 39 years, I feel I'm sad all the time for no reason. Those around me tell me that I have too much, but I cry almost every day. How can I get out of this state?"

Material things and family can't fill the emptiness from the inside because a part of you is missing. One solution would be releasing the mind. It likes depression. This is what it does best. Stop identifying yourself with it. I went through these states until I found out why. Then you can merge with the divine inside yourself. From this moment, you never feel alone again. Normally, you are happy for no reason.

If I tell you that empty people are poor, I don't exaggerate. It couldn't be more truth in what I say. I know my honesty is extremely painful for those concerned and certainly they don't like what they are reading now. But this way the awakening to real life takes place, and they won't live a superficial life in order to impress others.

How can you tell that a man is rich or poor without checking his bank account? A rich man is one who is full inside. That means they don't need surrogates to be happy and rich. They are rich, even if they don't intentionally show the world their wealth.

Growing the desire for luxury is the surest way to increase pain. Don't be the slave of the things you own. Even limit your needs. Spend your time looking for long lasting happiness.

It's not easy to think different, but it's not impossible either. It's up to you whether you want to be really happy or you are the adept of artificial happiness. What does artificial thinking mean? You think you're happy if you have a well-paid job, if you are married, if you have a house, a car and many children. It's a false illusion. Most people have found at the end of their life that this didn't bring them true happiness in life.

Happiness can be achieved by practicing self-control, cultivating the habit of living simply, but to think deeply, spending less money, even if you earn more. Isn't it better to live simply and soberly and become richer in reality?

How do empty people behave? Someone makes a confession on a social network: "My mother asked me to help her with something important to her, but my plan for tomorrow is different. When I said I couldn't, she said that we were family and family is the most important and if I am not there for her, I don't love her, I don't care about her and so on. It sounded like emotional blackmail to me. What shall I do, shall I give up my important plan for her or not?"

Adrian: "If tomorrow you won't be able to help her, would you be sorry? Can your plan be delayed?"

Dona: "Your mother is a priority, because she is the most important person, she brought us into the world and she loved us every minute from the moment she gave us life!"

Adriana: "If you are close to her and your plan can be delayed, then do help her; you never know when it the last time is and you don't know how hard it is to be far away and not to be able to be there when she needs you. If you can help her... do it."

Alina: "You are also a member of the family, an equal member... sometimes we can't be together, even if we are members of the same family, we need our freedom to follow our own path. At the end of the day every plan can be «negotiated», at least a little bit. Are you a good negotiator?"

Daniel: "Get to an agreement and see what the priorities are... mom is the only one that could understand you."

Enache: "If she had already phoned, what other call are you waiting for?"

Isabel: "It depends on how much time has passed since the last time she asked for your help and how important the reason is and if she normally appeals to sentimentality. If some time has passed since she last called, if the reason is important to her (it doesn't matter you put it on the ninth place) and if you're the one who can make your mother happy, DO IT! Because some years from now, you will tell us how your mom went to heaven and how you didn't have enough time and enough patience to listen to her and how you would now give anything to have her next to you. It's my opinion."

After the answers people give to questions, I feel like they are programmed like robots to save those around them. They cannot save themselves, instead they jump for others. An interesting approach to life. People are programmed so that they are afraid of their own shadow. They fear death as if it were such a sober event. They anticipate death and they tell you how sorry you will be you haven't helped your mother ten years ago. I notice that people have in their soul only regrets and disappointments. Where is the joy of living?

Where is that awareness when you know you are God and all those around you are the same? When will you see a person as something eternal and infinite? When you will see them with their true value without having to try to save them or pity them. They can save themselves, sit still, and stop worrying about it. The power is in their hands and they can use if they want. But how can they save themselves if they are programmed to shout out loud "Help! Help! Help!" to the left and to the right? Give them the chance to find out who they are and what a treasure they're hiding inside.

Emotional blackmail is so subtle and normal that most don't even realize that the umbilical cord wasn't cut at birth. Neither parents, nor children are aware of this. You shouldn't wonder why you are not able to have a full and balanced couple relationship or you're not able to be a strong person inside. Because you are emotionally blackmailed. You have no personality, no self-love you and then you will always be last in your life. You haven't learnt to this age to say "Yes" or "No" firmly. Uncertainty and insecurity follow you at every step and this is reflected in the quality of your life. You'll never be able to reach a great goal if you're not on your feet mentally and emotionally.

Don't forget this divine law, which if it's broken brings a lot of pain and suffering into your life:

1. God
2. You
3. Spouse
4. Children
5. Parents
6. Siblings
7. Friends

What does this mean? The moment you break the divine law, don't be surprised if your life is not how you want it.

Let me explain in different way. The first is God. In the second place are you. In the moment you made compromises and you stepped on you, you've stepped on God. Why? Because God is in you. Another example. It happens very often that women forget this divine law after having a child. They annul themselves and God implicitly, and often they annul the husband, as the child becomes the priority. You shouldn't wonder then why the couple relationship falls apart and the husband is turning to someone else. Or another example—your mother asks you to spend time with her, but your husband wants the same thing. What will you choose? Remember the divine law if you want your life to be in harmony.

Another characteristic of empty people is this: they want to stand out at any cost. For example, if they have dinner with their family, everyone necessarily needs to know how well and how happy they are! I bet on anything that these people do such gestures to impress the others, to show them they are superior, when in reality is totally the opposite. They can barely survive and the small economy they hardly put aside they want to pull it out and show it to the world. My question is: why can't you be happy without showing to the world? Because you need a confirmation from the outside? Because you want to make sure that your family is on the right track? When such people label themselves this way, it is quite obvious to me that everything is perfect in their lives. Nothing is as they would have liked. They lie to themselves and then they inevitably lie to the others.

Why don't you first prove to yourself the confidence in you and your reality? Why do you waste your time showing the others how happy you are?! Prove it to yourself and you will see how the joy comes from within. It will not be based on surrogate images anymore.

We infatuate too much when, in fact, we are false and inauthentic. Posing beautifully, we create false images of who we are just to look good in front of others. True generosity and wisdom can't be seen on Facebook, in all photos and check-ins you can only see the interaction that we have every day with those we meet on our way. When you act in your relationships with others without understanding and love, that says a lot about you. The way you treat others talks about where you are as a human being. Show me how you treat the people around you, from the janitor and the beggar on the street to the directory, and I'll tell you who you are. There is no superiority and inferiority between people and hypocrisy doesn't hurt anyone but you.

It's so easy to realize how insecure people are about their lives. How? You ask them a simple question: "How are you?" The ordinary question that has many answers. Someone answered to this question automatically: "Okay. I'm doing the shopping with my husband." She shouldn't have mention she still has a husband, because he was near her and I knew they were in a long and solid relationship. You can feel a person's uncertainty in the vibration of their voice. When in a short sentence, the word "husband" is accentuated this shows fear or how hard it is to keep the family together. Clearly she makes a huge effort to keep her marriage.

Dear people, stop trying to be happy! Happiness exists within you and you don't have to make any effort to enjoy it. It's yours and nobody can steal it.

A psychologist, psych spiritual counselor, Bowen Therapist Licensed Expert explains the phrase: "Tell me who your friends are and I'll tell you who you are."

"This proverb tells us in a quantum understanding that we gather, we become friends with those who have the same frequency with us. If you have neglect, criticism, gossip in your intimate behavior—you with yourself—you will attract people who show the same characteristics. If you have understanding, love, peace and harmony in your life you will attract people who have the same way of manifestation. If you don't know yourself yet, one way to find out who you are is to analyze the people in your life, from your nearest reality. After doing this analysis, you will discover where you have to work with yourself and so you will grow and you'll make a quantum leap to a higher frequency stream of consciousness. If you want to know someone you get in touch with occasionally, a way to know them is to look at their friends. Good luck in working with yourself."

To be yourself in a world that is always trying to change you is a great achievement for those who have the power to realize the deepest level of their being.

When a person decides to make radical changes in their life, the entourage reacts, jumps, but not of joy, but surprised that one of theirs dares to overcome their condition. When you discover your vocation, when you start to do sports and eat healthy, when you start your business, others begin to sabotage you consciously or more unconsciously. If you manage to do what you want, they no longer have excuses. If you want to you help others, you are bound to succeed because only by example you can educate them. Without the power of example you don't have the necessary credibility.

Be what you are and say what you think because who will be offended it's not important and who is important will not be offended. If you think so, consistently, things will improve. You will stop betraying yourself. And, when this treachery will end, it will not be so easy for others to abuse you or betray you.

Most people spend their day doing many unimportant and petty activities to relieve their tension (gossip, surf the net, smoke, watch TV, have little fights, give advice). Few people are focused on very high priority activities that lead to goals. Where do the two roads go?

Slowly and surely you die inside if you become a slave of habit, following the same path every day; unless you change your existence; if you take the chance to build something new; if you don't talk to people you don't know.

You die a little bit when you turn the television into your guru; when avoid passion, when you prefer the black on white situations and the dots on the "i's" instead of a whirlwind of emotions, those emotions that teaches your eyes to shine, the sighing to smile and which frees the feelings of your heart.

You die slowly if you don't leave when you're unhappy in your work; if you don't risk certainty for uncertainty to fulfill your dream; if you don't listen at least once in your life to "responsible "advice. Who doesn't travel dies a little bit; who doesn't read; who doesn't listen to music; who doesn't seek the divine within themselves.

It dies a little who destroys their love; who doesn't allow anyone to help them; who spends their days complaining about their own bad luck and the rain that it never stops. It dies a little the person who abandons a project before it began; who doesn't ask because they are afraid not to embarrass themselves and who doesn't answer when they know the answer.

We avoid death a little, always remembering that "being one with God" is not a metaphor or an elusive star. Another feature of the empty people is this: pretense. Yes. It's a real finding. When you lose your social status, people treat you differently. When you have that social status, everyone wants to be around you.

In vain you try to build your masks; there will be people who simply don't like you. Don't put masks on or else very few people will stay with you until the end of life. Is it worth building different faces, to be angry, to hate? Those who really know you won't forget you; those who have forgotten you had never known you.

Why do people get sick? Because they are empty. There is no divinity inside them. Cancer and difficult diseases occur due to heavy emotional shocks (family death, maximum frustration, violent divorce etc.). The past that can't be forgotten gets us sick. This is my opinion.

Someone else asks: "But why do children get sick?" Some children have incurable diseases because they have chosen this experience before coming here. They need this experience at a soul level. I know it's not an agreeable explanation for those who go through these situations. One thing is clear: there is no question without answer. Most times we want to hear only what we know or our mind can conceive. To be rich, beautiful and healthy is not bad, is a service that you do to yourself, to the society and all those who surround you.

CHAPTER 5

WHAT IS LOVE?

"Always remember that love never judges, it doesn't ask and it doesn't make claims. Who do you love this time of your life, but you still judge? Remember that judging closes the heart and blocks your love channel. The love that is capable of judgment is a love of the mind; it's not true love, real love, from inside your heart. Rather than judging, isn't it better to open your heart and accept the one next to you exactly as it is? Instead of focusing on the things that separate you, shouldn't you better focus on things that unite you and keep you together? Today look at the people around you and bless them with all the love you are able of giving. See in them the things that inspire you, you enjoy, and that bring you close to each other. Always remember that whatever you focus on will prosper. What will you choose today to see in the people around you?"

To love is the very law of life. It is the most sublime action that a human being can do. Love can accompany all other fundamental actions. If you learn with passion, with love, you will memorize easier and you will understand more easily. If you listen with love, you will hear more and much better. If you speak with love, your words will be given an unimaginable force. If you go to sleep with love in your soul, your sleep will be as restful and deep as a child's. If you think when you are filled with love, your thoughts will gain depth and brilliance. Thoughts that are built with love will be brighter than the sun. All these and more arise when love is present in your being.

Love is the best medicine. Any pain occurs where there is no love and no recognition of Love. When you learn to get back to love, you remember Who You Really Are. And when you know who you are, you realize that you are already perfectly healthy, complete, radiant and bright.

Love is everything. It's not only a spiritual word used by you to seem interesting, nicer or better. It is more than your mind can imagine. Love is a way God expresses Himself through you. I often hear, read books or various articles that talk about what love means. There are so many definitions given to this concept.

Dear soul, love is a way of being. You are love. It is a way of living. Your presence exudes love where you are without having to do anything in this regard. I have gathered so many life experiences that I saw and felt with all my heart how love manifests itself in the true sense of the word. It is a blessing that the God inside me gave me many opportunities to see the world and enjoy it. I allowed my divinity to be a messenger of love.

The joy in my soul is so great that I want to share it with you. I am love and from my plenitude I give love to all the people I see along the way. I say what I feel in my heart with the desire to pass on this information that can change your life.

The source of my happiness is inexhaustible because it comes from my being. I am not afraid that once scattered around me, I won't have it anymore. It isn't a treasure that must be preserved and kept secret lest anyone to deprive me of it. It is a diamond every human being owns. It just needs to be discovered and shared.

I will illustrate this concept called "love" through concrete life examples. Behind every experience is a wonderful gift that I allowed myself to collect. I gathered so many gifts from these experiences that, at this moment, I feel a complete and perfect being. I lack nothing; therefore I'm no longer looking for that something, because I know I am everything.

Determined to change my lifestyle, I decided to leave Romania to take a German course in Germany in a beautiful city called Augsburg. I've took an intensive German language course for beginners. I achieved level 1 and 2 after I passed the language exams. The experience was divine. I had 30 colleagues from around the world. Each person was unique, with a definite lifestyle, with their own mentality. My best friend from that course was a Catholic nun from India. Communication between us was very funny because no one from that course knew German. Everyone spoke their mother tongue and some of us communicated in English during breaks. We understood each other eventually. The body language and gestures helped us a lot to be able to communicate between us. The teacher was German and had a unique style of teaching. He didn't communicate with us in English because his purpose at this course was to teach us to speak German. He had a sensational teaching style because he had different techniques to ensure that we understand what he says. He was authentic, doing this work with passion and he was very happy when he could see our progress with each passing day.

During breaks, each tried to explain which country they come from and what was the purpose for coming to Germany. Each showed on the map where they came from. Some came to this course because the company sent them here. The company they were working for was expanding its business in Germany. Others came to Germany because they had found a life partner. Some came to this course out of passion to learn another language. My best friend from that course, the nun from India, came to Germany because the Catholic Church sent her to a church as a missionary. From Monday to Friday she was at the school and on Saturdays and Sundays she worked for free in retirement homes and children orphanages. Her life was dedicated to people.

I had learned German alone in Romania six months before going to Germany. When I went on the course, I already knew the basics of German grammar. A course module lasted two months. After three months, I decided to go to my friend in Austria. Because I was the best in the class, the teacher awarded me a diploma stating that I successfully completed the first two levels of the language course.

Austria also impressed me in a very pleasant way. Besides being a beautiful country, the people there are absolutely fantastic. As proof that man sanctifies the place, it is obvious that the country's image corresponds to the profile of the people who inhabit it. Love for others is obvious in the behavior of people towards everything around them. I have some very pleasant experiences.

Once in Austria, I inevitably met other Romanians living there. If you don't know them from Romania, you have the chance to become friends with them very quickly. So I quickly made quite a few friends.

One of them was already settled there for ten years. His way of thinking was different from the one I had. He was thinking exactly like the people there. He was behaving and acting according to the mentality of the people around him. He told me one thing: "Carmina, if you want to stay in Austria, you must change your way of thinking. Here you can live well only if you comply with the society you live in. it's the only way you won't feel like a stranger in this country."

He lived in a village in Austria, he had a house there. At first, I thought he was living in the countryside because he couldn't afford to live in the capital city where life is more expensive. My surprise was to see that the situation was just the reverse. Rich people live in the countryside. Only they can afford to buy houses and they want if possible to avoid congested areas because they love nature.

He told me how wonderful people are, and the joy you feel just because you live among them. He was very busy and he worked a lot. For this reason, he didn't have time to deal with his house where he had to do a lot to fix it. The house needed a complete renovation. His neighbor of 65 years of age was retired, and he offered to do the roof and the fence for free. His only desire was to have all the needed materials so he can get to work.

And he was very surprised too by the attitude of his neighbors. With how much love they give unconditionally. He told me how retired people do charity work for the sake of feeling useful. For this reason, they feel young and strong, albeit at a fairly advanced age.

They acted like carefree children and they give you the feeling that their life is perfect. It is. They live in the present moment without thinking about tomorrow. They have the inner certainty that all will be well and there is no point in worrying about something.

You shouldn't be surprised if you see a 50 years old person driving around in a children's car. Your first reaction is one like, "This guy is insane! How did he think at his age to get into a kids' car and drive around? Doesn't he have more important things to do?" It's the reaction I had when I saw this. My friend smiled at me and said: "Do you know who this man is? Learn not to judge people at first sight by the way they dress or what they do! "Wow! I said in my mind: "The way I look at people it's not very nice, educate yourself and look beyond what your eyes meet!" Embarrassed by the comment received from my friend, I said, "Who is this man? A simple man from the countryside!" He smiled at me again telling me: "This man is much more than it seems. He is the second important person in the Vienna City Hall. That night he invited us to have lunch with him in his garden. They are very curious by nature when they meet a new person and he wants to know more about it. My friend translated our conversation. In Austria they speak a German dialect and therefore I had the feeling I didn't understand what they say.

I felt like in an interview. He asked me so many questions that within one hour, he knew all about my life. He was very impressed when he found out about my studies in economics. He was surprised! He praised me while I sat at the table with him and other neighbors. He said he was sorry I don't speak German fluently because he wanted to have such co-worker at the City Hall. He asked me if he could help me somehow, and I said I'm just visiting and my goal now is to learn to speak German. I knew the grammar already very well.

I was surprised by the people I met there. How much dedication and love can people give! Incredible!

Another thing I would like to recount is the clear proof of love for people. I drove on a country road somewhere in Austria. On the way a terrible accident had happened. A very young girl crashed her car into a tree. Because of the speed and lack of experience, the accident was fatal, from my point of view. I was convinced that she is already beyond the visible world. It was a surprise when I saw that in five minutes the firemen, the ambulance, the police and a helicopter came to the spot. An army of people was around the girl. I don't think it took more than twenty minutes, and she was already on the surgery table. She might not have the chance to recover completely, but for sure this soul was saved. I was surprised how people acted in an emergency case with speed and responsibility.

My holiday in Austria came to an end. From here I went back to Germany. My friend really helped me to find a job, as a house maid. My desire was to meet new people.

The fear of the unknown is one of the biggest fears a person could face. Once you overcome this fear, your life can change radically. Nothing bad can happen to you, because God guides your steps, you're never alone if you learn to have a direct nonverbal communication, through feelings, with the divinity inside you.

Again, I had the opportunity to meet sensational people whom I had learnt a lot from. When you meet such people who by their example prove it that life can be lived differently, inevitably, your curiosity is even greater.

I enjoyed every moment I lived next to other people. I watched them, I admired and I respected them for who they are and for how they behave with the people around them.

This doesn't mean I had no challenges in my journey. There were many, but I learnt to live being in permanent action. In every challenge I saw a great opportunity to overcome my limits.

I have always been free to make choices. I did only what I felt in my heart. I chose only what I thought it could really make me happy. Life is a beautiful adventure if you can look at it this way. Compromises have no meaning if you want to be truly happy.

My journey continued. I arrived in the Netherlands. A wonderful country. I lived among these people for eight months. I had the opportunity to meet love in all its forms. I mean that pure and authentic love. There were many things that surprised me very much in terms of freedom. The freedom to be what you feel and what you want. You don't feel constrained by anyone or anything.

The joy and simplicity with which people live is enchanting. Instantly you fall in love with these human angels.

Once, I thought excessive freedom takes you wrong paths. But I found that it actually gives you the chance to be who you really are. You don't need rules and restrictions to be a good person, with integrity, who has the capacity to realize what is good or bad for them.

Here I saw clearly what unconditional love really means. I saw how it is to live this way. Living among them, I saw that it is not so complicated to behave this way. For a long time, life for them is not a drama or a disaster. There are not led by old patterns and beliefs that cause them pain.

The way of thinking is different and, therefore, life is lived at a different level. They don't criticize and judge people by appearances. They don't put any labels. On the contrary, they have the ability to understand beyond what human eyes can see. Here I also received some interesting life lessons that helped me for my inner change.

I hand the tendency to judge people who do various activities. For example, prostitution. I received comments on how I used to think. I felt a little offended. Then I realized that in fact they live on another level of consciousness. Love is so great that judgment, malice, envy and greed don't exist in their soul.

Women and men have a very high self-esteem. No one wants to use you in a way that it will hurt you.

I often hear the question: "Can a man and a woman stay friends after they break up?" My answer is: "Absolutely!" I have seen many examples of this kind. It is possible, there are many people living this way. Which means that true love lives in their hearts. They are a perfect expression of God.

Children are educated in a different way. Families live in a different style than the one I knew. First, small children are taught to be responsible for their life. Parents don't sacrifice for them. They give them freedom of choice from the moment they ask for their rights. For this reason, when they become adults, their life is not at all complicated. They don't look for a life partner just because they feel weak. They are with someone just because they want to share the love at the highest level. They are honest to each other and when they no longer feel fulfilled together, they give each other freedom without drama and suffering. Each of the partners is convinced that there will be something else in their lives. They're at peace and happy with themselves.

Children are not a burden for their families. They are allowed to experiment at an early age. Parents don't intervene in their lives unless they are asking for help. Children respect their parents unconditionally. They don't expect a bailout from their parents, perhaps at most, emotional support.

Only if you live among them you can tell what love is in the true sense of the word. Practically—not just theoretically. Then I arrived in Ireland. I really appreciate the people of this country. I love the Romanians very much, I don't discriminate between nations. I appreciate them and respect them because they are fair and very diligent.

I had a beautiful experience in this country too. People are very welcoming and very excited by the beauty of their country. At first, I didn't see it as beautiful as they said. Probably because it rains ten months a year and it is very cold. They love nature very much. A tree, a hill, a flower impresses them at maximum. In time, I discovered myself the beauty of Ireland. They have magnificent places. Landscapes you can't see in Romania.

They fill so emotionally fulfilled that they see beauty in everything. Don't imagine they live in luxury houses and they have very expensive cars. Not at all. Even if they were to have all these things, I don't think they would be any different of how they are now. They love simplicity. Their happiness comes from within. It is not connected with the material possessions.

Why do they live better? Because they have love in their hearts. Where there is love, there is God.

There I worked for in a house for few months. The reason I left was one that will surely surprise you.

I worked for a rich family. They lived in the countryside, although they also had a residence in the city. The reason they chose to live in the countryside was the silence and the peace offered by the surrounding nature. No chaos, no noise, no jams.

The person I worked for went to a party to a good friend. Being distracted, he forgot that alcohol and driving is a problem. He drove his car while inebriated. The police stopped him. They registered a very high level of alcohol. He was sent straight to prison. He was there for few days until he bailed out; the amount was quiet high. His driving license was suspended for 5 years. That's why he had to move into an apartment in the city, close to his work place.

What do I want to say with this experience? It's not the only one of the kind. I could give you more examples. The police didn't take into consideration who the person was and how important the person was in Ireland. The laws and the rules are the same for everyone. It demonstrates the high level of civilization, respect and love for the others who could be in danger because someone acts recklessly.

England is one of the countries that charmed me. The people are the wonder of this country. As an observer, I became aware why I was in that place and why it was necessary to get there. At the beginning, my mind left with the purpose of having a long term relationship with a person dear to me. And then my mind came with lots other reasons. I will work and I will have enough money to live a beautiful and full life. At the end of the experience, I realized that my soul didn't go there for the reasons my mind thought were very important. The purpose was divine: to learn what love means and how it manifests every day. Wow, what a revelation!

It's not a secret that the work I did in England was less usual for a woman. I washed cars, I cleaned and polished them. From a car you didn't want to get close to, I was transforming it into a shiny new one.

I worked for different car brand showrooms. But how did it happen to get to work there when I don't have a passion for cars? The circumstances. For me, all cars were the same: with 4 doors or 2 doors, with 4 wheels and a steering wheel. I thought that if I have so many luxury cars in my hand I will fall in love with them. I still haven't discovered a great love for cars. In my vision, they are still the same: a car is good because it makes your life easier and more beautiful. It helps you get faster to where you need to go and your comfort is greater. In conclusion, the car is an instrument that helps you fulfill your human necessities and that's all.

The next question in my mind was: what was the purpose of my experience if I didn't fall in love with cars? What did I get out of this situation? Surely the purpose of my soul was different. That's right; you guessed it, dear friend! I, as a person, got richer; my vision of life is much wider than before.

People surprised me in a way that I cannot put into words. There are so wonderful that I always want to be around them. They are a perfect manifestation of God. You feel blessed and loved by the whole universe.

From them I learnt how to be love and how to live with love.

Although working under less elegant and comfortable conditions, I was happy knowing what kind of people I'll meet. At first, I couldn't understand why they are so happy when their work is so uncomfortable. Under no circumstances they came to work with designer clothes, with expensive and fancy shoes. Their dress code was as ordinary as possible. The work was quite difficult. The physical effort was to match. For this reason, I couldn't understand in my mind why these people are so happy. How they come to work with such a great pleasure, knowing that most work for money, not because they are head over heels in love with cars.

They didn't have any secret that I had to discover. But simply through them God manifested Himself, He was taking the physical form.

At first, I thought that I was fortunate to meet nice people gathered in the same place. But along the way I realized that they are all nice. Perfect copy of each other. Wow, what a discovery! Being in the midst of love without you knowing it. Amazing! To be among these human angels, dressed in dirty overalls and boots that weigh several kilograms. Every day is a holiday for them; they enjoy it as if tomorrow will never come. They live in the present moment without thinking about how to do this. They enjoy every moment without reading hundreds of books about it. They love life without seeking God somewhere specific.

The goodness of their heart is like a ray of love that comes up in your life. Inevitably, you take the mood of the ones around you.

My colleague from work was 58 years old. She was working with her husband who was 61 years old. He was always smiling. He was dancing between cars when he wanted to take a break from work. Every evening he went to karate and the next morning when he came to work, he was telling us what he did the night before. Ordinary and unimportant things for the rest of us who were looking for happiness elsewhere. She told me that she has a beautiful house. Don't imagine that she owned it or that it was a luxury villa. Not by a long shot. She was happy because she had a garden where she could have a barbecue. She loves animals and nature very much. She is charmed by this.

One morning, she came into work and told everyone she was a little tired because she just came back from the seaside. She didn't get the chance to get home because the two days off were too few and she had to take advantage of it. I said she can rest only when she gets back home. Very cheerful she said she has no time to rest because tonight she'll go swimming. Folks, we are talking about a

58 years old woman that felt like she was 20 years of age. I took her as example because she was the only woman in that garage. All my co-workers were the same. They were all telling us how they live life moment by moment. Whenever you were within their coverage, they asked: "Are you okay?" You received this question at every step, even from people who you didn't see ever before.

If you were telling them that you were looking to move closer to work, they read the newspapers for you, giving you advice and didn't know what else to do to help you. If you wanted to take some time off from work to get to the bank to sort something, everyone knew that. They asked you if everything is OK and if they can help you with something. You felt like in a big family, where you, as a person, were on the first place. The work came naturally, without too much effort. The bosses are the best friends of their employees. You can hardly figure out that there is boss in the room. Only if you ask. Otherwise, you don't know. He is your best friend, because he is directly interested in your life. Not only the work that you do there.

I was very surprised of how disabled people are treated. How easy they are integrated into society, how happy they can be at their working place.

For few days I worked in another garage. All my colleagues were very nice. They brought me coffee from the kitchen where they had their lunch. I didn't dare to feel like I was at home because I was new to that garage. As I was only visiting them. The big boss of this company had the habit to sending us where they needed us. When a person suddenly got sick or was not feeling well, we replaced them. Therefore we were walking from one place to another.

In the three days I worked there, I thought a person was more distracted than all others. Only in the last day I realized that was a disabled person. His behavior was a bit strange: he only worked if he was in the mood, he was helping me clean a car door, and then he was going to another colleague and helped him to clean a window. He always smiled and he was always happy. I didn't understand how the company kept a person who worked only when they were in the mood. Up to a point when I saw couple of things he did that made no sense at the time. No one joked for him to react like that. His colleagues, who were working busily, left their work aside and began to act like him. Again, I realize how the true love manifests. People around him behaved so that he doesn't feel that he had any health problem. The society you live in helps you have a happy life. By the way they behave, they prove how much they love you. Being sick, you don't even realize this. That boy came to work just because he felt very comfortable there and he couldn't wait to meet with colleagues. His life was beautiful and meaningful.

So many things surprised me that I will need hundreds of pages to recount in detail how the love for people, nature, animals and everything around manifests. In England I lived in the same house with a family with an autistic child who was nine years of age. The parents' desperation pushed them to make the decision to move to this country.

The expenses for the child were high. The state didn't even provide the minimal amount of financial or physical help. People around them marginalized them and made them feel like a family that had a very big problem. The main reason that the family decided to move to England was: they really hoped to give this wonderful child a chance. As you know, autistic children are geniuses, not children with major problems.

Their desire was to integrate the child into a normal school. If he isn't able to cope he will be moved to a special school. It depends a lot on how the child manages. This child was absolutely perfect because of the day by day work, done by his mother. In Romania no one ever helped them in this regard. People felt sorry for her to have a child who was, as they thought, so ill. The school didn't really have people specializing in this field. She spent a lot of money with the child's sessions. The association to which she belonged to was simply gathering the files of the children with autism. Other than that, nobody really felt responsible for this child. It was up to the parents to cope financially, emotionally and psychologically with their child.

They took the first steps in this regard. Of course, they were helped by the people they met here in England. People very sensitive to the problems of others. They cannot live if they see someone around them suffer. They get involved and they seek for solutions.

They had to wait for some time until their file reached the English authorities. It took a while for them to analyze the exact stage the child was at and how many people he needs around him. It was a big meeting attended by the parents, the child, a translator and a few specialists who analyzed our little prince. They asked the parents the most ordinary things: what he eats, what toys he likes, what makes the child happy, if he goes to the toilet by himself, what sports he likes etc. A team of experts with a hundred questions about the child.

The care of these experts who will handle the case of our little genius was: "What if somehow the child won't like them? What if he doesn't adjust to their presence?" How to behave with him so they keep him happy and he doesn't feel he is a special child? In their view, our main character was completely normal; he just needed more attention from the people he interacted with. So, dear friends, the English authorities are trying to find the best solutions for this miracle child.

Speaking about England, I don't want to forget to tell you all the other things that surprised me. I don't mean that they have highways on hills and bridges under the mountains, but I want to talk about the way they love nature and animals. Driving on the motorway, I could see sheep grazing in the fields, cows and horses with coats on. Not because it was freezing, but only because it was colder than normal. So their beautiful animals won't miss the comfort they deserve.

Whenever I come home to see my parents in Romania, before me appear people for whom previously I couldn't have love and compassion. I felt sorry for them because they are very poor and beg for money. Now I look at them with love. I felt the goodness in these people's hearts. A few days ago I went to the supermarket and a beggar asked me for money. The shop assistant gave me a lighter as gift. When I left the supermarket, I gave 5 Lei, (approximately $1), to the beggar. He was very happy. After a few days, one morning, I went to the nearest store to my home. It was raining very hard. I waited a few minutes for the rain to stop. It didn't. I took the umbrella from the drawer and decided to get out of the house. When I went out, I found that it wasn't raining very hard anymore, it was just dripping. Then the rain stopped. Preventively, I put my jacket hood on the head and I started off. The story repeated. This time I met a beggar who asks me to give her money for bread. I told her that I'll give it to her when I get back. I bought a pack of cigarettes and got again a lighter as gift. I was very happy. At eight in the morning to get gifts already. Wonderful, I thought in my mind. I gave the beggar $1 and she said it's not enough for bread. I pulled out of the wallet another $1 and I gave her a total of $2. It was an exchange of energy. I received a lighter and then I gave back something. The question in my mind was: How much pension does this woman have if she doesn't have enough money for bread for a whole month? I took only two steps and someone else stops me on the street. To tell me that I was his favorite and he greatly admires me. He wanted to know where I was for so long because he hadn't seen me in a while in the area. His voice was quivering when speaking to me. He wanted to invite me for a coffee. I explained to him that it's not possible at the moment because I have a boyfriend. I got home very happy because I finally learnt the lesson of compassion without me feeling affected by people who choose to play so difficult roles in this life.

After a few minutes, it started raining very hard. I said in my mind: "Rain loves me too! It treats me like a queen! It stopped for me." Surely, you will say that it was pure coincidence. That may be so, I don't argue that. But the joy I felt in my heart was indescribable. To feel how people around you that don't know you give you their love, to feel how the nature loves you and that you have the Universe at your feet. It's sensational! I felt the presence of God in those people, in the rain and in my heart. What can make you happier than that? If you don't believe in miracles, perhaps, you forgot that you are one of them. Your birth is an undeniable miracle.

What it means to live at the edge of life? To think your happiness and joy come from the outside: money, cars, houses, positions, life partner, etc. it means that God gives access to these treasures only to some. Go down deep and there you will find the essence of life: joy, peace, true love, forgiveness, fulfillment etc. "An unsearched life is not worth living" someone said. Wise men don't even call it life, they call it sleep. When you don't live your Life, you have no control over what you live, Life lives your. You are at its mercy.

The energy of Love and Light, the Creator's nature, doesn't get into conflict with anyone or anything. It purifies everything, cleanses everything, heals everything, and lifts everything up. Energy is a precious gift given to man. Energy helps you to act, to enjoy things, to work, to express yourself the way you want, to have growth, to go forward, to get results and succeed in life, to love, to write, to learn, to help your fellow people, to help yourself, to smile etc. Energy gives you the opportunity to do what's nice and good for you and the other people.

You can only find the greatness and beauty of life by living in love, choosing happiness and discovering its essence. Life is eternal, dear, you're here to discover yourself, to find out who you are and live experiences that in a form of disembodied spirit you couldn't be able to have. You are here to love, to laugh, to be happy, to be joyful. You're here to be healthy, to have true love relationship, to have abundance and to share with others. You're here because you chose to be here when you come down in the flesh, you knew the rules of a wonderful life. You knew you had unlimited power, you knew that the universe gives you after what you deserve, by your vibration, you knew that you will attract exactly what you are, no more, no less, you knew that you have a mind which is the perfect instrument for materialization, you knew that when someone offends you they actually show you a part of you, you knew that what you feel and what you say are true, you knew you have your inner universe where there is everything you want, you knew you're perfect as you are, you knew that if you allow the Life Energy called God flow through you, you will experience a dream life! You knew these things and yet you let yourself covered by your mind which instead of helping you and be a fabulous tool, it has come to control you. It's never too late to realize this. You're free, unlimited and love. What could you want more?

How do you relieve your guilt feeling that doesn't allow you to be loved? In my second experience in Ireland, I found some good examples. While cleaning a house, I broke by mistake a crystal ball. I found out how much it costs: 500 Euros. I don't feel guilty at all. It was a story with a divine purpose. The owner said that so he'll call the shop in New York to see if the crystal ball was insured.

The other day, in another house when I was wiping the floor, the bucket of water fell on the parquet in the lobby. The owner was at home. I closed the kitchen door and she didn't see anything. In conclusion, I don't feel guilty at all for this incident.

In another house, the shower cabin fell when I wanted to clean it. I am not to blame that owners don't buy quality items. Why is this happening? For sure you guessed the answer.

This is what happens when you decided to do something with your life. When you have chosen with all your heart a great goal in life, all criticism, judgments and guilt get out of your life. Once accepted, they go away. When everyone seems to be against you, you have to be your best friend.

In conclusion, I feel like a millionaire and 500 Euros doesn't even matter. For sure the situation will be sorted somehow. If they blame me, this means I didn't get rid of this aspect yet. If the criticisms of others affect me, it means I still identify myself with that aspect. I think I'll give them each a Nobel Prize. Thanks to them, I fulfill my great dreams. I love this job, it fascinates me, and it is an inexhaustible source of inspiration. And I get to know myself better. Honestly, sometimes I don't like what I see at myself, but I am learning to like everything, to take me as a pack with light and dark.

Let's not forget one very important thing: people tend to throw their projections of themselves on others. For example, if someone tells you that you are "weak" or "envious" in fact, they think that about themselves. Or if someone tells you you're "stupid" it is their unconscious opinion about themselves thrown over others. Ideally, you should not identify yourself with other people's opinions. Everyone should know they are a wonderful being without confirmation from the outside.

Stop wasting your energy trying to defend labels; you can invest it in something creative or valuable. What others think about you is entirely their problem. They don't relate to you, but to the image you have of yourself, and you understood once and for all that you are not an image. They are responsible for the way they perceive you. They reject you for what they think you are, just as they praise you.

Carmina Harr

Your challenges, your wounds and sufferings that arise in the relation to the others are a very good opportunity for you to get back on your way, to get back to yourself, at your real Essence. Don't look at those who from the outside seem to have caused your suffering as if they were "guilty," they are souls like you with whom you had a contract to help you on your way.

What do I have to learn from experience in Ireland? What does it show me about myself? Certainly something I don't want to accept about myself. Once I played the role of the savior, I let myself in last place just to see others happy. Now I experience the same thing. I clean houses to make people happy. Simple? Right? What should you do to make yourself happy? You value yourself. You are aware you are always self-worth.

I chose an experience to show how much I love myself no matter what happens outside. People who speak to me in a disparaging tone, people who abandon me, people who don't keep their word, etc. And all this happens only so I fall in love with myself, and to create another reality. When you go outside your comfort zone, you meet all your sides. Everything around you is a huge mirror reflecting what you are not even aware of.

Only after you know who you are, do you come to accept easily what others criticize about you and to take only what fits in your everyday transformation. People, things, events, situations will always show you images about yourself, what you are inside. What you have inside as experience, as vibration in every cell of the body. You need people around you to show you who you are and what's inside you. This is how love manifests itself.

You are what you see in others. When someone behaves badly with you, you could be happy they showed you how you behave with yourself, and actually, how little you love yourself and how you punish yourself. To be able to see the best in the others, even in times when they show you their darkest side. This is true love.

Someone says: "I am overwhelmed by my life; I am exhausted because I continually sacrifice myself for my children, my siblings, for my spouse, my parents, for my in-laws, and my colleagues; in fact, for anyone who asks me for help. I want to be a good person and help everyone, but I can no longer cope. If I refuse them, then I'm selfish. What can I do to be at peace and happy and have time for my needs?"

Unfortunately, the term "selfish" is misunderstood. It's the point everything starts from. You didn't come here to save the world, but to save yourself. Your ego successfully plays the role of the savior. You are really selfish when you play the role of a victim pretending that you help the others. You do not actually save them; on the contrary, you harm them. You don't allow them to discover their power. They will always be victims. To love them truly means to help them to see their greatness. From here they can handle it.

Help without sacrificing yourself. Help because it is easy to make this gesture. One is to help someone because you can do it and another is to sacrifice yourself saving the world so you don't seem selfish. Define in your mind clearly the notion of "selfish" and you will see you will perceive the situations that occur in your way differently. You'll have more clarity on them and avoid confusion.

Someone makes the following assertion: "Help your friends when in need if you want them to become your enemies." The role of the savior doesn't help anybody, really. This is a very deep awareness of life's experiences. This is why sometimes we get something else instead. It's like a warning. It's good to remember this when you feel that you have enemies around you. In reality, they do not exist. Their role is to focus your attention on yourself.

If you want to help a friend, do it in a way you don't take over their burden.

I chose not to play the role of the savior because I realized that means not to honor the God inside me. We are equal and the savior creates the superiority status. Every one of us lives the experience they chose, maybe just to discover who they really are. Allow everyone to find out the power they have inside and no longer feed them with the energy of the victim. I know you feel sorry for people in need, but you don't help them with anything if you confirm their impotence. Instead, you'll really help them when you trust that they will be who they really are. True Gods.

Is your life tumultuous? Are you shaken, literally and figuratively? Are your relationships shaken? What you do professionally don't pay off anymore? Why are all these happening? So you get to know yourself much better. You don't see what you are fro so much ballast, from so many things that you still keep inside in yourself and in your life, things that no longer serve you. And it's time to do something with what you already have, to allow what is beautiful to materialize, to allow your desires to come true and to not be affected by other low energies. You are alone now, this process of self-discovery you have to do it by yourself. Please don't try to get others out from the pit, to teach them what to do; it's a time when you can help yourself; and you, by your example, can help others. Each person saves himself or herself.

When you find yourself in a difficult situation in life, when you feel that you have no chance to escape, when you don't know what choice to make, listen to your inner voice and trust that everything will be OK. You should have this inner dialogue: "What should I learn from these experiences? Why are they always around me?" They dissolve only when you understand their purpose. Otherwise, they repeat indefinitely, other characters appear, but in the same context. We treat the problem at the root, exactly inside our being. Someone said to ask the support of the Universe when we are in a difficult situation. But you must not forget that the Universe gives you exactly what you emanate. You give revulsion and despair, the same you'll get back. He gives you exactly what you hold inside so you can see exactly what conscious or unconscious command you give. If you emit chaos and despair, it's what you'll get back. You give love and compassion and you get them back tenfold; perhaps from whom you least expect. A man may be a tyrant to others, but act like a gentleman with you. What you have reflected on them at the energetic level, is what you get back. For this reason, love transforms everything.

Give yourself time this evening (every evening, or at least when you feel you are far away from yourself), give yourself peace, understanding and love. Put your mind at rest and allow it to translate what your heart says, be present and detached and listen.

Someone wonders: "What will happen if true love costs money? How many people will pay for it? And rest assured, I ask rhetorically because true love costs nothing and yet too few receive it in their life!" I notice this confusion is always made. People think that love is not about money, as money is something very bad. I always hear this phrase, as if people have to choose between wealth and love. Likely they try to find a reason for poverty to feel better. Many will choose love in the detriment of money. I was thinking the same once. In fact, this how I made my choices in life. I no longer wonder why the money disappeared from my life, although I once had it. I didn't treasure it and loved it the way it deserved. But I realized at very deep level that Love is everything, including abundance. True love comes as a pack. I think that we have many beliefs that create our reality.

A friend who loves you from the heart is one who regardless of age and situation, manages to make you realize that your life can be beautiful indeed if you are able to choose from it only what can make you happy. It is the one who doesn't encourage you to play the role of a victim, but on the contrary, they honor you without stepping into your experience.

True friends don't get upset with you, even if you had the courage to tell them an extremely painful truth. This way, you determine them to be totally honest with themselves. Of course, if you make this choice. Although I remember that I often had a divergence of opinions with them, they love me unconditionally. A friend full of love always appreciates sincerity, no matter how cruel I am. I am very happy with this reaction. I'm a little nervous when it comes to checking my friends. I have no regrets when I lose an inauthentic friend. I love authentic people.

I know I have explained in my first book about the vital role that gay people play. On Facebook I have found an interesting debate on this controversial subject. A young woman was searching for desperate solutions to fit into society and to live a normal life. This time, I will take a concrete example. A case study in Romania.

The question is this: "I am a young woman of 26 years and I am lesbian, and my life is a nightmare: my parents have disowned me, the church denied me, and I fail to have a stable job and a stable relationship. I know that all these are caused by my sexual orientation, which I didn't manage to quit, even if I really tried. What can I do to accept who I am? Without judging myself."

The answers to this question are:

1. Marcela: "Accept yourself as you are and you will be the happiest."
2. Laura: "Look inside yourself, not outside. When you will love yourself the way you are, the others will love you too and not the way around."
3. Adriana: "I don't think you have anything else to do: just love yourself and accept yourself, or it won't be You anymore. In our country, it will take time and several generations of people until the mentality will change. People are used to judge and categorize someone without even having the curiosity to know them, to discover their soul. They just put labels. It is painful that you have to suffer and be repudiated by a sick system, unable to see the truth around it. What is more shocking is that you say "the church denied me," I can't help but laugh, because

isn't the church supposed to love us and accept us as we are?!? Now what is it doing, judges people? Who gives it that right? I love you and I accept you, my dear, and I respect you for your courage to tell the truth!"

4. Veronica: "Your sexual orientation should ne only your business. If you have intellectual and professional qualities you shouldn't have problems getting hired (in theory). Any direct or indirect discrimination against an employee or potential employee based on gender, sexual orientation, genetic characteristics, age, nationality, race, color, religion, political opinion, social origin, disability, family status or responsibilities, affiliation at trade union activity is prohibited, the law says so, but the practice is killing us. In my experience, I tell you there are many people who get employed without having to declare directly their sexual orientations, so go ahead, fight, it's none of those "outside" business what are you doing in the house/bed."

5. Lavinia: "You gave your own answer: stop judging yourself! It all begins from here! If you judge yourself, how can you expect others to not do it? And, apparently, you're so focused on it that you think that everything goes wrong because you're a lesbian. Stop judging yourself, smile and learn to love yourself because you're wonderful!"

6. Roxana: "Why do you judge yourself? Who loves you and wants you close, they will love regardless of your sexual orientation, religion etc. So just be yourself with good and bad; people will comment anyway if you do either good or bad."

7. Ovidiu: "I think it's best to stay as you are and be confident. I don't think what happens to you happens because of your sexual orientation, but rather that you put the problem in a way that doesn't help. Yes, in our country people look weird who those that are not like the others, the majority, but that doesn't mean you can't live your life."

8. Dorina: "First, you have to accept and love yourself as you are. When you are at peace with yourself, you won't think that the others judge you or you won't care anymore."

9. Marina: "All that happens to you have nothing to do with your sexual orientation. I go with the herd, I don't get out of the society patterns and I had a parent who disowned me, the church turned its back to me when I was in pain, my jobs are a string of failures, and I better don't talk about my relationships. In conclusion, self-confidence, the confidence in the divine being inside you makes everything and not "the faults" of any kind. It's awfully hard to accept yourself as you are when everything that happens makes you think you're defect, but if you can see your defect as quality, it's ideal."

10. Lavinia: "First step: stop judging yourself. If you are not at peace with yourself, why do you expect others to accept you? The confidence you show will make people criticize you less and accept you easier; tested technique, applied, approved by myself."

11. Me: "It's a lot to say. First, we learn to love the people around us. Lesbians and homosexuals play a very important role in balancing the energies. We should honor them for their difficult role they have chosen in this life. The good part is that they are easily accepted by almost

everyone, with few-large exceptions. They are pioneers in changing the mentality of the place where they were born. My respect for the important role they play."

12. Ciprian: "I don't know what to say, but I don't get you."

I want to tell you that nothing is what it seems. Certainly, at a soul level, she played many masculine roles as evidence that the male and the female are in total discrepancy inside her. From my point of view, she has to accept the feminine side that she hated in other lives. She despised so much her feminine side that now she plays a dual role. She has to accept herself, to love herself so much, as to reconcile with her feminine side of her being. As I said in my first book, there is a major discrepancy globally between feminine and masculine. Women are not actually treated as men's equal. There are still many countries where women are degraded and can't have important positions. Yet their role is only for procreation and housework. At Creation, lesbians and gays balance the energies. When everyone will be able to balance the masculine and feminine within themselves, they will be complete. It means that they merged with the divinity within themselves and acts as a true God. At a soul level, nothing is wrong or incorrect. Each plays perfectly the role for which they came to School Earth.

In this life she should find out who she really is. She is an angel who came to do the work to widen the Creation for the Spirit's sake. She chose this difficult role because she knows that she can face the challenges. She chose her parents and the country where to be born. At a soul level, she knew that they were going to help her a lot to learn about things that she wouldn't experience if she wasn't in this human body.

If in this life she will succeed to love her feminine side in order to fully accept herself, it means that she had reached the purpose for which she came. If she fails to accept herself, she will definitely repeat this role. Many others and I, highly evolved souls, played such roles. Basically, I played all possible and impossible roles, imaginable or unimaginable. This is how a soul evolves. When we despise someone or something, we don't accept a part of us as part of the whole.

When she accepts everything she doesn't like, in fact she approves what she doesn't want to see at her. Society's marginalization only reflects what she has inside (deep-rooted patterns and programs taken from family or society). Once you know who you are, you believe in yourself, no matter what others reflect. So the new neural programs get implemented. If you react to criticism, you do nothing but to give power to the old pattern. Let it die slowly and surely.

Many people believe that the criticism is constructive. My view is clear: "Never criticism will be constructive." Its purpose is to feed the ego and to destroy the self-love. Critics accuse themselves and search for a reason to expose the accusations to the first person who comes in their way. Perfectly true! They throw their projections on others. They throw all their frustrations on others.

Your misfortune is that you are in their way, which then becomes something other than "training" for yourself because you think you are defective or incomplete. Do you want to be happy? Choose your friends wisely. It is very important that you choose carefully with whom you spend your spare time. Simply get rid of people who criticize, and do nothing else but stay in the way of your happiness.

Living with "love" every moment means to greet everyone with a smile, even if your heart is torn by pain, to forgive all those who think you are evil, to try to be happy even when everything seems sad.

"The true elixir of life is Love that pours over everything. It is the source of physical longevity. The aging process is always caused by the lack of this Love."

An example of this is the lady I lived with in Ireland. She is 75 years old and she is charming. Soon she will turn 76 years old. She is so happy and lively. She looks so beautiful and so well, that you could barely give her 50. She doesn't have a spouse. As proof that happiness comes from within, she doesn't not rely on people outside. She has three sons. And she is extremely proud of that. She is an example for me in this respect. You can see that her inner beauty is reflected on the outside. Her kindness, calmness and joy are contagious. Her presence in my life is a blessing. She is very active, very hardworking and often goes on vacations or various dance competitions. She is part of a dance group. I guess they are all of a similar age. I have no words to express the elegance and uniqueness of this divine being.

At first glance, you tend to say it's normal to be very happy when your life is simple and easy. But the real life story of this lovely lady is not taken from a fairy tale. She had a violent husband. She raised her three children by herself and she managed to take possession of a house. She also has a holiday house by the sea where she spends the summer. She manages to live in the present moment with such ease, being connected with the divinity within her. This is the normal behavior when you are one with the God inside you. I say she's an alpha female. What do you think?

Never judge anyone because you never know how their life is or what they go through. In this book I explained in detail this "phenomenon." Once understood on all sides, it is very easy to manage and change what's inside yourself and you don't want to see.

If you understand that the life you live is love itself, life has no concept of "good" or "bad" and you realize that it is entirely your creation, you prone yourself to instant fulfillment and peace. Your soul doesn't live in duality. Remember, the strongest statement is: I am! I assume you already know who you are! I don't doubt it for a single moment.

CHAPTER 6

WHY KEEP QUIET? DO YOU WANT TO BE FREE?

"A gentle look says everything. Sometimes it's better to keep quiet. Just to observe without saying anything. To look with gentle eyes. What else could you add to this moment?"

Great truths are found in deep contemplation. Listen to the silence and you'll understand. "He, who doesn't understand your silence, probably won't understand your words."

Everyone could be "a genius in manifestation" if they had their mind free. As long as the mind is occupied with drama, the person has no chance to find their purpose for which they were born in this life. Each of us has a divine gift waiting to be discovered. That requires introspection.

Often silence is golden. Countless times I found that it's better to shut up than to talk. Why? Everyone is unique. I understand that each has its own way of thinking. In silence, each of us can find themselves. The mind is silent so the heart can talk. You look at yourself and you look deep inside your being.

The truth of your soul is not identical to the others'. In silence, you find all the answers to your questions. It's a divine moment. It is in vain to try to convince those around you how you see and define God. How many ways God can manifest? It's a simple question. Every person and situation is a perfect expression of God.

Whenever you ask others what you have to do in a certain situation or how to solve a problem you are facing at the moment, it means you don't have enough confidence in the God inside you. It means that you are still looking others for the answer; your mind still has doubts about how you live. Stop it! Stop! Shut up! Feel! What does your soul want to tell you now? Did you hear it? It just whispered in your ear that it loves you and enjoys that you've realized that it's always with you. Celebrate this magical moment! The power is in you and you were constantly seeking it outside. You're not alone! Are you happy about this awareness? Definitely yes! But please, shut up! Don't impose your deep awareness to others. Why? This way, you walk far away again. It's a shame! You just connected with the divinity in you for a few divine moments. Shut up and create a deep and intimate connection with it. Rejoice in the depths of your soul. People outside will see your face radiating happiness. They will realize that you have something that makes you so happy and they will definitely ask you the secret of your happiness. What do you say? You've discovered the God inside your being? Better not. It's hard to understand these words with your minds. You can answer this way: the weather is nice! I'm happy to have met you, etc.

Every soul must reach this deep awareness individually. Some will need to be hold by hand until they discover the magic of it, and then you let them fly free. Support them! But don't force them to keep up with you. You know that sooner or later they will learn everything they need to know.

Keep quiet and enjoy life! The joy will be enormous when someone will ask you to speak. You feel like you cannot stop what flows through you. You bring joy to where you stepped. God blesses everyone through you wherever you go.

Why do you tend to speak without stopping yourself? It's the mind that wants to look smart and interesting. It's another one of her manipulation tricks. It wants you to believe that you are spiritual so it could block you on your way to your deeper awareness. It's sneaky! It's sly! It's manipulative! And brilliant. Love it for its slyness! See it as it's playing like a child. Enjoy its presence. Celebrate with it this present moment.

I ask one question. Why do you think that you are the only one who has the ultimate truth? Because you feel it inside your being. Surely, this is the answer. Stop one second and ask yourself: "Why do I think that the others around me are just rambling with what they say? Why do I think others around him are false prophets? Didn't you think they are perfect exactly as they are? They also resonate with a certain category of people. Stop trying to put labels on people's foreheads. I remind you: you don't possess the absolute truth!!! Only the truth of your heart! I don't need to repeat that you shouldn't impose it anymore on others. Allow others to discover themselves at their own genuine pace.

Why do you want to tell the world what makes you so happy? Is it because you cannot manage the happiness invading your whole being? And you want to share it because otherwise you will explode? You may feel this.

Everyone should be aware that they are a link and a very important part in God's great creation. You are born of infinite love; you've never been and will not be separated from God.

Be present in your heart every moment. We are interconnected, there is no separation.

When your mind is quiet and there's no noise among your thoughts, you are in contact with your divine essence and you can take wise decisions for you and your evolution. When you have inner peace, you can observe yourself and evolve in the direction your Divine Self wants. Realize deeply that you're here on this planet to manifest your divinity in the material concrete plan. Meditation is a very good technique that could calm your mind and allows you to connect with your Self when you feel disconnected from your divine essence.

Silence commands respect. In a room full of people and a heated discussion the one who doesn't talk is the most esteemed. Contrary to popular belief, the power doesn't belong to the person who manages to speak first, but to the one who manages to keep silence the longest. Speaking immediately awakens the critical spirit of your interlocutor.

"Don't try to look for words when you run out of words. Allow yourself to be silent, for this silence speaks for itself." To write is to listen to what your Self dictates. Shut up, listen and write.

Why shut up? A moment of silence may be worth a thousand words. Love is silence. It is worth all the words put together. A hug is an "I love you" whispered by your soul! Spend some time in your company. There are divine moments! You can learn more about you; just listen to your inner voice. Put silence louder and listen to what your divine Self tells you.

The society puts the label of "introvert" to the one who pays a special attention introspection and silence. Some people find introvert people odd because they don't think and act in the spirit of the flock. They are so authentic that they do just what they feel.

Let's see how a psychologist describes the characteristics of an introvert.

Myth no. 1—Introverts don't like talking

This conception is false. Introvert people prefer not to talk if they have nothing good to say. They don't like to talk about things that don't interest them. Invite an introvert person into a discussion on a topic that they are interested in and you'll see how you won't be able to stop their avalanche of words.

Myth no. 2—Introvert people are shy

Shyness has nothing to do with being introvert. Introverts are not necessarily "afraid" of people. What they need is a reason to interact. It is in their nature to not talk just for the sake of talking. If you want to talk to an introvert, you have to begin the conversation.

Myth no. 3—Introverts are rude

Most of the time, introverts don't see the point in all social amiabilities if they are not necessary. They prefer to be realistic and honest. Unfortunately, this isn't possible in all cases, which determines some sort of pressure that they find tiring.

Myth no. 4—Introverts don't appreciate people

On the contrary, they appreciate very much the value of the people around them. If you are lucky enough for an introvert person to consider you a friend, you can be sure you have a loyal ally for life. Once you win their respect, being a quality person, for them you are the best!

Myth no. 5—Introverts don't like getting out in public

It is totally false. These people like to go out in public only if they feel that the other people resonate with them. They also avoid complications that can occur in a public place. They accumulate information and experiences very quickly and as a result, they don't feel the need to stay there for too long. They're ready to go home, to rest and process all the information; in fact, rest is absolutely crucial for the introvert.

Myth no. 6—Introverts will always be alone

Introverts feel perfectly comfortable when they are only with their thoughts. They like to think more, to dream, to meditate and to have problems they can work on—for example, to solve puzzles. They are not dependent on the presence of others. But they have moments when they feel incredibly lonely if they don't have someone with whom to share their discoveries. Eventually, they yearn for a genuine and sincere connection with one person.

Myth no. 7—Introverts are strange

Introverts are often individualists. They don't follow the crowd and prefer to be judged on their lifestyle. They believe in themselves and therefore, most times they dispute the rules of "normality." Their decisions are not taken based on trends or popularity.

Myth no. 8—Introverts are "geeks"

Introverts primarily solve the problem from the inside, paying particular attention to their thoughts and emotions. It is not that they would not be able to be attentive to what is happening around them, just that their inner world is more challenging and rewarding and therefore they prefer the "breaking" from our world.

Myth no. 9—Introverts don't know how to have fun and relax

Introverts prefer to relax at home, in their intimacy or in nature, not in crowded places. Introverts don't like adrenaline and unpredictable risks. But they love the change. If you are talking around them too much or there is too much noise, they are giving up. Their brain is very sensitive to a neurotransmitter called Dopamine. At introverts and extroverts the dominant neuropaths are different. They charge with energy if they are in a fun place with people who enjoy life. They avoid depressed people because they transmit a bad vibration.

Myth no. 10—Introverts can overcome themselves and become extroverts.

Introverts can't "fix" themselves. They deserve respect for their natural temperament and contributions to the human race. In fact, one study (Silverman 1986) showed that the percentage of introverts increases with the IQ. In silence, the self "wants you." In silence, everything is heard clearer. When you stop the outside noise, you can hear the internal chaos, but also your true voice and so it begins the cleansing at all levels.

Why be quiet? When the mind is very quiet and silent, God communicates with you. You feel His presence every moment of the day. You see Him in people, you read Him in the books and all around you. The state you have is amazing when you leave yourself in the hands of the divine inside you.

I want to talk about freedom in the true sense of the word. Financial freedom, emotional freedom, freedom of thought and freedom to express your opinion.

Freedom in relationships is a subject that I am particularly passionate about. What you can do to have a fulfilled family life. I don't talk about the first five years of relationship when the partners are deeply in love, but how to be happy at least 30 years with the person you feel that part of your being. That person who complements you, balance you emotionally so you have the power to feel fulfilled in all areas of life.

It is very important to know what it means to be a complete woman or man. Everyone, needs to educate themselves individually, they need to know how to act especially if they didn't have the opportunity to see it in their family or society they live in.

It is no secret that the man thinks and acts very differently from the woman. To create a balance in the relationship, each needs to know how to act and what to do to maintain a balanced and beautiful life together.

It's an authentic woman the one who knows what she wants in life, who knows how to make conscious choices, and doesn't let herself manipulated and controlled by her partner, by her boss or by the society she lives in. she thinks freely, and acts according to her inner voice being true to herself. She doesn't lie to herself about how she feels, she has the power to recognize that she is frustrated, angry and unhappy and she is looking for solutions to reach the balance with herself without having to blame those outside her. She has the power of decision, from the ordinary things to the ones that contribute to her happiness. She has a point of view on what is happening around her and especially on her life.

To be a woman is an art. It's more than wearing heels, cleavage or perfume. Elegance is a quality both physical and moral, and has nothing to do with clothing. Femininity and beauty come from within. It's a mindset.

Who is the Woman? She is a queen who inspires and brings new life on Earth. She is a queen who rules her kingdom with dignity, whatever and however it may be. It's a model of inspiration for all others. A Beauty! Dare to open new paths, to be ahead of everyone and be a model of beauty and attitude all around! Dare to feel like a queen every day of your life!

Have you ever wanted to be a super woman? Have you ever wanted to be the absolute woman, free, the synthesis of all women inside yourself: the lover, the mistress, the inspiration, the magician, the hero, the mother? The woman who doesn't look for a man to feel complete, but is looking for him in order to give him, and celebrate together, her own completeness.

The man dreams of finding the perfect woman: he wants the woman to be feminine, to be a housewife and a mistress, a queen and a child. Men have always been instinctively drawn to the one woman who embodies all these as only she can lift the man and help him to gain power and to be whole. Maybe for the world you are just one person, but to one person you are the whole world. "The most beautiful nights reach perfection when in the silence of the night you hear and feel the heart of the loved one like a drum beating deep inside your chest and your soul ..."

The woman can be satisfied with one love, completely fulfilled, because she doesn't look at the man's body, she looks only at his inner qualities. She doesn't love a man with a beautiful muscular body, she falls for a man who has that certain something—something indefinable, but amazingly attractive—which is a mystery to be explored. She wants her man to be not only a man, but an adventure in discovering consciousness. Because of her serenity, her gentleness, she can fulfill a man's life tremendously. She can surround the man's life in a very soothing, comfortable atmosphere.

In my view, a strong independent woman doesn't mean a woman who borrows masculine characteristics and thus becomes stronger. A complete woman, full of personality means a woman who honors her femininity and at the same time doesn't compromise on the quality of her life, in her relationships, with respect to her lifestyle or dreams and needs.

"You can be a scientist, or an artist, but don't forget you are a woman. Don't become part of the men's gang."

A strong man is essentially a free man in every respect. He has the conqueror instinct from Mother Nature. He is more rational than the woman. He sees life from a different perspective. For him financial security is very important and he is very protective. The view of a rich man: "If women did not exist, all the money in the world would be meaningless."

What's the difference between a woman who can have any man for a relationship and one that, regardless of beauty, intelligence and social status seems to put off any man? The first category has a unique lifestyle; she is not desperate for a man. In contrast, the one in the second category is so unsure of herself that she could sell her soul to be with the man she wants.

The woman who is waiting for the "unique" and "true" right person may end up on life's waiting list. It's like waiting for redemption.

Since always, the man and woman try to love each other. She usually wants everything now, the man wants first to be accepted and loved because he wants to conquer.

Two people fit very well when they are of the same nature. They get along in the long term if they have the same values in life. The moment when one of them no longer evolves, the other is losing. At some point, they reach a huge discrepancy, and the two find out they don't have the same views anymore, the same tastes and preferences. So the quarrels and misunderstandings occur in a long term couple relationship.

Each of them must have their own personality and have an independent status, even if they have common goals. Neither of them must be annulled as a person when they live under the same roof. They respect and help each other in reaching their professional and non-professional goals which they have in common or separately. Of course, the alpha woman is an independent woman, not dependent on her husband. That's called emotional and financial dependence.

I know from experience that less active wives in the social life of these powerful men, in time, fall into the second, although they seem to be on the first place. I saw such situations all around me. To keep your number one in the couple's life for as long as possible, it is necessary to avoid as much as possible marriage routine. For me, marriage means the lack of motivation for women to do anything, thinking she has everything and it doesn't make sense to reinvent herself.

Marriage in medieval style means the place where both must make concessions. And that leads to frustrations over time. And frustrations lead to "mismatches of character" and, indirectly, to separation. Like my cousin says: "In the beginning between us was chemistry, now it's all math."

Lasting marriage is an art based on tenderness, touch, intimacy, physical and emotional support, freedom. Marriage is not a prison, pressurizing the other, terror and not least it is not physical and verbal aggression. Let's make every marriage a garden, where our dear flowers, our children, can grow in harmony, freedom and security, and we can merge into each other in a celebration of the divine union of two spirit-soul in this journey on the beautiful planet Earth.

Marriage also means safety. The alpha man is a conqueror and after marriage he doesn't think it makes sense to try to impress. The alpha man is free, creative; he cannot be locked up in a prison. On short term, yes, he wants it, but on long term, he will change because he is in constant change. You as his life partner, you have to be one step ahead of him. Come up with new ideas. Even if he doesn't put them into practice, at least it shows him that he's free.

"The real woman is the woman you want to hold hands with on the street, the woman you to sleep next to, not only to lie down with, it's the woman that makes a cold morning seem warm, the woman you want to spend all day in bed with, just to be able to see her there with you ... just you two, the two of you. It's the woman that doesn't make you want to seem a different person than the one you are, you don't want to impress her with what you're not ... you tell her straight who you are, what you want, how you want it, it's the woman you are always naked next to even when you are dressed. She is a woman who understands you, caresses and tells you a good word, from the heart. She doesn't want you to be the prince; she doesn't want you to struggle to impress her to win her heart. She wants you exactly as you are. The one she fell for. Authentic. The woman you want to discover every day, you want to enrich yourself a little with her richness. It's the kind of woman that when something happened, when you have a problem, she will look into your eyes, she'll caress your face gently and she will tell you that as long as you are together, any problem can be solved. It's the kind of woman who makes you think and that's good. She makes you think you are a happy man. That she has chosen you, you are hers, all the others had lost this war and you are the only one who won it. She may not have been your first love, but she knows for sure that she found her prince!"

My opinion is that there are professional mistresses who will always play only a secondary role in a relationship and they will be mistresses only by chance or occasionally. There's no shame to be a mistress at a time, but don't be in this position forever. A real woman will not be content to be kept secret while another woman receives "applause" and the admiration of others. "Sometimes, in the woman's mind, strange ideas sprout. Why will you want to marry your lover?!?! Live your adventure and leave him where he belongs if you started on the road to adventure." The wolf changes its hair but not its habits.

You, the real woman, if you want you can play all the roles for your life partner. There's no need to limit yourself. I assure you of this if you still have doubts. Be authentic; be creative and full of life!

Because the topic became too serious, I want to cheer you up and to laugh with all your heart. A friend tells me at one point: "Older people say that a woman never forgets the men who were great in bed, and men never forget the women they couldn't have! A bit naughty our elderly."

"After she finishes her confession, the priest tells a young woman:

— Go with God!

Looking around a bit confused, she asks:

— Which one of them?"

A friend asked a man, a manager: "Why can't you do more?" His answer was: "My mind doesn't let me!" Of course, it was about sex. Forget the mind, was her reply. Overcome your limits!

One indisputable truth: "Man is born between a woman's legs and for the rest of his life he is struggling to get back there, because there's no place more beautiful than home." These are pamphlets. Treat them as such.

A very dear friend makes a few confessions that are worthy of note: "Recently, an elderly man told me he is mad that young women now walk almost naked etc. I asked him why he doesn't enjoy seeing something beautiful. Only because he can't have sex with them anymore? He couldn't believe what I said. He tells me, "So you know, women who want to have sex with a man who rejects them for whatever reason, don't forget and don't forgive. I had such experiences with few women over the years.

You know, I said it to many. The man is obligated to try and accept if he is rejected. Many women I know told me in my youth, women I didn't have sex with and I met again after many years when I was no longer interested: "Why didn't you tell me you admired me? I didn't notice that you had a crush on me." So the man should try politely. In general, they easily forget a rejection, especially if they often propose. Men are like coffee. The best ones are warm, strong and keep you up all night."

"A man who knows everything about all women doesn't know anything about one." My opinion.

Therefore I advise you to have 100% confidence in what the woman inside you says, to impose your standards with which nature has endowed you to make the world a better place. Don't compromise, be rough and impatient with the irresponsibility of men and reward their honesty and openness as you like.

Only when you don't know your true value you make compromises in order to get attention, appreciation or love from others. But because of the awareness that you compromise with yourself, you will not be satisfied, no matter how much you get from others.

When we talk about romantic relationships, we implicitly talk about sex, eroticism. One of the great disappointments of a man after he "chased" a woman is to discover she is inactive in bed, moans, she is silent, she is not moving properly, she doesn't even make eye contact with him. Believe it or not, in reality, there are many signals that show whether your girlfriend is active or not in bed.

A woman who dances has rhythm, suggests power, vibration and creativity and is another sign about how she moves in the bedroom. So watch her dancing and you'll get an idea of how she moves between silky sheets.

Although you see a woman who sexually vibrates or has some of the qualities listed here, don't forget that these are just some signals; it is not clear evidence about the partner's sexual abilities.

Many women love their man, but the sexual opening is often restricted by education, religion, previous experiences, physical problems etc. This is how you get to divorces and mistresses.

In parallel, please think well and analyze with maximum objectivity what makes your femininity "cry," what prevents it to manifest? Is there something in your life, a thing, a person who makes you forget you're a woman with needs and enhances your desire to ensure the comfort of all, except for you? Something that prevents you ask for your right to tenderness and love that you deserve?

Take advantage of the opportunities of this period, be honest with yourself, "shake up" the past, take the bull by the horns and redo your life! Healing will come by itself. What will you choose?

Self-respect means attitude. It is the feature that you should cultivate. Its purpose is to help you not tread on your soul, avoid compromises and be present while doing conscious choices for the smooth functioning of your life on Earth. When you respect yourself as spirit, mind and body, you will make the right, correct and necessary choices for your growth on all levels. Self-esteem is the basis of a happy life, full of accomplishments and divine creations.

Growing and maintaining a solid self-esteem is actually a process of weaning—relearning. And as you already know, the weaning part is the hardest. You must get rid of subconscious patterns of thought and behavior that you have repeated and reinforced over a lifetime, and such a process doesn't happen "overnight," but gradually.

Which is the lifestyle of a person with a high self-esteem? How can you build a solid self-esteem?

1. It's never the end of the world when you fail.
2. You are constantly preoccupied of growing the level of your self-esteem by achieving small results.
3. You listen to inspirational music.
4. You read valuable books which help you change the way of seeing life. Books about people who made their life a masterpiece.
5. You identify your own path in life; you follow it step by step, going towards achieving your goals and dreams.
6. You do breathing exercises with the help of mediation or you can use other simple techniques, for example going out in the park. During the conscious breathing, revelatory ideas occur to you. Geniuses that discover and created amazing things, created for themselves a unique and proper environment.
7. You spend time with positive people who have a goal in their life.
8. You are righteous!

9. You are determined and you ask respect from the others.

10. You are responsible for your decisions.

11. You live in the present! In other words, be present in your life!

12. You have a good image about yourself!

13. You love yourself!

14. You totally trust yourself.

Which is the biggest obstacle that you overcome when you were looking to grow? Poor attitude! The attitude of inferiority! Refuse to be your own opponent and cease to lead a battle with yourself. This can unlock enormous amount of the potential that lies within you and you can channel this energy to more useful directions than judging yourself and constantly criticizing yourself.

Set limits and make sure they are not "broken" by others. When something is important to you, when it's something you don't like or it's not useful to you, make it known. People in your life, friends and family, need this information to know to protect your space and personal values.

"The first thing is to deeply accept yourself. Each feels inferior in some way. The reason is not accepting the fact that each is unique. There is no question of superiority or inferiority. Each is part of a category that is their own and no comparison comes from here. And I cannot imagine a being that has everything in this world. Some didn't hesitate to try, but failed miserably. Just be yourself and it will be enough."

The way you see yourself is what you project onto others. The more beauty you see around you, your life will become more beautiful. Choose consciously to see beauty all around you. This attitude will influence your whole life, because beauty is the most important need of the emotional body.

Your life can change from one moment to another depending on what you choose to see. Nobody can make you see things, people or situations differently than you want. Low self-esteem is one that you position you in conflict with your inner state of well-being.

Respect is of two kinds: self-respect and respect for others. But, remember, you will never receive the respect of others if you are a person who doesn't respect themselves. If you try to start with the second option, you will fall deeper into the abyss. Once you have increased you self-respect, you can go to the next step. To win the respect of the others.

If someone doesn't appreciate you as a person, that doesn't mean everyone feels the same way. Do not underestimate yourself. Do not waste your time with people who don't appreciate you. No matter how good you are with others, you will always find someone to criticize everything you do. Ignore him, smile and move on. As you know, people can't read you mind. How could anyone know what you think if you don't express out loud? Whatever you do in life, you need to communicate with someone at some point. The secret is to be able to communicate, so you can express your thoughts clearly and bluntly.

In order to love others the way you want, you must first give up on any mask and open your soul to embrace love. Even if there is a risk of getting hurt you have to be sincere and genuine. To support the ones you love, it's necessary first to support yourself long enough to become their element of stability and balance.

It's time for you to say loud and clear what you feel and what you need. It's time to decide for yourself and to not let others choose your fate. And that comes from the lowest level, of family and couple relationships, of friendships, to the highest level, linked to your country and beyond. Have the courage to say and to argument what you think. Each does what they can with their life, what they want so they have the life they desire. Simply, express yourself with love and detach yourself.

Authenticity is your own beauty. "The art" of authenticity is the courage to be vulnerable! Yes, you understood well! Perhaps you and others don't like to be vulnerable because you consider this as a weakness. It's just a belief taken from the society. It is true that vulnerability is a part of you that feels like shame, like fear. It's just one facet of it. On the back, the vulnerability is the birthplace of love, joy, beauty, creativity, inspiration, and belonging. The final goal of authenticity is to practice it so it teaches you to live with love, happiness and contentment to feel total fulfillment.

"Authenticity is a collection of choices we make every day. Choosing to be honest with ourselves and with the others. Choosing to leave our own self to be seen without shame."

Why don't you meet the right man? Because you're not mentally and emotionally ready for a big love. If you don't love yourself, it is impossible to offer a sincere and true love. Because you have not learned anything after the last parting. The failure of the previous relationship, instead of motivating you to look at the relationship with yourself, it makes you still look for salvation in the arms of a man. Because you're just as desperate as in the last relationship. You look for balance, happiness and joy in a relationship with a man instead of being a woman who can get all those by herself. As long as your happiness will depend on a man, I'm sorry to tell you directly, but you will always be unhappy.

If you don't love yourself, how do you expect a man to love you? If you don't learn to accept and cherish yourself, you will always be condemned to beg for the love of a man that can confirm you that you deserve something. And when his love for you is gone, everything collapses around you. Do you really want this?

In fact, the question in my mind was: why the wife of a powerful man fails to be number one for her husband for all their life together? Although she was the best when he married her. That's clear. From my point of view, the answer is this: "She, the woman, has much to do and learn. She doesn't know how to keep their relationship beautiful for 30 years." Everybody knows the nature of a powerful man; it's no longer a secret. For this reason, I believe that women have to be educated if they want to have a fulfilling life. Also the powerful man must know how to keep the woman next to him, not only because it's convenient, but also for pleasure. It's a game, in my opinion, which must be known. Avoid routine and monotony. Then fighting and the rest that lead to rupture. They both need to create a balance in their personal life if they want to have a fulfilling and happy life ever after.

I want to remind you that a woman who forgets about herself, dedicating herself body and soul to her family and husband, considering him more important than God, thereby creating a too close and possessive link, ultimately, can have the surprise of losing him.

"Being in the care" of a man restricts your emotional and spiritual development. It's comfortable, but it leaves deep scars in the long term. You're an adult, not that helpless baby in the care of your parents. Maybe you are already 40 years old and you act like a woman that has no help from life or the men in your life.

In other words, the disoriented woman who hasn't found herself has a hell of a building site in her soul. Who could work there, that's the question?! The more you are able to function independently in spite of the behavior of other people and environmental changes, the stronger you become.

Between the "porcelain" woman and the "free" woman is an abyss into which, ironically, the men jump. The deep free space that allows discovery. The deeper the gap, the more curious men are to find out what's there.

"Keep your eyes wide open before you get married and keep them half shut after marriage." Success in marriage is much more than finding the right person. It is to be yourself the right person for the marriage to work.

Being loyal to someone is one thing, but to believe that the person belongs to you, totally forgetting about yourself, is something else. The very idea, that vision creates the promises of a lesson that the Universe wants to show you that no one, absolutely no one belongs to you, but we all belong to the Father. In a marriage, it's good to have a partnership, to have cooperation and joint action, the good of each being targeted equally.

When you offered from your fulfillment, even if the other leaves, you remain whole. You know your value doesn't consist in his presence and if he's happy somewhere else, let him go with peace in your heart. When you are complete and whole, SUFFERING disappears. I mean you love and you share love, you don't need something in return, you don't feed your energy from others. A man tells me his opinion on this wonderful awareness: "It is difficult, however, to be indifferent in a situation where you gave everything. It's for the great souls."

Someone says: "I got divorced a year ago and I still live with my former husband. I don't love him, but I can't stand to be alone. I am afraid of loneliness. What shall I do?" I automatically translated this phrase like this: "I can't stand myself, so I can't stay with myself even for a second."

A man's love is a surrogate who replaces the divine love in every woman. This is why many women suffer. This is called "love pain."

You value yourself as much as you appreciate yourself. When you are happy with yourself, you don't need anything from the other and you don't even expect something from them. You don't live for anyone else. You don't live for a Man. The man is not the Woman's Universe. Live for Yourself! It's easy.

The hard part for the betrayed woman is to understand that it is impossible to have next to you a man who loves you very much if you don't love yourself above anyone or anything, unless you give back what you get. It's not so hard to give love day and night. If you think this is impossible, then expect to always be cheated on. Just to put salt on the wound, I come with the following finding: first, you become what you want from a man. The beggar status doesn't serve anyone and you have absolutely nothing to gain from this. Decide at this time to become what you want to have in life. Don't linger on it. Make this choice and your life will be exactly as you desire. There are no problems without solutions. There are only life beliefs that limit you and don't allow you to be who you really are: a real woman, strong and full of life.

In other words, the woman of today is confronted with two situations that give her a headache: 1. She wants a man but she can't have him! 2. She has a man and she doesn't want him!

If you give your freedom in exchange for financial security, you play the role of a victim. Instead, if you give your safety on freedom, you feel truly happy. Be honest in love. Don't measure the love that is given to you so you give back as much, but give love from the plenitude of your heart.

The story with the "headache" is not a good excuse for not making love, because the endorphins released during sex have analgesic effect. The kiss improves the appearance of the skin, helps blood circulation, prevents tooth decay and relieves headaches. And the story of "poor me" or "it was for the best" doesn't characterize the woman who knows exactly what she wants from life, the woman who trusts herself very much.

I find it very strange when women hate each other. I could never understand this. I'll give an example that is very common in real life. If the woman is cheated by her lover she is seeking revenge on the other woman. In my case, when my ex-husband was in love with another woman, I found it anomalous to take the other woman's eyes out, although I had a thousand reasons. He was the problem. If it wasn't "her," it would be another woman. I saw even more interesting disputes between women. Unfortunately, we have no spirit of solidarity. That's why, women are so oppressed, exploited at work, at home, in society.

Psychologically, a woman feels in competition with other women when she has a sense of inferiority and I slacking self-confidence, which determines her to behave like a lioness. Because of fear! To not lose her husband, her job, the house, the kids, etc. A woman who loves herself and knows how much she is worth is convinced that she will find better opportunities. She accepts "failure" as a springboard. She doesn't run after anyone and she doesn't insist to be friends to anyone. Be yourself, do your job and work seriously on yourself. The right people, those who really belong in your life, will come at the right time. And they will stay.

Question: "Why are women jealous of other women, even if they don't know each other, and basically between them there is no direct conflict of interest for men, territory or attention? And still the hatred is at maximum level. I would prefer answers from women who understand the phenomenon."

The answer is obvious: "Very low self-esteem! Only then you can envy other women! A woman who doesn't trust herself sees danger in every woman! Everything happens only in her mind!" How could you be authentic in a relationship when you're not true to yourself? Every time you lie to someone, you lie to yourself. It is a great loss you don't have the courage to show yourself as you are. Why are you afraid? Of accusations and judgments? Of abandonment?

The less you trust yourself, the more suspicious you are about the others. The less you accept yourself, the less you accept the others. Where are the jealousy and the desire to possess born from if not from the lack of self-confidence? I learnt over time that jealousy is simply self-disguised insecurity.

This situation of belonging to someone, of being psychologically fed with energy by someone, of depending on someone always involves anxiety, fear, jealousy, guilt. A mind overwhelmed with sorrow will never know what love is. A state of suffering, sentimental or emotional, the pleasure and the desire have nothing to do with love. My advice: "Don't expect to get something in return for love. Realize deeply that your harmony comes only from within."

A strong man who works for what he has will not tolerate eternally a woman dissatisfied with herself. If I were a man, I'd fall in love with a woman who would make me feel comfortable with myself and would help me get to the surface my hidden potential and who has the ability to see beyond what is visible at first glance. I could love the woman who wouldn't want to change anything about me. I'd be madly in love with her if she would accept me and would not change anything about me. Because if she does it, I won't be the man she fell in love with. Then and only then I will feel chosen for what I am, not for what I have or what I can do.

Despite the old proverb "Don't take the problems in bed with you," many men still continue to sleep with their wives. Your attitude towards the situations that arise matters enormously. Adopt a positive attitude and nothing will stand between you and what you want!

A woman can be both feminine and strong. What does that mean, to be a strong woman? To honor your feelings and to have the courage to talk about them without apologizing or trying to control the others' reactions. A strong woman feels good about herself. She doesn't need someone's approval to be happy or loved.

Question: "I am married for 15 years and I have a 15 year old daughter, but I am unhappy with my marriage. I have had a deep loving relationship with a special woman for over 5 years, of which my wife knows unofficially. I wanted a divorce many times, but my wife threatened to kill herself because of me. Now, the special woman told me that she can't accept anymore to be only my mistress, so she gave me an ultimatum to file for a divorce. But I am afraid to have my wife on my conscience and to leave our daughter without a mother. What shall I do?" Mihaela: "When you got involved with the other woman, what did you expect? To work out with both of them? Did you think that you could actually cheat on three people? The wife, the mistress and yourself, why don't you just leave your mistress? Why give in to the emotional blackmail of your wife? These are questions you must answer to; why did the mistress accept the situation for five years and now suddenly she no longer wants to. Many, many questions, and until you will have answered them, you won't have peace and you won't know what decision to take. Let me tell you an old teaching I learnt early in life from a woman who is no longer with us: no wife is good as mistress, and no mistress is good as wife. So think!!!!!"

Irina: "No, she won't do it, she just threatens you. It's good to teach her to be free and independent and so she can be happy; and, finally, tell her flatly. It seems that she is blackmailing you obsessively and it's not good for either of you—especially that the child is old enough to understand what's going on and she doesn't expect anything good from you. So be brave, a man must be brave and have dignity. It's not enough to be called a man, you must also act like one or maybe you like it like this way and you are comfortable with the situation?! Something is not as you say it, I think you want to feel loved by two women and that's meanness, not manliness."

Mihaela: "Leave them both now you realize their lack of character. They both threatened just to impress you; they are only able to live in the shadow of a man, take a holiday and go somewhere alone for few days and put your life in order."

Sofia: "Everything comes at a cost in life, and you pay the price sooner or later!!!"

Mihai: "Think: the wife is God's gift!"

Marina: "As you have already realized, you are being manipulated by the threats of the two women. At first, you say you are unhappy in your marriage, do you honestly think your happiness will come back when you enter into another marriage with the same kind woman? You don't need to choose either with fear, you have to pick something out of love, but first you have to discover that something. Good luck!"

Edy: "Bad, bad, bad... if, indeed, he cared for his daughter, he couldn't have a mistress. He is only afraid not to have his daughter in his life (that if the wife would do such a reckless gesture). It is difficult to educate a child, better relax beside your mistress. My opinion—divorce, or stay with the mistress. From two he should choose one; smart women don't take this step especially for a man who cheats on them."

Dana: "You can't build your happiness on someone's pain."

Stela: "If your wife knows about the relationship and after long discussions she doesn't accept her fate, she is selfish. Because you don't love her anymore and she knows it."

Nela: "You live in classic triangle: two women and a man, I recommend you read S. N. Lazarev who says that this triangle can't be broken until God allows it. It is dangerous if the man forces the break up."

Adrian: "What matters is the family above is everyone's interest (mother is addictive to the husband, the husband is looking eroticism elsewhere, the daughter, we don't know how much she understands from what happens); because the girl needs both parents and she is not in a position to choose, the primary interest is the one of the child's. Some people can have better relations separately than together but no one told this to the 15 year-old girl."

Me: "It is hard for women to understand that they can't keep a man by force! There are so desperate and they have so much disrespect for themselves that they prefer to live in their own hell. I wonder: when will the Romania woman learn to love herself, to trust herself and be confident that she will always find a man to love her? Do they still have more children in order to keep a man next to them? I have seen many cases like this one."

Me: "About ten years ago, I experienced myself this strategy, but in a different context and I can say with certainty that it doesn't work. Instead, I realized that as long as you play the role of victim, it is impossible to be happy. Self-esteem is totally missing and you lower yourself to emotional blackmail because you don't have the power to look at yourself in the mirror."

Daniela: "The mistress is a regulation, now she pretends for him to take on responsibilities in the relationship with her. Until now she fulfilled all his requests, which he wasn't able to get anymore from his relationship with his wife. Be sure that if he was to move in with her and he was to discover all her defects, he would appreciate what he lost. A statistic was made showing that men are happier in their first marriage than in those that followed."

Me: "Not always the relationship with his mistress is a regulation. It can be very serious. For example: my ex-husband married his mistress shortly after and they have a child together. Just that they got divorced after nine years. I think it was true love (looking at it as an observer). This statistic is very good. They have enough time for regrets. God bless them!"

Most of the questions include the answer. When you're an observer (without being emotionally involved), you realize it easily. But when you are involved in the situation, you forget about yourself, you are disconnected from the inner source and you cannot have clarity.

Normally, a mentally healthy person will never cheat if they have what they need right next to them.

What does a man want from a woman? Curious by nature, I asked a man directly to know exactly how it is. Not that I didn't know the answer, but I wanted to have a confirmation from him. His words are memorable: "To find the same woman in the bedroom with the following roles: good mother in the relationship with the child, excellent cook, loving wife and mistress in bed." And what should the woman ask in return for these requirements? A house with a swimming pool? A comfortable car? To travel around the world? I am just asking! I think: if the woman gives everything, it will only be correct to receive everything! The appreciation is not enough! The facts make the difference!

Freedom of thought is another interesting topic for me. It is necessary to have the courage to express your opinion on any situation in your life. Certainly, every time you have an opinion on what you eat, where you want to spend your vacation, how you dress, what you want to do in your free time. You must have the courage to be honest with yourself and tell others how you feel. If you always please others, you get to emotional self-destruction. You collect in your life just failures and floors. You create yourself a less favorable image to those around you. They perceive you exactly how you think about yourself. They can't do it differently. For them, you are exactly what they see.

If every person were to learn to have a mind of their own, certainly, the level of individual living, and then the mass level, would be much better. For example, when you are asked for an opinion about the fate of your country or about the fate of your city, you must have a personal opinion, not one borrowed from those around you. The most important is to think at your own good. If you're OK with your decision, certainly it will be OK for those around you.

Naivety in any area of your life is expensive. The lack of information in one respect costs. It will only bring a minus into your life. One day, we will all live the same way. Therefore, it is extremely important for you to make considered conscious choices in your favor. Freedom of expression is very important when you want to be truly free, happy and authentic. "Most of the people are afraid to say what they want. That's why they don't get it."

Travelling abroad in recent years, I inevitably have borrowed from the mentality of the people in these countries. An authentic and free woman is that woman who is honest with herself and has full confidence in her. She has the courage after ten years to say to her life partner: "George dear, I don't love you anymore, even though you have a few millions euro into your account, but we should still be friends, and we will still support each other in our plans." It's exactly how real men with high self-esteem and a modicum of backbone think too. Therefore they are happy every day, even if they are 70 years old. They feel young; they enjoy life as if they were 20 years old.

On this occasion, I want to reveal a secret from the art of seduction. I needed ten years to find it. Better now than never. Eventually, experience is the mother of wisdom!

The secret that is not written in any book because it's considered unimportant or it crosses the line of common sense is as follows: in a couple relationship, always the one who is very good in the art of sex subtly manipulates and leads. There is no balance. It's a miracle if that happens. It's a way you fully enter into the human heart, in the best sense of the word, but often can be used for other benefits. When you are emotionally manipulated, there are consequences. The most important is to have total control over your feelings and implicitly over your life. You learn all your life. Not from books, but from real life.

Not by chance there is that true saying: behind a powerful man, always, but always, without exception, there is a strong woman. Not necessarily from a financial point of view, but from the inner strength point of view. Under any circumstances behind a strong man you will not a woman who will play the role of victim and complains constantly. If there are such women, certainly, they are on the last place in that man's life.

1 million euro question:

"If behind a strong currency
There is a highly developed economy,
Who is behind a strong woman?"

Behind a strong woman, there will always be, without exception, a man at least as strong as she is. It's the inner strength that comes from your Self. Live with confidence. You hold the greatest power in the world: the power of Your Self! "Be yourself, everyone else is taken."

Reality confirms this statement: "President X came out with his wife one evening to dine in a restaurant to break the usual routine. The restaurant owner has asked permission from the bodyguards to come close and greet the president's wife. And so it happened.

When the restaurant owner withdrew, the president asked his wife: "Why did this man want to greet you in particular?" His wife answered him: "In my adolescence, this man was in love with me."

The president commented: "This means that if you had married him, you'd be the owner of this restaurant today?!" To which she replied: "No, honey, if I be married to this man, he would be the president today!"

Women love men. They look for them, they want them, they need their strength, the emotional and physical balance a woman has when she is with her man. Men love women. They look for them; they need their presence, their femininity, the softness of their skin, the warmth and intimacy that they emit, the idea of motherhood and protection that a woman instinctively exhales. We are different, but we need to complement each other for a full and balanced life.

In my opinion, the only thing that really matters at the end of your journey on this earth is how deeply you loved and the quality of love you offered.

When you enter into a relationship, get in full of love and enthusiasm, willing to share with the other one the love that you are. This is a dream relationship to last. A relationship where there is no jealousy because love could never be jealous. Love is extremely happy when the person you share it with feels good next to someone else. Love restores freedom.

"Do you want to share your love with someone else?—Yes!—Perfect! You're free and I am happy for you! I love you, and your happiness is my happiness." It would be great to say this to all people you enter into a relationship with, but wish to share their experience with someone else too. That's what I do and believe me, I feel great! Someone else can't give me what I have to offer to myself. There was no one who could give me what I feel now when I now know who I really am.

You will find everything you want to find when you stop looking. Then you will realize that you never looked in the right place. You will never find outside yourself what you'll only find inside yourself.

Love, my dear friend, is to give and receive freedom. It means to give power to others. In the act of love, there are never guarantees. If you seek for approval or favorable response, you can't love freely. And if love is not free, it is not love. It's like going to the market where you can haggle and negotiate.

I believe that if you realize that the most precious and powerful gift you have are your words, maybe you won't be using them against yourself. I also believe that the energy and the power of your thoughts are in the words you use, the power to communicate, and create events in your life. Tell yourself every day: "I love you!"

Beliefs act as a filter on a lens and can change the way you see the world, and the biological system adapts to these beliefs. When we truly admit that those beliefs have such power, you hold the key to freedom. When you trust Life, you know that you are always where you need to be and when you need to be. You can't get lost or be late.

You have the freedom of thought, the freedom of choice and the benefits of an education based on your own aspirations. You are free in politics, religion, free to believe what you want, free to choose your business, profession or occupation. You are free to accumulate and to have any property you can acquire. You are free to choose your home, to marry, to enjoy equal rights for all races, the freedom to travel around the world. You are free to choose your own diet and what clothes you wear. You are free to set any goal in life for which you are ready.

An interesting question from those who live their lives with rules and restrictions imposed by others. If we are free, then who rules our life? They fear that too much liberty corrupts and they become lustful. Paradoxically, freedom is the only one that gives you the responsibility to think what is good and what is not good for you. You don't need rules to know how you want to live every day. You have the Divine Consciousness. That means you have the sensorial experience of feeling your existence. It is integrated into your being and requires more and more awareness. You stop defining yourself as that empty person, led by others because he doesn't no know which direction to take. Now your only guide is your Self, the God within you. "Home" is not in a celestial palace, it's within you. This explains the fact that a person with his Consciousness integrated in his being cannot break ATMs, cannot kill, cannot hurt anyone; he has no longer low vibration. He is love.

The state of consciousness. Consciousness is awareness, not thinking. Consciousness is profound wisdom. When you have an experience of consciousness, you almost can't explain it. The state of consciousness should be flexible. In most people it is rigid. You cannot open your conscience through thinking. Many people think of enlightenment. Consciousness is multidimensional. You can have several states of consciousness. Mind does not like this. When consciousness is combined with experience, you have something almost indescribable. Consciousness is like an empty vessel ready to be filled with experience. Then, conscience knows awareness. Consciousness doesn't care if you had pleasant or unpleasant experiences, it only cares about the experience itself, it doesn't judge. Go into a state of consciousness. You can't go wrong with anything. Breathe and allow your consciousness to expand. It asked you to invite it into your physical body and into your mind. Allow yourself to open your consciousness. Only a brave person goes beyond thought. You ask yourself: "What will happen if I will lose control, will I lose my mind?" You will get where you want. There are no thoughts in consciousness. The mind is complex, consciousness is simple.

CHAPTER 7

SOUL MATE. HEALING SOUL. TWIN SOUL

"When you wish to feel someone you love next to you, just close your eyes and feel their presence. Breathe, open your heart and make complete silence. Then let yourself feel their smell, warmth and energy. Stay with your eyes closed and talk to them. Tell them you feel them close to you and enjoy this. We are with each other all the time; just most of the time the lack of the physical presence makes us forget this. Because we are not physically together, this doesn't mean that we are far apart. We are all interconnected. We are all at the same time, in the same place. In the Spirit's dimension, time doesn't exist. When we connect to our True Essence, we feel as we all get together. We feel like we are one. So, whenever you miss someone, just remember to close your eyes and feel them. Remember they have never been away from you."

Two people living with the God inside them can only have a very good relationship. That doesn't mean that you wait for the other to make you happy. From here there come so many disappointments, misery and drama. Then you think you have chosen the wrong partner and that's why you're not happy. You're looking for another partner and, after a while, you feel the same emptiness and the same lack of fulfillment. But the problem is not that partner, but the wrong perspective on life, because you think there is a half that can make you whole. One of the great illusions most of us live with. Perhaps you ask me why I am writing again about this topic. Because I noticed that there is a lot of confusion.

I want to settle things from the beginning. This topic applies only to people who know who they really are, who have done the intense work with themselves, who are complete and are aware that God manifests through them. With this deep awareness, we understand that we only have life partners. Some of them, if we want, we can call them soul mates. This phrase is well known and I choose to use it in a completely new context. This soul mate is not just half of your heart. It is the sister of your soul that enables you to evolve very much at a heart level. You can even have more than one soul mate in a lifetime. They reflect the parts of you that you have to face in order to evolve. The biggest blockages, fears and limitative beliefs that control you will surface in a relationship with this soul which is a huge help for yourself on the road to fulfilling your personal destiny.

Couple relationships between two independent partners are more satisfactory, realistic and functional than those where we have all sorts of unrealistic expectations from the other one because we consider the partner our "soul mate."

There could be three categories of potential boyfriend/girlfriend, husband/wife:

1.   Soul mate
2.   Healing soul
3.   Twin soul

I use generically the term "twin soul" for the person who is already complete. I also use generically the term "soul mate" for people who feel incomplete. These concepts created a lot of confusion: soul mate, twin soul. You are your own soul mate and you can enjoy a free relationship, without security contracts, without expectation, without needs. And it is valid for each of us! Te healing Soul is the one that meets yours to give you strength and power when you're exhausted by the karmic experiences.

Many of us are with a soul mate or with a healing soul with whom we have a united karma. If you have to pay for a negative karma, you will be with a soul mate; if you have a positive karma you will meet a healing soul. We can be together for a lifetime. We free our karma or not, we learn lessons that help us evolve. From the moment you decided to say "stop karma," you start evolving rapidly. Soul mates can really help us. They are those people you feel you have known forever and they are simply part of your heart. You feel a very deep inexplicable connection. Life is difficult and complicated next to this soul. Including at the soul level when we can talk about unsolved problems. In many previous lives, certain lessons remained unsolved or unlearned, some debts are still not paid, and certain relationships hadn't been consumed, and the soul feels the acute need to finalize something. Sometimes, no one understands why out so much passion into a certain cause or hobby. If you have the feeling that you have to finish something or to end a situation or a relationship with someone, then it's probably because some "doors" hadn't been closed properly. Most times, the unsolved businesses can stop you progress in other areas of your life. Everything that happens to you is part of a puzzle, and "the pieces" must be seen as a whole, not separate.

Imagine a woman who, in a previous life, had a husband who was quite possessive and domineering. For a while, she accepted it, but at some point she decided enough was enough and broke off the relationship. A short while later her husband committed suicide. The woman had remorse. She felt she was to blame. Shouldn't she have given him another chance? She felt this guilt for the rest of her life.

In another life, they meet again. There is an odd attraction between them. At first, the man is extremely charming and she is the center of his attention. He adores her. They begin a relationship. But this time, he becomes increasingly jealous and possessive. He suspects her of adultery. She finds herself in an inner struggle. She is angry and upset that he accuses her unjustly, but also she feels a strange obligation to be forgiving and to give him another chance. He is a hurt man, she believes, he can't be helped if he has this fear of being abandoned. Maybe she can help him get over it. She justifies his behavior this way but, in fact, she allows the violation of her personal boundaries. The relationship negatively affects her self-esteem.

The most liberating choice for the woman would be to end the relationship and to go on her way, without feeling guilty. The pain and the fear felt by her husband are not her responsibilities. His pain and her guilt led to a destructive relationship. Their relationship was already emotionally burdened because of a previous life. The purpose of this reencounter is for the woman to learn to let things go without feeling guilty and for the man to learn to stand on his own two feet from an emotional point of view. So the only real solution is to end the relationship. The solution for the woman's karma is to free herself from guilt once and for all. The mistake she did during her previous life was not that she abandoned her husband, but that she felt responsible for his suicide. The leaving of his wife in this life confronts him again with his own pain and fear, and it offers him a new opportunity to face these emotions better than trying to get rid of them.

How do you recognize that you are in a karmic relationship? The other person immediately feels strangely familiar. Quite often, there is also a mutual attraction, something compelling in the air which urges you to be together and to discover each other. If the opportunity is available, this strong attraction can turn into a love relationship. The emotions you experience may be so overwhelming that you think you've met your twin soul. However, things are not what they seem. In such a relationship, there will always be problems which sooner or later will come out.

What is Karma? In Sanskrit karma means "action" and is the equivalent of what Newton called "Every action must have a reaction." When we think, speak or act, we initiate a force that will act as such. This law of cause and effect doesn't act on us as a form of punishment, but helps us along our journey to evolve and learn.

I noticed that many people don't really know what that term means. Some of them are running when they hear this word. Others don't believe that religion hasn't said this before. It's perfect as is. It is not wrong or correct. It's just is. Eventually, every person will reach this awareness by themselves at the right time. I use this word because people often use it in their communication.

The perspective, from my point of view, is this: "For those who have chosen to live "the royal life," meaning that we are one with our Soul, it means that we assumed all other aspects of life. For example: from what I know, from many lives, I was a handsome, arrogant man and I used women. In this royal life, being a woman, I had several failed relationships, inexplicable from a human point of view. Everything at the soul level is right. From the moment you connected with your Divine Self, you are the Creator of your Life. It changes the equation of the problem. Karma vanishes.

The preset destiny exists up to a point. It can definitely change if you take over the responsibility for your life and you don't live it to the wind. Then you become the Creator of your life: "How you make your bed is how you will sleep!" When you quit damaging relationships with others, you have time to stand on your feet and think about what really helps you. You feel free and full of energy, vitality, spontaneity, luck and success everywhere. You are the one who deserves all the best.

In my vision, "karma" means those dark aspects of you that want to come out to be forgiven, accepted, loved and then released. These issues can mean deep wounds from your present life, or, in the broadest sense, these issues may come from previous lives. To better understand this term, I will try to explain in words how I see it. I need you to use your imagination to understand beyond your mind what I mean.

Source = Universe = Creation

Spirit = Your Soul = Your real Self = The divinity inside you = The God inside you

The Old Man = all the lives you have had up to the moment of your awareness of who you really are

The New Man = the divinity within + the Old Man transformed

False Self (Ego) = the Old Man (mind + body)

Real Self = all your sides = all your lives = Mind + body + Spirit

The Real Self gathers all your experiences to reach perfection. It aims to evolve so much as to reach the stage in which to declare sovereignty. Now, the Old Man merged with the divinity within and became the New Man.

The New Man is permanently connected to the Source that created it. Now, you are one with the Universe. You're part of the whole; you don't feel separated from God who created you. If you become truly sovereign, you're out of the laws of Karma, so depending on your beliefs, you create your future.

From this moment, your old identity has disappeared. You don't look for a relationship to fulfill you. You don't look for the need to be happy. You're already happy because God lives inside you. You are balanced. You are at peace. You are love. It is very difficult to explain in words with your mind everything that happens at the Spirit level.

You should cease to be the Old Man and be who you are, in fact, a new creation. Choose to become the New Man. As long as you identify yourself with the Old Man, you will fight with all human things; you will never have peace, because you are a slave of worldliness. You should be born again, otherwise you feel condemned to suffering and pain and you don't even realize this, but you feel a deep void in your heart. "Nothing is as it was and will never be ... But this is a wonderful thing! What does the same joy of a year ago mean today? What does the peace of yesterday mean today? You're not the man of a year ago; you're not even the man of yesterday. You are the man from now! Every day is a new life. You have the power to choose what you are now!"

In other words, the soul mates once lived with a strong love, so pure that they were destined to meet again in their present life; their deep love is a continuation of their previous one. The continuation can be for a short period or for many years, depending on how much karma has to be consumed. Soul mates separate permanently when they fulfill the purpose for which they met again, even if in those moments of rediscovering each other everything seems to last forever. It's an illusion that hurts.

When you meet your soul mate, you have a strong sense of familiarity, as if you know them for a lifetime. Instantly, a deep unexplainable connection appears, one that transcends physical attraction, and the signals that you will form a couple are growing. This strong feeling, inexplicable in words, I felt with my friend in Holland. It was a healing relationship. In a healing relationship, partners might know each other from one or more previous lives. But in these cases there isn't an emotional karmic burden. A characteristic of healing relationships is that the partners respect each other as they are, without trying to change each other. It is freedom and peace in the relationship. There is a heart connection between them due to the fact that they don't take with them the other person's emotions or their personal mistakes. From an emotional point of view, both partners are independent.

Twin souls—complete. Such an encounter has the characteristics of a magic meeting, where communication is open on totally different ways than before. They can't in a relationship of codependency, based on ego or the perception of a "need" believing that the other one makes you whole. Both souls often face separation in space and time while strengthening their connection to the spirit and each one finds its strength and mission which they came with in this current life.

This time their goal isn't to start a family or practicing a trivial job. Each of them has a life mission to be discovered and implemented. The purpose is bound to make major changes in people's lives. They bring joy and happiness to people around them. They support each other, but they are independent.

They can have children, but in this case the child is a free soul experiencing what they want. Communication between the three of them will be like between three adults. Each with their own personality, they express how they feel and how they want every moment of the day. The child in this case is not a burden. I could say that they can grow on their own. For them the love from the parents is sufficient. Adults know who their child is and what their purpose is. For this reason, they trust him, no matter what choices they make in life. There are three masters, three complete souls. Father, mother, and child.

If twin souls met at the wrong time, there would be sparks. Certainly, it would be a world war. It is an illusion to think that if you find your twin flame, your life has found its meaning. I remind you that you still have a meaning in life. Remember this!

It is an illusion to think that if you met your twin soul, you will automatically have that idyllic love stories. It is your perfect mirror. So the first step, and the most important one, is that you become as you want your partner to be. An important lesson that you have to learn in a couple relationship is independence. If you are dependent to your partner, you become like a burden hanging on their shoulders and they get to wish to get rid of you. On the first level of personal development is our ability to handle thing, to take care of ourselves, to survive in the midst of the world.

Every person's path to them self, to the divine love inside them, the higher unique Self, I think each of us discovers and understands this through different ideas, through diverse ways of expression.

In other words, the twin soul is a person who knows who they are, is complete and has solved all their previous inner problems. They will meet with a complete person just like them. They will form a couple to another level. From their plenitude they will give unconditional and pure love. They are free and open to each other.

The two partners see each other as pure souls and not as individuals, masks of the soul. On this level, you see beyond the face of the partner, you see directly their soul. Now your mind is no longer interested in the little things, because you solve quickly and with absolutely no effort any material or social problems you may have.

If you want a life partner better than you had before, I give you the secret recipe: become yourself better, happier, more satisfied with yourself and they will come in your life as fast as you want them. Free and true love defies time, distance, religion and any obstacle. Why do people want to fall in love? Answer: "To know a part of themselves through a partner."

From the perspective of unconditional love, the couple relationship is the choice to spend your life with one of all beings on this earth. There are many potential partners. It is an honest choice to love one person in a different way than all others, in a close, intimate, passionate way. The communication is nonverbal, with great passion and love. Choosing a partner is based on resonance, compatibility, special attraction understanding, friendship, trust and everything you know a successful relationship means. A free choice, by mutual agreement, on indefinite term. At one point, the limit will still be required by the evolution of each person involved in this relationship. If the two partners don't evolve at the same pace, the two people no longer resonates as in the beginning, then separation is inevitable, without feelings of hatred or revenge. When love was given without conditions, after separation remains love based on compassion and understanding. Instead, when a couple's relationship based on conditional love ends, love is replaced with hatred and contempt.

In conclusion, the couple's relationship based on unconditional love is a unique relationship between two drops in an ocean, with the possibility that the two partners will get back together when they will feel it in their heart. The reunion is magical, like they were on a long vacation and now they returned.

Your Twin Soul already exists. If it didn't show up yet, it doesn't mean you will be alone, jut that your trust in its existence is very weak or it doesn't exist at all. Believe in it and you will meet it in this life. Be sure of it. Meanwhile, get ready at all levels of your Being to receive it in Your Life.

Through your soul, you can meet another human soul. You can feel it, even if you spent just a few seconds in the presence of that person. And even if they are away. Through meditation, you can have direct communication from soul to soul. Bear in mind the following statement:

"Darling, I love you! I love and I want you in My Life. I don't need anything; I just want to give you everything I Have and everything I Am. You are perfect for me, and your simple presence in My Life makes me happy. I know you are somewhere in this world, I feel you and I am ready to have you next to me! You are perfect for me, I am perfect for You. I deserve you and you deserve me! I deserve and you deserve all the love and happiness in the world!"

Or you can say this statement:

"Infinite Universe, I meet and I share my life with the ideal man. He is single, free, in perfect physical and mental health, he is faithful, funny, gentle, friendly, he loves to dance, to travel etc. Our paths meet and we will be in love in no time!"

How can you tell if a person is right for you? Just one look is enough for you to know with certainty whether or not they are the perfect person for you at the time. You look them in the eye and you feel as an unseen hand caress your soul. There aren't eyes that attract you through a particular form or an unusual color, eyes with long eyelashes and beautifully arched eyebrows; they are those eyes that show peace, sincerity, confidence. That look pours onto your soul and caresses your heart with thousands of fine feelings. How many destinies have been changed and troubled with just one glance. One writer says: "The power of the gaze has been so much abused in love stories that it started to become incredible. Few dare today to say that two people fell in love because they looked at each other. Yet, this is how love begins; just like that."

Our loves with healing souls or soul mates life partners, matures with us. And we learn, in time, that true love is about giving. True love doesn't hurt, and the measure of love is not pain. Those who live healthy loves don't twist and turn on the floor in pain. There is no "but" in their relationship, no "however." They give and receive equally, maybe not always identically, but what is missing in one is completed by the other. Healthy love is not the one that drives you crazy and stirs your soul, it is the one that develops naturally, goes through all stages and gathers everything into a whole. True mature love doesn't annihilate every trace of reasoning; it opens your eyes to new horizons. It broadens your vision, it doesn't narrow it. This is one of the features a twin soul has, a soul that has completely integrated the masculine and feminine inside itself. But in order to recognize it when you meet it, so you don't pass without seeing it, to appreciate it at its true value, you need all the other pseudo-loves. Because, unfortunately, we don't learn otherwise than from our own life experience. Experience is the mother of wisdom, and through it, our soul evolves and reach perfection.

An authentic love relationship feels from the first moment when the two interact. There are those exceptions when the two resonate and stay together without feeling the need to seduce the other in order to get their attention. They don't feel the need to pretend they no longer love each other because they were angry if the other one came home two hours later than they promised. Without tricks and other strategies for staying together. There are women who set a goal in their mind: "I love him and he will be mine at any cost." Now, a "fight" starts for attracting the man at any cost forgetting who she truly is. The price will ultimately be paid by her when her partner is not as she wanted because she can't change him with projections of her own mind.

How can you tell if you are ready to meet your twin soul? If they also did this inner work with themselves. The answer is simpler than you can imagine: Everything that is Down is also Up. The Divine harmony and love descends on Earth through twin souls. Blessed is the one who now meets their twin soul. Because the Chosen one is the one chosen by the God inside you, they are not chosen by the Human inside you.

As you know, your divine origin implies that you are all, man and woman, and that you are whole and complete in yourself. No soul is meant to be the half of another. The reason for the existence of twin souls is not to learn something. The purpose is simply joy and creativity. Twin souls have no function within duality. You will meet your twin soul when you will transcend duality, when you will identify yourself with the God inside, who is whole and undivided and who is able to take any form or appearance. Twin souls meet again on their journey back home. "Home" is your divinity. What binds the two of "you" is something beyond duality, something previous to the history of duality. Both "you" have experienced the limits of duality to discover gradually that your essence is not in duality but outside of it. After having gone through all the highs and lows of duality there will be a time when you will meet your twin soul. Because they are on their way home, twin souls feel inspired to anchor the energies of love and unity on earth and they do so in a way that matches their own unique talents and skills. This way, the love of twin souls puts the milestone between "being one" and "becoming One." So, twin souls when they meet are already two creative wholes.

In a world too obsessed with relationships, where it is believed that relationships are the key to happiness, someone must say just balance everything that the real I you can discover only in the moments of solitude. In the relationship, you reflect parts of the soul, emotions, thoughts, ideas, with your partner, but in solitude you reflect the real you, the one beyond the soul, emotions, thoughts. From my point of view, it is necessary for any sincere truth seeker to offer themselves daily moments of solitude to reflect. After such moments you can relate with others completely differently, fresher, calmer, and more aware of yourself.

The mentality of absence results from your perception that you're not worthy of love. If you don't feel worthy of love, you'll project this on the outside. Do you feel wronged? If yes, then you will project missing parts in your life. Only someone who feels wronged will be wronged. To end this mentality you must forgive the past. It has no effect on you anymore, because you've released it. Without forgiveness, it's impossible to get out of this mentality. And to forgive, you must become aware of all the ways you feel pain in. You have to recognize the pain. Then you can forgive it. Hidden wounds have hidden agendas that keep us hostage into the past. Experiencing the absence is not God who punishes you. It's you, who show yourself a belief that needs to be adjusted. Be willing to face your fears and feelings of worthlessness and lack of value and He will help you see the divine spark that lives in you.

"Loneliness is the spiritual condition we are born with, that natural and true condition. With time, we forget it, we grow and it becomes increasingly strange to us. Sometimes we find it again, but now we are afraid of it because we have become strangers. Now we run from it, although we should look for it again, because only through it we can hope to find the truth."

If you get on the train, it doesn't mean that your god is the rail. In the train of life, the God is YOU. The train will go in the direction you want from the line NOW. All aboard, please! I went to all the stations so far, but still I continue my journey to the destination! You are the creator of your own destiny and you're here to build step by step the playground where you can celebrate What You Really Are.

Solitude is important. It allows you to recharge, to get a fresh perspective, to get in touch with your own feelings and to hear your own voice instead the voices of others. It allows you to think more deeply or stop your thoughts, if that is what you need the most. It allows you to be more proactive than reactive and it reduces the stress caused by your busy schedule. It is important to spend time alone to relax, to create, to meditate, to concentrate or to just be.

The reason you are alone is far greater than you can imagine. Behind solitude is a divine gift. After long searches on the outside, you'll realize that you were actually looking for you, the real YOU. From this moment you see the relationships differently: from Self to Self, not from human to human.

Solitude is actually the test of happiness. If you want to check whether you are happy or not, then stay alone for a while. "You cannot feel lonely if you like the person you're alone with."

From my point of view, the divinity doesn't protect you nor gives you advice. It just is! Guiding you. That's all! You have free will if you want or not to listen to your inner voice to. The mystical living of deification rebuilds the being in the plan of consciousness and makes it aware of what it IS. This is what I believe now. I don't know if I found the right words to express what I felt. Words are just too limited.

The union between a man and a woman is like the union between Sky and Earth. And they last forever thanks to this perfect communion.

When two people love each other, two worlds put together their wealth and eternity. Sun and Moon attend this birth in love and hope to find an answer to their expectation, a miracle. Therefore, every love is unique and its promise is like the sunrise. Divine love triumphs over everyday reality, over theories, over the prose of the lifeless common sense. It speaks the language of the ones mad for God, of those who breathe in spirit, of those whom the human love teaches to love God. God's love and people's love are not two loves, but two sides of the same love. Love itself is the deepest thirst for Truth; it is the voice of the being itself. Two united souls are not afraid of anything. With understanding, peace and mutual love, lovers live the miracle.

The most beautiful of all things in life is to meet another human being whom to spend your life with. The relationship is becoming deeper and stronger. With the passing years, it is becoming more beautiful and special. Love between two people is the most wonderful thing. It's a godsend. Love cannot be found if you seek it with desperation or if you wish and pray for it. The day you will not want anything from a partner, only to share with them all you have, then you will give wholeheartedly. It is a divine accident that occurs in your life just when your Self feels ready.

Love

By Carmina Harr

When I think of you, I feel like flying.
Love is so strong, that spreads over sees and countries
Words are too few to express what my soul feels
You are part of my inner universe and this matters greatly
I feel you close, and the distance in time and space is an illusion
I love you as much as I love myself

I cherish you as much as I cherish myself

You are my perfect mirror and I thank you

I love you because I am you, because we are one.

I, or you, it's the same.

Open the door to love and stop thinking

I wait for you with passion and desire.

Have the courage to say YES to love without fear and dread

Have the courage to be you, the authentic you, the one who allows his heart to express freely

Have the courage to share the love hidden inside you

Don't think too much, there is no point

Feel, go deep inside yourself and discover the feeling you never had before

That feeling that gives you wings and confidence that everything's possible.

Allow the God inside you to meet love

Allow Him to be one with You

The unlimited you, the endless you

I want to know you beyond what I can see

I want to feel you beyond what I can feel.

I want to be what I have always been.

Divine being, great and radiant.

It makes no sense to plan when and who to fall in love with. You can try; you can say that you will not be enticed by this magic. You can say that this sweet trick is for naive people. When you least expect it, you find yourself in love. You see yourself happy, fulfilled, and complete, you breathe just to satisfy your soul, living your pride aside, making room for a true love.

On Earth there are many kinds of relationships. Many of these involve a very deep intimate connection with souls from the same family or from families of similar souls. In some cases, the partners were brought together with great intensity because this is the only way that the souls involved will make a commitment to each other. The commitment in a relationship is not always a good thing, but it is often necessary for the partners to learn soul lessons that couldn't easily learn by themselves.

There is only one way you can find true fulfillment in life, and this is to learn to love and accept yourself. Having this base, the relationship stops being traumatizing. This because you don't expect so much from it anymore. When you know how it is "to be together" with yourself, it's not that difficult "to be together" with the other one.

The longing you feel for a man or for a woman is nothing else but the longing for yourself. This person reflects in you this deep love you feel in your whole being.

Being the ideal partner for you, it means that your love relationship with another ideal partner is one of sharing. Two divine and complete beings meet to celebrate life together.

When you discover that you are the perfect partner, you simply fall in love with you, with the God inside who thinks, feels, and speaks through you. The discussions with others will be this time from Self to Self, not from human to human. Love will be from Spirit to Spirit, not from body to body. When you merge two souls through love, the energy produced creates miracles. This is how masterpieces and inventions are born and the vibration of the earth rises. Therefore that energy isn't lost, but something is created out of it. Creation increases, awareness grows. What could this mean? Our spirit lives in the human body on Earth. The more humans will realize this, the more heaven spreads on Earth. This way, Creation broadens.

And, yes, you meet the man or woman you love, not as a need, but as a joy to share love together, not to feed energetically from each other. There will be no need for contracts and vows, each will develop independently, freely and honestly in harmony with the other. Every day, the lover can renew their vows of love with this magic: "I love you." Every day, I love you and I show you this, not just at the beginning. You can say every day to your life partner: "Today I also choose to live with you with the joy, love and happiness I have to share."

"Love is the only religion, the only God, the only mystery to be lived and understood. When you understand love, you understand all the wise men and mystics of the world. It is not difficult. It's as simple as your heart beat or breathing. It comes from you; it's not given to you by the society."

A friend says: "I know many Gods. The wind, the rain, the birds, humans and all you see is the divine manifestation of God. My gods are real and they are around me, they can be seen, touched and known by everyone. My gods are kind, good and wise, loving and faithful. Each person who taught me and shared with me uncensored and total love, every soul who believed in me, who didn't promise me the kingdom of heaven and immortality in exchange for kneeled love, but who gave me the most sincere and good moment from what they had—is the god I believe in.

Each soul that does more than says, more than seven days, that isn't selfish and possessive, that doesn't threat and punish, that doesn't want praises, is a path to heaven and a God in making. God has a plural."

CHAPTER 8

THE DIVINE SELF

Now you are ALL. Not just a part of you. You are what you like and what you don't like at yourself. You are complete. The sky, the earth and everything visible and invisible lives inside your being, but your logical mind can't understand all these!

Of all the lives you've ever lived on this planet, this is the life that will bring the change. This is the life you prayed for so you discover who you are. Some of you will say: "It's too late. My body is worn out. I am not capable and the required level to do these things. I'm too old and too naive." Well, what do you want to do, to complain or to change the situation? Perhaps that is why you sit and read this here and now, Light worker!

"Incarnation wasn't designed as a trap, or to last forever. It was conceived as game, as an adventure, for the Man—God to be able to practice his creative skills and explore Life. Unfortunately, you have let yourself locked in so deep that you become the people of insecurity, people of fear, of vulnerability, people of death. You learnt death and you forget Life. You learnt suffering and you forgot joy. You learn the man and forgot God—sublime intelligence that allows you to create the illusions you want."

As you already know, a person is made of: Body + Mind + Spirit. Some people know how to explain easily and clearly what happens inside our body. Others are good to talk to about how our mind works. And others know what happens to our Soul. When your mind merges with your spirit and your body, everything is transformed. Your mind and body raises to a very high level of vibration. From this moment, your Self lives inside you, through what you choose to experience as a human being.

As long as you have human form, your goal is to reach the highest possible levels of consciousness and personal power. Spiritual awakening is a signal that you're ready to learn more about your true identity and to move into an active state of co-creation with the Universe.

What does it mean to be human? Is when the sky meets the earth, the water with the sun, the sun with the moon, and all forms of life find their meaning. The Man—God is the Creator.

You don't even realize the power within yourself and how many things you could do with this power coming from your Self. You can achieve anything you want, any dream of yours, no matter how big it is, can become reality if you believe this.

All geniuses allowed their Divine Self to express through them, to create through them, to discover what the mind cannot conceive. The man is the one who puts into practice what the divine transmits.

This confusion was created: you wait for God to give you what you need. Don't struggle too hard. I say something else: nothing falls from the sky. You are also God, God manifests through you and you act. The Divine Self tells you what to do, guides you, but doesn't do anything in your place.

If you don't know exactly what you want from your life, if you don't have a dream, you can't create the wonderful reality you want. Action is very important. Act to achieve what you want.

Most people ask God to tell them what to do and to guide their steps. The question is natural. Which God will you ask? The one outside of you? Or the one from inside you? You are the God that you pray to. Do you pray to yourself to have a better life? And yet you do nothing about it? You're free as a bird here on Earth. You create your reality.

The Divine Self can support you in choosing the easiest ways for you. Now your Divine Self merged with your body and your mind. You are ONE.

You have the free will, you experience what you want, and the God inside you supports you anyhow. He loves any experience you have.

This idea of letting God do everything for you, is like you are waiting for miracles to happen and you do nothing. It's like you wait for someone to create your own reality. And in fact He is inside you, He supports you and you give the orders, you make the conscious decisions. He guides you through intuition, instinct and all sorts of messengers that come with the information you need.

I think many people realize that God is inside them. They know they are a divine being. But I feel as though they project God outward when they say: "Relax, he will bring you all you need." How to stay relaxed when you see that nothing happens? I just wonder!

A human angel expressed God very nicely: "As long as you have your eyes open, you see God Himself. He is not something, He is everything. Everything you see, and everything you don't see, is God. All, without exception. God is the screen you just read this text on. God is very text you're reading. God is you; God is the paper napkin you wipe your nose with. God is the flowing river. God is the bird that sings. God is in everyone. God is in all living things. And none of the above sentences is true because God is not only in all creatures. God doesn't represent only all people. God is not just you. God is not only the tissue you wipe your nose with. God is not just this text. God is not only this screen you read.

God is the infinite enumeration of everything there is. Not everything taken as parts, but each taken together. This is God. This is what He looks like. Exactly as you see it whenever you open your eyes. Every moment of your life, since you're born until you die, you see and you feel God. However, many choose to never be aware of Him.

As long as you imagine God as a separate entity, whose will makes things exist, you will most likely feel unfulfilled. Fulfillment comes inevitably with the understanding that God is everything. When you constantly see and feel God, how could you be unfulfilled?"

Your Self wants to know what it's like to be human. It wants to know human pain, wants to know how is to suffer. It wants to know what it's like to write a book, sing, or dance. It wants to know the pleasure of drinking a glass of wine, and having a bath. It wants to know what it's like to have a body and a mind. It wants to know how it feels to drive a car, how it is to enjoy life in every possible and impossible way. It was separated from you for a long time and it longed for all the things you can do in the human body. You're probably wondering: "What does my Self mean with this experience?" It wants to say only this: "Hello, X, you're alive!"

Life throws you up and down. It throws you in the abyss, or it can put you on top of the mountain. When you are on the bottom of the abyss, don't despair, and when you are on top of the mountain, don't get dizzy. The danger when you are on top of the mountain is incomparable bigger that the one when you are on the bottom of the abyss. On the bottom of the abyss you will manage to find the resources to save yourself out of desperation, but if you get dizzy on top of the mountain you can only fall. And the fall can be for good, you might not be able to raise yourself up. Only together with your Divine Self you can stay on top of the mountain forever, where you actually deserve to be.

For the God inside you, it doesn't matter what your mind thinks about life. It doesn't matter what you experience. For the God inside you is a joy; and to your mind—a great sadness. Your mind can live with joy too after you change its old programs.

When you're in that state of euphoria, you feel like flying, when your soul is flooded peace, He expresses through your mind, He provides your ideas and you write them. Stay in that stream, without pushing yourself, without allowing your mind to analyze. Only after that, you can read with your mind what you had written, correct it grammatically and give a physical form to your masterpiece. It's too simple for your mind to understand how God expresses through you. It's so simple!!!

How can we avoid or remain as little as possible in a state of pain?

When you hurt yourself, are you happy? When you're starving, are you happy? When someone else gets hurts, you happy? No, the human side doesn't enjoy it. Angels laugh when they see how hard we play life. And they can't understand why we don't choose something else. It takes these harsh experiences, so you wake up and discover the God within. On the other hand, where your attention is, your energy is. When you think something hurts and you keep thinking of it, the pain becomes more visible. It hurts more. If your thoughts are full of love, it's impossible to attract such situations. You are on different frequency.

There are two phases:

1. when you are disconnected from the Source. Your Self watches you. It's always with you, but you don't know it.
2. when you are connected to your Self and you recognize it as part of you, knowing you can create a different reality. You have the power of your life through it.

How is it when you feel rejected? Self-love helps you again, doesn't it?

When you are rejected this shows something about you, it shows you how much you reject yourself, how much you detest yourself, how much you argue and blame yourself. Rejection has as purpose "to bring you as close to yourself, to your divine essence." Don't be afraid if someone abandons you! Often people refuse "expensive" things because they can't afford them!

People will abandon from the greatest love at the soul level until you manage to have a wonderful relationship with Your Self. Looked in the mirror, abandonment shows you that you are on the last place in your life. When someone you care very much for, simply gets out of your life, remember that: "The leaves fall in autumn, not because they want to, but because it's time."

A person who is connected with the Divine Self and lives consciously every minute knowing who they really are is more powerful than a million people who are not aware of themselves, of their true divine part. So it's easily explained the creative power of the Genius, of the true Creators that can change the lives of millions of people, who make revolutionary scientific discoveries that help raise the level of consciousness.

In your interaction with the external environment, during your life, you always receive messages from Your Self. Whether they come from those you interact with, whether they come through media, books or through nature, the fact is that the universe sends you signals every time. If you consider them or not messages, whether you take them or not into consideration, it depends on your free will. The more aware you are of your divine essence, the more you conscious you become. The various messages continue to come to you trying to show you or to teach you something. It matters less who "the messenger" is, the most important is the information from its content, and the mood the information received gives you. The Universe offers you this way of communication with itself, with yourself from the perspective of your interconnection with the Source where you come from.

Dear friend, what is the point of your unpleasant experiences? Certainly, it is necessary to learn one of the most important lessons that you have to use going forward forever. When unpleasant situations occur again in your life, there's only one question you need to address: do I listen to its truth? Or do I listen to my truth? Each time, choose to listen to your truth. At some point, people won't come to you reflecting your helplessness, fear and mistrust which are reflected on the outside of your being. Being permanently connected to the Truth of Your Heart, you will be stronger than the millions of people around you who are disconnected from their inner source. You have total confidence in yourself, no matter what happens around you.

When someone says: "You didn't do anything with your life! Where are the results? In vain you read books about wealth, abundance and success." This time, choose not to get angry, laugh and answer: "I am very happy with my life. Where do you see that I have a problem? I changed my mind and this is the most important. It is the supreme wealth I own at the moment."

There will be people who will try to increasingly annoy you. Be aware of it! Don't fall into their trap! Prepare yourself mentally and emotionally to celebrate the meeting which will bring into the light your weaknesses. The best response to a verbal attack is this: "I am very pleased with myself and how I think. This is the most important for me. The rest doesn't matter!"

A friend expressed very nice precisely what I said earlier: "Make peace with the truth of your heart and do everything that is in agreement with this truth. Nothing can shake the complete clarity and confidence in what you really feel when they exist. No more plays are needed on the outside; no combat scenarios, and contradictions, no chaos are required anymore when you are completely at peace with what you feel, and what you have done. We live too much at a personal level instead of realizing that the words coming towards us are not accidental and the conscience always speaks to the conscience. Each message you receive is from your true being for your true being. When you understand that it's not about me and you, but always you are me and I am you, you can really see the truth and the illusion dissolves." You're not your mood, your limit, your helplessness. You are defined by other things. You're not the people around you. You're not what they think about you. You're not even what you thought someday. You are now one with God. There is in you a universal consciousness that is in resonance with the consciousness of the Universe.

Trust that everything you live is part of your ascension and allow your pure divine Spirit to guide you in this life to live Heaven on Earth. Find yourself in all and everything and feel the union with All That Is.

You need patience, consistency and eagerness to reach your maximum potential, to wake up to life the treasures that God has placed in your heart.

Mentor, an addiction? Yes, until the moment of enlightenment. From that moment, you realize that you already know everything, because there is no question you can't find an answer to when you're connected with the divine spark within you and your mind emptied of everything it knew before.

Some say that as long as you identify yourself with the collectivity and its aspirations, you need a mentor in the true sense of the word. The collective influences found everywhere abundantly satisfy your need for knowledge and development. Socially, you will discover remarkable personalities of the moment, leaders of opinion, religious leaders, spiritual trainings that will give you enough support to feel safe. But if you want to stand out, then you can't be satisfied anymore with the opinions you hear on TV, with what some singer or a footballer say about life, with the collective advice and teachings on "the market," with the astrological recipes and spiritual advice that guarantees your success in... everything. When you first realize this, usually you feel a bit... in the air. You can't even believe the naiveties and superstitions of the crowd, but you don't know where to go either... and then you start looking, open your antennas and catch a signal to a target that still you can't define it too well. From this moment, but you should be extremely careful, because you're on your own, alone in a jungle where you will find it hard to distinguish right from wrong and the mentor from the profiteering.

"Whoever follows a Master is a victim! You are your own Master."

"I knew this for many years, when I was reading about Buddha who told to a close person who wrote everything Buddha was doing because he was watching him constantly:" You will be enlightened too the day after I leave from Earth." Then I understood the message that as long as you look outside and follow a master, you are not and will not be a Master! As simple as that.

So we shouldn't be someone's disciple, or follow devoutly some clairvoyant who is not above us (it's just a channel), to be ourselves, our own Master! Without studying, learning, attending workshops, without questions! And so it is!"

Everything that follows "I am" is the force with which everyone contributes to the materialization of their own wishes. Your words are the creative force of the Universe! I am Love, radiant Health, Divine Peace, and Faith! I am beautiful, special, unique, and distinct! I am a part of You!

Do you think of God or do you feel Him, experience Him? There are many concepts about God. Those who teach about God know the least about God, they teach from a book, not from their mind. People created the concept that God is a father and that He is far away. You cannot study God, you can only experience Him. You can't talk about this beautiful experience. In ancient times, there were no words for God because they couldn't talk about God.

You've searched for Him far away. You and God are the same. Your will is His will. What you want to do is what you call divine will. So you're never in conflict with the destiny because destiny is not pre-set, it is determined entirely by you, from the moment you've identified yourself as one with your Real Self. Everything you think creates your next moment. Every "now" moment is the product of the thoughts you've had a few moments before. This is the science of God. It's not philosophy if you want to believe that everything, in fact, is so simple that your mind cannot conceive it. Too simple and too easy to be able to understand this science of God.

Now you more deeply that it is you who create your destiny. And at this point I can make another choice, right in the middle of the actions where you are. You'll notice as you forget about yourself when you enter people's game. Without you wanting it, it attracts like a magnet. You forget about yourself, and then you come back to the center of your being, your home and where God lives. Many happen outside your world and you could get distracted deliberately by those who cling to the old you and are afraid of the possible changes for the better. Simply choose consciously not enter their game. For example, when pains of any kind occur for those who are in an intense internal evolution, there are signs that major changes occur in the body. The body simply needs to process and therefore it takes time to get to see the changes in you. With your inner transformation, everything transforms. Mind, body and Spirit will be at the same level and they will merge into One.

Where was the key to enlightenment hidden? It isn't hidden on top of the mountain or in the depth of the ocean or among the stars, because they knew that people will get everywhere. They hid it right inside the man, the place where they knew he will never look in. The surprise is great. Those who were looking for their own truth came to look inside themselves. It was the latter version that some have discovered it by chance, others have discovered in despair when they saw that no one answers to their problems.

Freedom and Enlightenment depend only on you; no one outside of you will offer them to you. Enlightenment is already within you, what you have to do is only to express it aware of this reality. Simple.

Contrary to the obvious impression, in the "present" there is no boredom. There is just interesting. The false Self tends to convince you that if you take it out its reality, you'll get bored. It is exactly the opposite. The ego never stops to give you a state of dissatisfaction or worrying which creates boredom in time. "Now" is just "to be." That doesn't mean doing nothing, but on the contrary. The actions are livelier, fresher, more careful, more intense, but in accordance with nature and the whole. Routine doesn't exist anymore because you don't have the feeling that you always do the same thing. Every action of yours is with the mood you have now. You are aware of every step and gesture you do. You can't get bored when you're in full consciousness

It's very, very easy to tell whether you identify with the False Self or with the True Self. If you are depressed, it is very obvious that you identify with your mind. You live from your mind, not from your supreme conscience. Mind = Ego = False Self.

When you identify with you False Self, you tend to run from the real YOU. You forget who you really are and you identify with your thoughts entirely. He is not the great YOU, but the little man trying to survive from day to day. You run from yourself until you're caught by all fears, frights and frustrations and you mentally succumb because the pressure in your head is too much.

You identify with your ego until you will fall so many times into the abyss that you will get tired. There are people who love this life, they feel only this way life is exciting. I honor them and I have compassion for them. Why? Because I know who they really are and I know they play this role until they will finally wake up. I did the same, so I have a great understanding of them.

Sadness doesn't mean depression. Depression is a feature of deeply negative people who see life in black and gray. They don't even realize it. They are deep asleep inside their grief. There are those who see no ray of hope in their lives. They live in their own hell. They struggle every day and grind on the inside until they reach exhaustion. Despair is the sister of depression. Looking from another perspective, depression is not a weakness, it's a sign that you tried to be strong for too long. But really, who did you want to give all your strength to? To your False Self! The True Self feeds only on joy. Joy is a natural state of the Divine Self. When you enjoy, you are instantly in touch with your Real Self. Joy gives you wings to want to experiment and to be present in the experience and the journey towards the end point of the experience. Allow yourself to enjoy it. Accept that joy is the natural state of existence.

Instead, sadness is a short-term discomfort. You are aware of it and it appears when a painful or frustrated aspect inside you suddenly come in your way for acceptance, love and release when you feel balanced and happy with yourself. Your mood changes suddenly. And quickly you return to your original mood. You know you're not that pain. You're Everything. You are awake and you are the observer of your emotions, your thoughts and how you feel every moment of the day.

Hell and Heaven are nothing more than your thoughts. They take you to Hell to visit your own Shadow, then to Heaven to see the God inside you.

In the first book, I explained how the Mind, with its scenarios, keeps you depressed. If it took hold of you, you need more inner strength to take your power back. After that, you're the boss; you command your mind, not the other way around. Why is it so important to release the past that belongs to the False Self? Because you left parts of your soul in that last life. Every pain you feel is nothing but a part of you that you left behind. Therefore you feel exhausted and powerless. You gave it to others and it's time to get your strength back. Healing yourself totally, feeling complete again, you can be what you dream to be. In this book, I wanted to illustrate how the Real Self manifests, what it means to live in the same house with God, how He communicate with you and how He directs your steps towards your Supreme Good. Thoughts of joy, peace, wealth and everything that means well-being come from your Real Self.

It's a controversial book for free minds.

So if you want to change your present, accept your past lovingly. This is the first step. The second step is to change your subconscious patterns. The third step: you create your present as you dream acting in the desired direction.

This book you are reading at the moment deals with the second and third step in detail. Be careful what I write because it's not a fantasy book, it's a book that offers clear and concrete solutions. And to not seem a storyteller who writes beautifully, I gave myself as example. I am very brave to reveal my privacy, my thoughts and what I feel. I am an open book to you, dear reader. I love you and I am at your disposal. Why? I write books out of love for people. This is my gift from God.

We have many things to learn from children. Up to 14 years, they are instantly connected with the Divine Self. After that, they disconnect from their inner source to connect with the mind. Parents require them to come back down to earth. The society imposes certain patterns that must be followed. At school, they form a certain behavior. The best child is the one who has very good grades, the one who uses the least their intuition and creativity. They are appreciated and congratulated for the rational use of their mind. I was a very conscientious student in school. I always wanted to be among the first and I exploited my mind to exhaustion, so to speak. I know I didn't use more than 10% of its capacity until the age of 30. It was only after that I learnt to explore more in accordance to my inner voice. I put it into practice in a creative way and I freed myself from the rational aspect that is far too limited. The mind is a wonderful tool if you know how to use it. Otherwise, it uses you. You have too many useless tools in your inner wardrobe to leave them in storage. Use everything you have on hand and see what wonderful things you can create. You'll surprise yourself. You will not recognize yourself. You will feel reborn with each new step you take in your life. Discover yourself and you'll be amazed. Work with You, with the great YOU.

How simple is Existence! It's so simple that when you perceive it directly without the explanations of your mind, you want to say: "What a fool I was being tangled in my mind!" And you laugh at your own stupidity. Existence is extremely simple! There's no need to explain why things are as they are. Explanations don't solve anything. Possibly they entangle things. Explanations destroy the direct perception of the existence. Through them, you give your mind more work. It will certainly create a screenplay worthy of an Oscar.

I didn't know that my Self was planning for me to be a writer; I thought I should be an accountant. My mind wanted very much for me to be rational, and my Self wanted me to be creative. Eventually, I forgot everything I once was, reminding me more and more who I am now. This is the main reason I don't regret for a single second that my old identity had disappeared. Do you realize what a huge ego I built in eight years of college? And how hard it was to free it? It was very painful. Why do I write? Through writing real inner messages come out of me that I might not hear otherwise.

You can graduate from school, but you're never done with your education. Education is an experience that lasts a lifetime.

The realization of the day: first thing you need to do is to rebuild yourself! Ignoring your self attracts many harm and danger that can be seen in the lives of human beings. When you're 100% convinced that you are completely balanced, when you live only in peace and love, be ready for the deepest darkness to surface. Parts of yourself you do not want to recognize. They are so dark! The spiritual tag hides behind big dragons. With this awareness, I try to free myself from this status. It's a big trap in which I was stuck for long. It's like a shell where you hide very well. But you'll see that when you get the courage to get out of it, experiencing life, not just paraphrasing about it, the situation is different. Certainly you are not going to like what you find because you were convinced of whom you really are. You will discover many patterns and beliefs you weren't aware of that imprisoned you your own trap.

Enlightenment is a natural process; you can't learn it from books or studying in various groups. It is too simple and therefore it seems very difficult. It is individual and unique. Acceptance, self-love is the basic condition of enlightenment, of exiting the victim status. Enlightenment is not a journey that reached its end. It means being conscious of the journey, of the ongoing experience.

An enlightened person is one who doesn't want to have followers or to have a statue made for them. The enlightened has one message: "We are all equal, we are all God." They can share how they have found God and they can help you find Him in your heart. Everything in creation is perfect exactly as it is in the present moment. Therefore, everyone is perfect exactly as they are and everyone has their own indisputable truth. You have two options: 1. Drama or 2. Joy. For both you pay a price. Each chooses what they want. It's so simple; everyone plays how they want here on Earth.

To materialize enlightenment is hard, is tough, because it shows you're your illusions. It rends all the identities. It breaks all falsehoods. It tears what you thought you are so you can really find yourself. Very, very few people have ever walked this road. Many people talk about religion, about God and virtue, and spirituality, about all the others, but few stop to look within themselves to their inner journey.

It's impossible for an enlightened person to wear the tag of the spiritual person. He knows he is "nothing" and at the same time, "everything." For spirituality is just a step to enlightenment if we allow ourselves to stop thinking and talk about God. The phases a soul goes through are these:

a) the religious phase when it's looking for God outside of itself. We experience this in many lives until our conscience opens up.

b) the spirituality phase. You are aware that God is more than just Someone who rules people's destinies. He is everywhere. Many lives you can play this part until you become aware at a deeper level that God is too simple to be analyzed.

c) last phase—enlightenment. You know who you really are, you know that you are God too; the thick veil between the visible and the invisible world disappears. You gain clarity. You don't play as tough anymore that you forget about yourself. You are one with your Self. He experiences life through you.

Over centuries there have been created beliefs according to which an enlightened person must be a freak, someone who lives in isolation and say philosophical things. His clothing shows it. They have followers. It's a false illusion. It's a subtle phase of spirituality, of mind. The mind loves to be spiritual. It's so cunning that many are stuck in the trap. When you no longer belong to a group or a way of thinking about God, you are on the enlightenment path. You feel your mind empty of all the information it once knew. You're not it or who you thought you were; you're the one that you are looking for over hundreds of lives. You looked so much outside of you until you discovered that you are the miracle, it's about you in the equation of life. Just imagine what an enlightened looks like: it's a person with a smile on their face who loves life, lives every moment as they feel, experiencing what they want, they are free. They love people and life. An enlightened person can be anyone who lives in the same body with their spirit. It's so simple that you don't even have to think about.

When do you realize that you're in the last phase of evolution of your soul? When are you enlightened? The answer is worthy of note. A revelation worth writing in large letters of gold: when you know all the answers to all of the questions it means that you are enlightened. Where do these answers come from? Not from me, not from outsiders. All the answers come from within you. I know it seems strange, but you will understand what I am saying only when you feel it in your whole being.

The great paradox is that an enlightened person is the one who never thinks. This is the beauty of the game.

A human angel says: "Every time you say that your place is not where you are in a particular moment, let this thought go. You've never been and will never be in a place that isn't right for you. You are not there for nothing; open your heart and your eyes so that you may see how your life is a teacher and provides you with the wisdom and the clarity that you miss. When the time comes for you to be in a certain place, you will simply be there. You might not know how you got there, why you are there, how things happened, but certainly everything will lead you to understanding. There is one understanding you're looking for all your life and which hides behind every experience, the understanding who you really are."

A friend says: "I just experienced this State. I would like to keep it forever. It's a dream, it's wonderful. (On my way to the train station all traffic lights were green)."

Victor: "How did this happen?"

Violeta: "«This» meaning what, Victor?"

Victor: "The STATE."

Violeta: "I don't know exactly. It is created. It comes from within. Each discovers their own method to create the connection. I just woke up like this morning. Oh, yes, and the intention before going to sleep!"

Aurelia: "Keep it and feed it permanently, enjoy it and attract with your magic state the materialization of a dream! It is the right moment!"

Violeta: "Thanks, Aurelia!"

Aurelia: "Kisses, good luck!"

Lucian: "What state? What drugs do you use?"

Florin: "I want the one with the traffic lights."

Me: "Being aware of Yourself (of Your Self), you noticed the magic. You are wonderful!"

You are Conscience. The world is only a holographic projection of this conscience. Everything is in your mind, in your brain and you are the one who can decode and rebuild your inner world. And the way you do this decoding and reconstruction process generates the reality you live.

Consciousness creates reality. Consciousness creates the appearance of the brain, of the physical body and everything that surrounds us, which we perceive to be real. There are seven levels of consciousness. How can you tell if you're on seventh cloud? At the last level of understanding, you know that you are God.

The roles you play are as shields behind which people, pretending to be busy, defend their lack of accountability. Roles that tell you you're still incarcerated and you still have unhealed wounds. Play your role, but don't identify with it. The role of being spiritual wears this mask.

In a holographic universe, even the time and space cannot be perceived as fundamental things. A concept that space doesn't make any more sense because, in reality, nothing is separated; the same as time has no meaning, because everything happens simultaneously. At a deeper level, reality is a super-hologram in which the past, the present and the future exist simultaneously.

The material world is an illusion, and although we think we are physical beings moving in a physical world, even this is all an illusion. We are only receptors that "float" in a huge ocean of frequencies and what we extract from this ocean and metamorphose into the real world is nothing but a channel extracted from the many channels of this super-holograms. This new face of reality is called the holographic paradigm. This paradigm can explain the mysteries that couldn't be understood with the help of science and have been classified as paranormal. Thus, in this universe, the individual brains are actually indivisible portions of a larger hologram in which everything is connected to infinity.

An enlightened person says: "Master, you are in this world to become the Man-God. Or to become the Man-God you need to uproot all laws, all dogmatic beliefs, all ritual practices and to be limitless in your thinking. If you want to own unlimited freedom of expression, an immortal body, peace and joy, you understand that your life has absolutely no borders. Understanding this, it will happen, for everything you want to become and you recognize as truth, will become effective. Thus, it is the only law to be accepted in your kingdom."

Someone wonders: "In the morning, the first thought was the question: "How is it possible for humanity to know, having physical experienced, just the planet Earth, when the universe is so vast? How is it possible that we, all people living now on this planet, not be have reached farther than this planet we live on for few thousand years?" I went farther than this planet; I met other dimensions, what about you?

Every word, every sentence, every idea is a part of the great "I" =the God inside = my divine Self. My soul is there. My books are alive. I am an earthly angel. Earth Angels, besides their personal mission, choose a global mission. This global mission is to provide a service to the world.

"Because of some (so-called pioneers) for about 2,000 years now, we are running on the same spot (see religions of any kind). It is true that they bind us with our own chains of ignorance and therefore is even sadder. But man was created to evolve and sooner or later they will regain the brilliance they once had."

When you are Co-Creator, it means you are aware of what's inside You, around you and everywhere in the Universe, in this dimension and in the other dimensions of your being and your existence where there is an Omnipresent, Omniscient and Omnipotent Power, which when you are Aware of It, with Its help you can create your own reality, it can bring into manifestation everything you need to experience What you Are in every nanosecond of your existence. To love is a quality of the Soul, in the subtle body it is a harmonious energetic center and a high level of consciousness, and more than sure in this state of awareness automatically attracts towards you all the similar things. You Co-Create whether is benefic things for you and the others, or not. The moment you state and assume your Personal Power, you become aware that through the power of your mind and your emotions you can create Hell or Heaven. Learning to meditate, you can enter this state of awareness where you can free old limitative beliefs, you can become aware of aspects of your Self that don't belong to you and you can create a new reality. It's more than important to be aware of this Inner Power and that what you look in the outside is inside yourself.

CHAPTER 9

WHAT DOES MIRACLE MEAN?

"There are two ways to live your life! One—to believe there are no miracles, and another—to believe everything is a miracle."

It was scientifically discovered that human DNA is practically surrounded by a field which can transform matter. And that once this matter transformed, it stays this way. This is power! And you still wonder what you're doing here? You start putting it all together and you make the connection with all information you have in the present moment. And again you will notice, without being surprised, that you are a real miracle.

I am very happy to have received this gift called "Life." Although I remember sometimes I quarreled with it, life loves me unconditionally. It's a gift with a special dedication. I feel spoiled by life. I am and that's all that matters. I'm here now together with my Self in human manifestation. The rest is history.

I love this life because I understand its meaning. Life is so beautiful that I cannot express it in words, I can just feel. Feel with each passing day how many beautiful things await for you, how many loving and wonderful experiences are here for you. It only takes a conscious choice on your part. Think and feel with your whole being the wonder of life. The sun that shines, the rain that pours love, the rivers running smoothly, the sea which loves us, the strong mountain showing us that you can move it from its place if you have faith as big as a grain of mustard, the books that teach you to discover yourself and to grow, the success stories that show you how people managed in situations where no one expected them to. All these happen so YOU can see it's possible. There is no impossible. I'll say it a thousand times. I feel this.

I want you to feel it. I want you to come one day and tell me: "I did it! I have everything I want, I have a wonderful life, and my life is paradise!" I know this is my mission, to prove that it is possible, and beside this to encourage you to discover the dream, life.

A clinical psychologist, accredited by the College of Psychologists in Romania, psycho-spiritual counselor, Bowen Expert licensed therapist (master 2 level) accredited by the Bowen Therapy Academy of Australia says:

"Dear creator friends! Today I invite you to start your day with the statement: "I have always been creative intelligence." Saying these words slowly so to permeate every cell of your body, you activate in you the state of genius and creative intelligence, condition yourself to maximum efficiency in everything you do. When you are creative intelligence, the solutions for the experiences and situations you're going through occur and you download information from the upper streams of consciousness. In the state of creative intelligence, dilemmas, problems and scenarios disappear from your head. Choose to be creative intelligence for a magnificent life."

The miracle is the fulfillment of an impossible goal in terms of thought, motivation and action of an individual or group of individuals. The fulfillment of the impossible objectives is possible as long as the goals and methods to achieve them don't violate the Universal Law, God's laws and the rights of our fellow human beings.

To have a goal in life doesn't mean to dream, but to turn your dreams into reality. Blessed are those who dare to dream of a wild goose chase and are willing to pay the price for turning them into reality. The price is not so high. You must change your mind and to believe in yourself.

As far as I'm concerned, I choose not to be an ordinary person. I choose to be an extraordinary person. I am looking for happiness, not the safety from one month to another. I want to assume calculated risks, to dream, to build, to fall, to get up as many times as I needed, and to succeed. I refuse to sell my desired life for two bucks. I don't exchange my freedom for fear and my dignity for a mediocre opportunity. I will not bow to a guru or disciple, no threat will overwhelm me. My richness consists of verticality, pride and courage to think and act on my own. So I can enjoy the benefits of my own creations and to face the world with courage, saying: "I have done this."

The miracle in itself is self-knowledge. To know yourself so well as to make sure that anything is possible if you really want it. The power is in you and you can do anything with it, you can create what your heart desires if you believe it with all your heart. The God inside you will guide your steps exactly where you need to be so you can fulfill your most ardent dreams. Just be decided that this time you picked your own destiny in your hands and that you are responsible for it 100%. Educate your mind! That is your only responsibility.

How certain are you that you will succeed? Do you have that inner conviction to help you ascend the pinnacle of success? Do you choose to be a loser or a winner of your ideas? Are you determined to overcome the fear and the anxiety so you become an extraordinary person and make a difference in this world leading by example? How brave are you? Let's see. I challenge you to overcome your limits. Now it is the time to act, don't procrastinate! Act! Don't let obstacles block you. Don't let difficulties discourage you. When someone really wants to get something, they are willing to risk their life for this ideal, this is how sure they are they will succeed. You decided not to give up in until you achieve your goal, what your heart tells you relentlessly. Trust it and continue what you're doing. Take the first step towards your dream. Persevere. Agree to play any role that doesn't violate your integrity and those around you to get where you wanted. With every day your wish should be more ardent and your self-confidence increasingly higher. When you're really ready to fulfill your dreams, nothing can stop you. You're the only one who puts obstacles in your way. You're the only one who doubts that anything is possible as long as you don't violate the divine laws making sure your honest goal represents love and care for people.

Opportunities are everywhere, at every step, you just have to take off the veil from your eyes and you'll see them. Extraordinary opportunities often appear as temporary troubles or defeats. It's just an appearance. Try to see beyond this veil. Form this belief in life that you can do anything you want; you can have anything you can think of. Even if you have nothing at the beginning, however, you have a burning desire to succeed in life, you have a rich mind and you are very confident. You own everything inside; you already have all the tools you need to act. You don't miss anything; you just had this false illusion that created your reality of the present moment.

The only cause of failure is that you retire from the game of life when you face a challenge. You're not persistent and you don't really believe in your creative force. You have great doubts about your inner power. Here is the time to work a lot. You with yourself. You are the treasure. You're everything you want from life. The quality of your life depends on you.

It's never too late. Real life begins after 40. Until then, you just research. Most people have come to have great success after this age. Until then, they have relentlessly tried different variations. Of course, there are exceptions.

Success and failure are two sides of the same coin. Behind the failure is success, and vice versa. I challenge you to see failure as something extremely constructive. It means you're on the brink of success. The more numerous your failures, the closer the chance of success. My life experience has confirmed this. There isn't the slightest doubt that the greatest failures in my life helped me to climb the heights of success. They pushed me increasingly higher. So high that failure now seems like a child's game. It is part of the recipe for success. It's simple, right?

The word "no" from someone doesn't necessarily mean a negation. Most times, "No" for me meant a masked "Yes." Every time I heard this word, my mind interpreted it as a determined "Yes." When someone told me that what I want is not possible, in my mind, I said: "So you think now, but I'm sure it will be exactly as I want. No matter how long it will take to prove this. I know this «No» is a big «Yes» ".

Wealth begins with a state of mind, with a definite purpose, with little or no work at all. You must be very preoccupied about yourself to find that spirit that attracts prosperity. Wealth doesn't come as a result of hard work and exhaustion; it comes from a hidden longing or an unexplored passion. Discover your passion, your desire, your genius. It is your responsibility.

Are you ready to risk everything for your burning desire? When your answer will be a definite "Yes" expect miracles. They are at every step if you truly believe in them and if you are convinced that life is a miracle. Everything in the universe is abundance, so we can ask for anything as long as we don't walk on someone's dignity and free will.

You are the master of your life; you are the boss of your soul because you have the power to control your thoughts and emotions. You are like a magnet that attracts to you people, special occasions that fit perfectly with the prevailing thoughts that govern your mind and soul.

Fears limit you, and stop you; they hold you back and don't let you out of your so-called comfort zone. It is much easier to take "I can't" in your arms, but in fact this "I can't" is "I am afraid." Try to do what you have set your mind to. No matter if you fail. It is important to try and to gain experience.

Only in the dual world there is good luck and bad luck. They are concepts invented by humans. When you live at the spirit level, these two concepts don't exist, there are illusions created by yourself which guide your life. So you have exactly what you deserve, exactly what you emit through your thoughts, words and actions.

If you characterize the experience as negative, it is 100% your own work. Luck will entail hazard, and there is no such thing. God doesn't throw the dice. Your imagination is the preview of your life to come. Whether you believe it or not. If you can't imagine what will come, don't ever expect to look in the mirror and see it.

Certainly, the question in your mind is: "How could there be miracles if there isn't luck?" The answer is as simple as can be. Everything is energy. You create a miracle because you believe with all your heart into it. Your energy goes to that direction, towards that dream or that frequency. There is no action that doesn't have an effect at some point and this will reflect on you. You can perceive this effect as positive or negative, but it still remains the effect of your actions and thoughts. Clarifying these very important issues, of course, you will be fully responsible for your life.

The miracle exists. I healed myself. If six months ago I was sent to the hospital for surgery, now I'm perfectly healthy. From the moment I found out, I knew that the first thing I need to do is to find out the cause. The disease is only an effect. I worked with myself; I have always thought I enjoy radiant health. And so it is!

Your greatest power can be your greatest enemy: your MIND!!! If you use it well, it will bring great success. If you use it wrong, it will make your life miserable. It's up to you how you decide to use it.

How can a dream become a miracle? Simple, if you understand the following scheme: your thoughts = what you say = what you feel = what you do. That means to be congruent. They are all on the same line. Total sincerity to yourself from all points of view.

If your dream is great, you have to be as great and in this way you can intersect. Your desire occurs very quickly in the physical reality if what you say, what you feel, what you think and what you do are at high vibration. Maybe that's why some of us are disappointed that the Universe doesn't give us what we ask for every time. Respect this secret which is no longer a secret. It is the key that unlocks all the doors that were previously built in and cemented. Eventually, dear friend, the work with yourself is the only salvation. Now you know what to do. No more excuses. It's up to you if you create a dream life or a mediocre one. It's up to you if you choose the miracle to bless your steps.

There are opportunities all around you. If you seek, you'll find them. You must direct your steps in another direction. Turn around until you are in the miracles' direction. They multiply as you find them and catch them. An opportunity is "a happy occasion," "a favorable moment." You have a great chance to do something with these favorable opportunities coming your way. You don't see the opportunities around you simply because you don't look for them. Out of habit, you probably expect someone to give you a tip. You hope a miracle will fall from the sky instead of doing something concrete to make it show up. Go to success, don't run from it.

Offer yourself the unique chance to see the opportunities in your life. Act with total faith, no matter how absurd is your plan.

"There is no impossible, only our limited mind sees that. Because we were programmed since early ages to believe only what we see in the physical plan. But what happens when we cross the threshold and look beyond the limits? Imagine a brilliant mind, an unlimited mind that once in contact with the Universal Mind, reveals ideas, thoughts, projects, people, magical and wonderful experiences. Imagine how through you flow the abundance, love, joy, happiness, health. Imagine how you succeed in everything. There isn't impossible. Always tell yourself: "I CAN! I WANT! I am a genius who changes something in this world. The first time, my world is changed by directing my thoughts and positive and magical feelings. Next, to change people's lives, I must be a role model in their lives. I can succeed! I can have money, I can have a wonderful job, and the opportunities come from everywhere. I just have to BE. To feel that I am in the right place and wait for the right moments. I can succeed! I have a brilliant mind and a loving heart. I am! Thanks for everything I have, all I receive and everything I will get ". Always tell yourself that you will succeed, repeat yourself constantly that you are brilliant. No matter where you live, you can be in Africa, the Universal laws are the same for everyone and if you are a visionary and you have ambition your dreams are much closer than you think. Everything you want already exists, all it needs is the right vibration and you will get there. And you can get that vibration through thoughts and feelings.

Meditation is often considered important to improve concentration, clarity and attention, but also for maintaining the state of inner calm. But it is also important for improving your state of happiness. That you can change brain structure through meditation doesn't surprise me at all. It is a joy to know that you can change how you feel and think today, what you want, actually.

In this world you have to make some room for yourself, to have your place in the world, to create opportunities and to exploit them to the maximum. Otherwise, no one is struggling to build you the well-deserved place in it. Once you are known, everyone wants to be with you as if you were not the same man as before. Suddenly, everyone has a benevolent attitude and meet all your wishes. What do I deduct from this change in the attitude of people towards you? Wealth attracts wealth, respect attracts respect. There's room for everyone in this world, there is no competition, each is unique and even if what they do is very similar, in fact, is very different in essence. Each puts their unique impact on their own creation. For this reason, envy, hatred or contempt makes no sense. That means that to move away from the success that awaits you knocking at its door.

Dear reader, what I have written so far aren't just words, I don't fantasize here, they are an expression of what I feel and I want you to feel beyond words what I wanted to say. What I have written so far are not only beautiful desires or thoughts or feelings, but my divine essence. Don't look at the form, see the content. Content without action is zero.

Once you start working on your mindset, on how you think and pay attention to your words, things begin to move slowly. You already get the attention of those around you, you have more energy and you can say that you are doing something. An action is worth 1,000 words, especially if it is a good one. Sometimes you are successful, sometimes you fail (a painful process), but from each you learn something, you learn to be better.

My dear, I tell you miracles exist. Surprisingly, I have a house and three parcels of land. In Hălăucești, Iași county.

The story is this: my parents supported my grandmother and my mom's sister during their life. On the death of my grandparents, the sister came into possession of the house and the farmland. Normally my mother should get it all, being the next in line. My parents have invested heavily there during their lives. But my mom says that she won't live for so long as to care about her older sister who is now 63. I paid for the documents and other adjacent expenses. Three parcels of farm land are passed directly on my name and the house and the garden will be mine. I don't have children, but I am supporting my aunt.

Incidentally, I am an owner now. I didn't even know my aunt has so much farm land. It's the first time I've heard this from my father. It's a miracle and I believe in miracles. I am the sole owner. Wow! I only found all this out last night. Incredible. I thought it was about three small plots of land. This universe is really cool! I am amazed!

Only last night I found all these interesting things from my mom. My grandma was a big landlord. Really cool! The Universe looked through all the family memories. Now I realize how rich my grandparents were. I had no idea until few days ago.

My great grandmother on my mother side had three brothers. Two priests and a cantor. As priests, they didn't inherit anything. All wealth was passed onto my great-grandmother, the only girl in the family. She had six children. My great grandmother shared the wealth to all six children equally. They were the first rich people in the village. At that time, priests were highly rated. Where did my great grandmother get this wealth from? The question in my mind!!! My mother told me that her grandmother was a very private woman, very quiet and didn't speak to anyone. My mother doesn't know either how she inherited all these from her grandparents.

And it's not an accident that I inherited all these. At the soul level, it is correct. It's an ancestral connection, I could call it karmic. Not by chance I came to this family. The uncle of my grandmother, my great-grandmother's brother, with a PhD in the history of religions, supported and developed the Greek-Catholics in Moldova. He was a Roman Catholic and a Greek Catholic. He was the first priest in Romania who sanctified mixed marriages. He wrote prayers. He was the director of the Theological Seminary of Hălăucești. He died at a parish in Buzau, while he was the parish priest. It's not an accident that I am the one who learns about the family's story.

Probably, many people will say: "It's easy for her. She didn't work for what she has received, she inherited it." But I want to clarify things for those who have this dilemma. What I got is right, even if apparently this legacy fell from the sky. Many years my work and endeavor were taken away from me. I didn't have any conflicts with anyone. I accepted it, although it was very hard. For this reason, for years, I gathered so many frustrations. Then I had to take a huge amount of work with myself to free myself from them. All my life seemed unfair. I didn't understand why some or others take advantage of me. I understand now. It's what I thought and the Universe fulfilled my wish. I changed my way of thinking and my attitude about life and the Universe is working hard for me according to my inner change. In other words: "What others took away from my divine rights, someone else gives back to me now." Strange but true. In the Universe, it doesn't matter who gives and who receives; it's a perfect balance.

Maybe if I were a man, it would be easier. The truth is that whenever I put my mind to a man, I lost. I'm only one, they are many. So to speak. Eventually, I will succeed in everything I want, even if the road will be much longer than it was necessary. I mean from a professional point of view. I helped and I forgave. I think that is the secret. I have never received anything in return for my effort, but it seems that the Universe is careful and gives you everything all at once. It's better than nothing. Better later than never. It is important to know the secret that now it's not secret anymore. To use it correctly in your favor and I guarantee you from my experience that your life can take a turn just as much as you have the power to imagine it and to want from this life. It depends on you how you live, how you think, what you want and what dreams you choose to live of the endless opportunities. They exist everywhere, at every step, but you must turn your face towards them. If didn't see them until now, I assure you that you sat with your back to them. You didn't have eyes for them because your mind was occupied with other things. Listen to your heart and you will not fail. Trust it, no matter what your mind says. Risk. Learn to take risks if you really want something in this life. To risk is a way of living. Learn with small tiny steps. No one is born knowledgeable. We educate and form ourselves during life. Everyone is free to educate themselves exactly how they feel and how they want. They are as free as a bird, nobody and nothing outside coordinate like they are puppets.

To receive, you should be generous in return. When you are willing to give what you want to get, naturally you will get it. When you give more than you receive, the dynamic of the Universe will work for your benefit and it will reward you in a fabulous way.

Do you feel annoyed by this expression? "Everything you do, you do it to yourself!" You give love, you receive love. The paradox is that it's very possible to get love in another form and from someone else. If I gave 30 years without receiving back from those people, I received unexpectedly from whom I didn't expect an inheritance and other gifts invisible to the naked eye. It may not seem fair in human terms, but at a subtle level is more than fair. This is just the beginning, to get what you have grown over the years in ways that your mind can't imagine. I call them miracles.

My grandmother died in January 2012. And I wondered why I got this legacy in September 2014, and not back then? Why didn't I know this before? And the answer came! Surprising answer, I was thinking about anything else but that. It has to do with self-esteem! How can you tell that you have high self-esteem? The Universe begins to give you more and more surprises. Opportunities and miracles appear in your way and you are amazed.

Look at where you want to be and don't waste a single moment complaining about where you are now. The Universe doesn't differentiate between thoughts that you have about your own reality and thoughts about the life you desire. Make your active vibration to be about what you want and observe how quickly your life changes to match your vibration.

I realized how fantastic I am: "While I cleaned houses in Ireland, I was daydreaming to be a millionaire." I had nothing to do with the present reality. It is imperative that you first design in your mind what you want to be, and then you become what you think about yourself. This attitude is called FAITH. When are you implementing a new program in your being? When everything you think is completely integrated into every cell of your body, when this program feels like a natural state. It's simple, right?"

Incredible! I chose to be a writer, to make a film in Hollywood and my mother thinks how great it will be if I will get a job as a saleswoman in a shop in Ireland. It is clear that we live in two completely different worlds. My friend said it well: "Surround yourself with people who believe in you! Thus, you consume less energy than if you are surrounded by people who criticize you without having results, resisting, being tempted to prove something to someone or making efforts to cover the voices that don't resonate with you." My advice: if you're going through hell, keep going! Go until you touch Heaven, and then tell us all about it!

People with low self-esteem can't praise or support those who are trying to do extraordinary things. In contrast, those who have everything they need inside themselves offer from their plenitude without fearing of seeming inferior or insignificant. They recognize their own value and they don't need external confirmation. They know that no one can take away their treasure from the inside because each owns it, but few use it. The person feeling valuable wants to have around them people with greater potential.

"Life itself is magic, and if you don't believe this, at least try to live it magical."

Each of us is a miracle! Every day is a miracle, and if there were no miracles, life wouldn't exist. When you are aware of something, the miracle already took place! You just have to truly believe in it!

A message of encouragement: "Be brave, I conquered the world!" I didn't say it, Jesus Christ did. I think He has more credibility than me. If you claim that Jesus is in your heart, then walk with Him. He's closer to you than you can imagine.

Someone makes a comment to this statement and says: "No good deed goes unpunished. The last man we thought was a good man, they crucified Him." This is what happens to those who dare to conquer the world. Many people will say it's impossible, when really, anything is possible. You, who read this lines, I am convinced that you are a genius, you're a miracle! Yes, you who now sit down with my book in your hands. I'll talk with you. With the God inside you.

A read book, another life. A tree will thank you for not dying in vain! It will continue living in that book that you hold in your hand! If, hypothetically, the world plunges into darkness, then it will live further in the book you are reading!

Someone might say: "The tree will thank you if you read the book on a book-reader or a tablet." But it's about the energy the book offers once printed. Everyone who worked on the book left their energetic mark in the book. The author certainly left her heart and soul in the book. The printed sheet has a different energy provided by nature. You can't imagine what powerful energy the book in your hand can send.

When the feelings of loneliness and desolation overwhelm you, take the child from inside yourself into your arms. Notice the pain in this child. It is longing for total safety, once known as an embryo. He wants to see that safety reflected on the face of your partner, on your child's face, on the face of your mother or father, on the face of a therapist. Then show the child your face. You have the face of an angel for this child. You can heal this child in the most absolute way you can dream of. Neither I, nor any other "master" is able to do it for you. We can only show you the direction. You yourself are your savior.

The miracle in your life can start right now. Write in a secure and valuable space how you want "your perfect day" to be. This is how you rewrite a new program in your mind. Many of these programs are implemented deep in our subconscious, manifested by the members of the family we belong to and their implementation is achieved through repetition of behavior models (word and/ or facts). These programs are accepted and recorded without any discerning. All these "programs" are "carried" and manifested unconsciously for very long time, considering that they are normal and natural to us.

Today is a new day. Today is the day you can start creating a new life that will fulfill you and make you happy. Today is the day you begin to free yourself from all your limitations. Today is the day when you can learn the secrets of life. You can change your life for the better. You already have all necessary tools for this purpose. These tools are your very thoughts and beliefs.

It is for the first time in my life when I seriously think how I would like my perfect day to look. It's time to think and to give exact details. My subconscious needs to know what "perfect" means to me.

My perfect day:

— It always starts with me.
— I love waking up every morning next to my life partner, the one a carry in my mind and in my heart.
— I drink my morning coffee sat in my full of flowers garden. I and myself. I look at the sky, I feel the breeze, I hear the birds chirping, and I enjoy the beautiful flowers around me.
— I meditate, to make sure that I am connected with the God inside me. If I am in peace and harmony with myself, I am certainly on the same frequency with Him.
— I like to take care of myself. A walk, a trip to the hairdresser, manicure, pedicure, skin cleansing are all essential elements for a beautiful and harmonious face.

— A good massage I will certainly receive from a person dear to me. A romantic place is balm for the soul.

— I allow the divine inspiration to flow through me, writing on paper all the information coming through me. The greater the tranquility of my mind, the clearer and more precise the information.

— My goal is to write the best books. I don't do this because I get bored or because I like to write, but because I have something to tell the world. I can't keep everything I know secret because my mission is to share all the messages coming through me so I can live a happy and fulfilled life in all respects.

— I dance. My Soul and I dance with joy because we found each other again after long searches.

— I love with maximum intensity. I give love because otherwise I will die like a flower that doesn't receive water. Love gives me wings and inspires me.

— Every night before bed, I meditate on the immortality of the soul. Meditation is the best healing and beauty treatment which you can offer yourself, because in meditation you are resting in the high resonances and harmonious frequency of Unity. And sometimes you have to enjoy by yourself. Aromatic candles, a glass of red wine and good thoughts about the wonderful future that awaits you. Pamper yourself with an evening dedicated to you.

How do I pray? Every morning and not only, I have created my own custom prayers. What is a prayer? It's not a request, you don't beg: Lord, give me health! Lord, give me money! Lord, give me a car! Not like this! The best prayers are the short ones that come straight from the heart and go like lightning through the brain. They are nothing but gratitude and thankfulness for what I have and what has not yet appeared in my physical reality, but already exists.

"Always be guided by the voice within you, and by the no one outside of you. There will be many people who will encourage you to do what they think is right, but the only truth you'll find is the one inside your heart. You can listen with openness and interest other people's opinions, but always check with your inner voice. To allowed yourself to discover if that thing is true for you. When your inner voice will be heard louder than the outside one, then you will know what to do and you will find also the resources and the inspiration needed to do it!"

Abundance is flow, the expression of the love we have for us. Who doesn't have abundance is so because they are not sure they want to live and then they have enough just to survive! When you choose life with confidence, when you choose to live, then you get abundance, it flows naturally, and it serves you. No matter how much you refuse to accept it, there is your inner world and this is in fact your whole world!

"Miracles don't come from heaven for some star headed, special and righteous people, etc. They are in all our reach. For their fulfillment, we need knowledge, desire, will and patience." The whole world steps aside in front of the man who knows where he's heading!

You create beauty in your life you through your attitude, your behavior through your actions. It depends on you! Trust me: "The greatest pleasure in life is doing things that people say you can't do." It's great to do things that seem impossible for most.

"Never, never, but never give up." Why do you think you shouldn't give up? If you do so, it means you gave up on yourself. It means you gave up on Life. It means you are dead, although you mime being alive.

A miracle you don't understood its true potential is: "No one on this earth is like you. No one has exactly the same desires, the same talents or the same memory. You have your individual way of approaching things. Your job is to discover your unique talents and then manifest them in your unique way."

Thought is energy. Thought is movement. Thought is real. Thought changes your life. Thought leads your life.

My new life beliefs are:

I can have everything: health, love and money.

I really deserve to be loved.

Money is a blessing.

Happiness is a natural state.

Life is simple and easy.

Anything I want comes easily in my life.

I can be successful because I deserve it.

The people who succeeded in life are connected to the God inside them.

I am very good in all life areas so I can act.

Love is joy, freedom and enthusiasm.

To get to do what I like, it is necessary to just start doing it. Things will untwine themselves naturally.

Work is pleasure.

If I failed, it means to try again but differently.

I can have as many friends as I dream of.

People are wonderful.

Anything is achievable in Romania and outside of it.

Love is eternal.

I am young and I have all the time in the world to do what I want.

You are born rich, you die rich.

I am rich, and happy.

I always get what I want.

Money is easy to make.

I am the luckiest person in the world.

To get something, you have to want that thing.

It's simple to change when I believe in it.

I can learn anything. I instantly retain the information I need.

Theory is only theory, practice makes the difference.

Life can be lived without compromises just on the liking of your heart.

People can't wait to help me and to give me their best.

Better rich and honest than poor and without principles.

Money makes you happy.

Always, without exception, take an action to the end.

All men/women are angelic beings who manifest free the way they want.

In a relationship, if I chose to be there, I love.

Life means joy, wealth, and fulfillment. This is my life!

People surprise me more and more because I believe in them.

I was born to succeed!

I have enough knowledge to succeed in love.

All great inventions were born out of progress's sake.

After laughter is more laughter.

Everything is free in life. It can be something cheap but very useful.

To succeed in this life, you must believe you can, you want it.

I am too good now, I am too happy. For sure something extraordinary is about to happen to me.

I am intelligent/capable/special. I always succeed.

A relationship is something divine, sacred.

You can earn as much as you want.

Everyone, with no exception, can live out of their passion.

People are good.

What I have to offer is priceless.

All people appreciate me.

The thoughts of today create your life of tomorrow. Each thought increases with each time you concentrate on that thought. One of the most beautiful meetings with myself was on one evening when I having a walk by myself. In a great location, outdoors. I lived a magical moment! I felt literally floating!

I stood in front of the fountain. It wasn't working. Less than 30 seconds later I hear a magnificent melody sang by Sarah Brightman & Andrea Bocelli: "Time to Say Goodbye 1997." In the next few seconds, colorful lights lit up and the water started to flow. At one point, I noticed the water was dancing in the rhythm of the music. I was alone in front of this divine moment. In front of me, there were terraces full of people. I couldn't believe the surprise. In the middle of the song I noticed a couple showed up enjoying this divine gift. I was with my half anyway. I think you got it!? Life loves me and sings as my heart feels! My Self told me: "When I am alone I dream of the horizon. And I can't find my words. Yes, I know there is no light in a room if there is no sun, if you are not here with me. It's time to say goodbye, I will go with you in places I've never been or visited before. Now we will enjoy them together. I will go with You on ships over seas that no longer exist. I will make them live again and enjoy being there with you. I will go with you. You and I." My self talked through that song, God talks like this in many ways. The song says many things: it's time to say goodbye from your old identity, now you are not the small person anymore, but the great YOU!

Love the God who created you, who is not far from you and do whatever you want together with Him.

Another miracle. A travesty, the woman with a beard from Austria, won the Eurovision Song Contest in 2014. "The beard is a declaration, a way of saying that you can do anything, no matter who you are and how you look," the winner declared.

Someone makes a comment to this statement and says: "Aliens invade us." And I add: "We are conquered by genuine people who have the courage to be what they are!" And the person responds: "That means we don't really show what we are...?" Good question! I never said that! I just want to say that I appreciate enormously those people who are not hiding and have the courage to show themselves to the world just the way they are! And they are not going to change to please others. I call them brave.

Are there miracles? Certainly! This time, the miracle was for a boy of about 20 who believed with his whole being into it! And because I'm an earthly angel, I was the intermediary of this miracle. But to better understand what it is about, I'll tell you the story from the beginning. As you already know, in Ireland I cleaned houses and offices. Saturday I work for a family with high social standing. Saturday, at the end of the work, her husband gives me two tickets to an outdoors concert in a huge park in Dublin. His wife and children were away on vacation, being alone he thought to give them to me. Holding an important position in the city hall, certainly, he had received them as a bonus. Initially, I thought about going to this concert with my brother, but eventually I decided to go alone because he was still working. All said and done. I enter through the park's gates and I saw the congestion, so I came back thinking I should go to a supermarket to buy myself something to eat and a juice because I knew it will be a long concert. I got into the supermarket and I remember I left my wallet at home. I didn't buy anything because I had no money and I returned to the concert. I smoke a cigarette in front of the park's gate. A 20 years old kid asked me if I have some tickets for sale. I said I had two. Amazed, he told me: I want a ticket. How much does it cost? I didn't answer the question. In my mind, I said 5 Euros. I gave him the ticket and he ran happy! Yes. I have given it for free. Then I walked slowly to the concert. I was scared of how many people were there. There were many policemen and guards. I stand in line and each person was checked from head to toe. I opened the bag and they start checking. What could I have? Specific tools for my job. The policeman told me that the object I was cleaning cookers with needs to be discarded in the trash because it is not allowed to go to the concert with it. I explained that it is a tool which I need for my work and I don't want to throw it away. Seeing me resisting, a gentleman intervened trying to explain. And at one point, he asked me how much the cutter was? I told him 8 Euros. And he said: "What do you want to throw in the trash? 8 Euros or 50 Euros worth a ticket?" Wow! I was shocked. I remembered that earlier I gave away a ticket. Incredibly, I had no idea that I had 100 Euros. I threw the cutter in the trash and after five minutes' walk I ran into different people who were checking the tickets. Seeing how many people are at the concert, I was scared. It was crowded. I watched them for a while, then I changed my mind again and I went back. I thought in my mind: it's too dangerous to be alone among thousands of people. My fear was this: how do I go back in the dark among thousands of people, knowing that fun also means lots of alcohol? And again I went back. I had another ticket. Someone asked me as I was walking out of the park: "Do you have tickets to sell?" I said yes. "How much?" I said, 25 Euros. "Do you have more?" In my mind: "Yes, it's with someone in the crowd." Going back home, I bought candies and a juice because now I had money and I bought a cutter just like the one I threw away a few minutes ago into the trash. I went home slowly, thinking about everything that happened. And then I realized: when you truly want something, a miracle happens. The kid, just as a miracle, received a concert ticket. This is how powerful his desire was that the Universe arranged this in his favor and I was the intermediary who didn't know why I was there. And I received the money for my sweets and juice. I love miracles because I know they exist.

Everything comes—you just create the conditions; everything comes—just clear the path.

Life is ready to happen to you too. You create so many barriers and the greatest barrier you can create is to run away.

Because of this, every time life knocks at your door, you are never there.

You are always somewhere else. You run after life and life chases you, and the meeting never takes place...

CHAPTER 10

HOW DO YOU BECOME A HAPPY PERSON?

The most beautiful love story is with your Self. This deep sense of love doesn't compare with any material thing or relationship. Once you experience this state, you don't want it to end, you want to always be this way and you can actually do it. You are free to choose whether you stay so or not. Your mind is empty, and the soul begins to envelop you in the fragrance of its beauty. You are peace, joy, love, you are light. It's truly you with no mask. Now you can fly to the highest peaks, you can do anything living in the present and guided by your Self. Now it's YOU. Welcome to LIFE!

The most important thing is to learn how to be in love with yourself. To like yourself so much, that you are certain you are on the right track in terms of your spiritual, physical and emotional development.

To love your way of being, to admire yourself for the courage you show every time you face a challenge from life. To be very proud of you because you had the courage to be who you really are, without hiding yourself seeming what you actually aren't. To congratulate yourself for how you handled a situation, because you had the courage to say stop to compromises so you can start a new life. To feel how every experience in your life makes you increasingly stronger. To have the ability to understand beyond what human eyes can see what your purpose is on this Earth.

Someone says, "For years, I discovered personal development and my life has improved a lot because I learnt to put myself first. And yet I am unclear: I still don't know the difference between putting yourself first and being selfish. What's the difference?"

The answers are:

Oana: "When you put yourself first, it means you love yourself, and when you love yourself, you love the others."

Oxana: "To put yourself in first place means to be selfish, and selfish isn't necessarily something bad, although I was educated to believe that. Between the brackets, selfless doesn't always mean something good! So it remains to learn (usually the hard way) what it means too much selfishness and a sound and justified egoism. Unhealthy altruism means to offer to take a friend from the airport on your only day off, and you also had to solve some urgent matters. Healthy selfishness may mean to reject that friend politely and to make amends that the next time you will be available. It is pure selfishness when you never bother to help your friends that you probably don't even have."

Manuela: "I felt it on myself, Miss Oxana! I like your realism!"

Marius: "Selfishness is to think only of yourself; to learn the pleasure of giving or helping without expecting anything in return. In this bad world, you are the good one, and one day you will be rewarded."

Marina: "Selfishness supports your ego; you put yourself on the first place for your personal 'rise'." Serving the spirit, you put yourself first to please the divine inside yourself which is linked with the other's divinity. Confusing, isn't it?"

Tiberius: "Selfishness can be a form of kindness with yourself, depending from case to case."

Laura: "Only when put yourself first you allow yourself to evolve to that level that makes you happy and your happiness reflects back to all those around you. Everyone will tell you that you are bright or that you glow or that your eyes laugh. That is the sign that you have arrived where you always wanted, you feel fulfilled, happy and you feel how the desire to share with others pours on everything. And guess what? That will make them happy too."

Oana: "I have no idea, I don't really understand the difference, but you might appreciate yourself at your real value, to be sufficient to know to appreciate yourself and to show your value. If you want everything to be in your favor, this looks like selfishness to me!"

Marius: "We all love ourselves if we take care what we drink, what we eat, we make sure we don't get hurt or fall—it means we care about us. Only unstable, pessimistic and unhappy people don't love themselves. And I also have a piece of advice: you need to learn to say NO and this doesn't mean to be selfish."

To fall in love with yourself and to live as you please doesn't mean you are selfish. You are selfish when you ask the others to live as you want them to live.

Enjoy your self-confidence you showed up until now. Congratulate yourself for having the courage to be honest about your feelings.

If you manage to overcome the trap of survival, I congratulate you! You're a very brave person who did everything possible to have a fulfilling life. The moment you are the most important, the Universe is at your feet. The God inside you will take exactly where you feel you deserve to be. You are your master and you order the life that you desire.

Being first in your life will automatically mean everything that is old will disappear from your life. Only the moment you released everything that hold you back, new opportunities appear. Chances and opportunities to reflect on how much you are worth to yourself. What you think you are worth, that is how much you have in life. It's a perfect relation between what you think you worth as a human being in this world and what you have in your life in the present moment. No I didn't like this awareness either. I accepted it and I continued to work hard with myself.

Do you have the courage to create the life you want? Do you have the courage to live the life you deserve?

I am impressed with how much effort some people do to be unsuccessful and unhappy. Always looking for evidence to support their limitative beliefs, they struggle with those who show them that there are other paths and that they can start from scratch, they work like little robots without thinking about the big picture and when they have free time to think, they fill with the TV, news, gossips with the crowd, anything, just not think for themselves.

Self-love is a prerequisite for a good life. Being in harmony with yourself, being proud of who you are, respecting yourself, you will not accept to be treated badly, to not be loved as you deserve or to wallow in improper relationships.

This because you are happy with yourself, because solitude doesn't scare you, finally, you'll be able to spend enough time with someone interesting who you love and admire: yourself! Declaration of love: "Every day I love myself more and more!

I love everything that is part of me! I love my body with all his strengths and weaknesses. I love my eyes that see these wonderful things and inspire goodness; I love the voice that always says, "I love you! Thank you!" I love my ears that listen to the voice of the God inside me, I love my hands working and embracing love, I love my feet running towards a new opportunity for success, I love my soul that helps me get the Divine information, I love my internal organs which help me to survive, I love my cells and I give them all the possible and Divine love that helps me stay healthy. I love my subconscious mind and the conscious one. I love my personality. I love my spirit, my soul and my heart that beats and gives me the chance of a new day. I love the God inside me. I love myself and I am a beautiful creature!"

Your life is a joy, a blessing! You feel how every step you take in life is guided by the God inside you. You feel how every thought in your mind comes from the heart. You feel how everyone you meet in your way is sent by God. You pay attention to everything coming your way. You know that God is there and wants to tell you something.

He whispers to you sweet and gentle to sit still because everything will be fine. Leave your worries to his will, stop stressing yourself and stop getting agitated; everything happens as it should be in your life at this time. You love your divine essence living inside you. You love yourself because you became aware of what a valuable being you really are. What a wonderful heart you have. You know you're worth more than your mind can imagine.

You are one with everything around you. Nature is part of you. There cannot be one without the other. There is a perfect symbiosis between nature's heart and your heart. It gives you the support and the energy you need at any time of day. It's a blessing to be in love with everything you see around you. You see the world's perfection in a way you could not see it before.

Your perfection is reflected in your reality. Yes, you understood well. You are perfect just as you are now. You shouldn't be slimmer or fatter, you shouldn't be taller or shorter, you shouldn't have a home with pool, and it can be a rented room. You are perfect just as you are now. You are a manifestation of the God within. What you do now, He wants you to experience it through you.

You are in love with the world that surrounds you. You can see the light in them and the goodness that fills their soul beyond prejudices. You love your passion and what you do with pleasure and ease. You are in complete harmony with your heart's desire.

How is it to be in love with God? It's a question with thousands of answers. Each can respond in a unique way. How do you feel when you know that divinity is part of you? Don't you feel like jumping for joy like a small child? Don't you feel like laughing with no reason? Don't you feel like bursting of happiness? That happiness that comes from your being, from your awareness, from your words and actions.

Don't focus on how people treat you. Focus on how you treat yourself. If you are in an abusive relationship, for example, don't focus on the behavior of the abuser. Look instead at your own behavior. Ask yourself if the decision to be with someone abusive is an appropriate way to treat yourself. Take the responsibility to love and care for yourself. Don't try to pass on this responsibility to someone else.

Your task is simple. Love yourself right now! If you forget, just remember your duty—and start to practice it. Tell yourself: "I have a responsibility to love myself now. If I don't love myself, nobody will. The love of others can reach me only if I love myself." The jealousy of the life partner derives from the fact that you're so emotionally dependent on them that unconsciously you make them behave like this.

Don't try to be perfect, it is an inappropriate goal; want, instead, to admit every mistake you make, so you can learn from it. Perfection is spontaneous and effortless when you tell the truth, when you give up the desire to impress others, when you abandon false pride.

It seems that the only wish of the Universe is for you to be whole, and this makes it relentless in sending us people who strongly exhibit these aspects that you deny or refuse to recognize. The first questions people ask themselves when they constantly search and research, when they look for something but they don't know exactly what, they want something but they don't know what it is: "What should I do to have the life I want? And very few of us wonder: why I want such a life?"

The most important thing you need to do when you came to address such questions is to answer them. Until you answer these questions, your life will not change. It will be exactly as you know it.

I assume you want to bring more value to your life since my book got into your hands. I'm sure you are reading it for a reason. You look for answers, for solutions, for examples. If you are one of these people, you've found the right book. It won't perform miracles just because you read it. I tell you this so you won't be disappointed when you're done reading it. Perhaps you will have some profound awareness into your being. It's great if this happens. But it's not enough. You must be determined to change something in your life. Maybe the way you think, maybe the people who surround you, may your dissatisfaction. Who knows!? Only you know why you are reading this book. I support you on this way because I opened my heart to you, dear soul. Together with you I answer these questions. But I really want to act on this too. I'm not happy with the fact that I found the answer to these questions. I want to bring into my reality all that dreaming.

To answer the above questions, it is necessary to start with the most difficult one. It is the question that unblocks you and helps you respond more easily to the others. It is: why do you want to be happy? Please be totally honest with yourself, without masks and other limiting beliefs.

First, I want to tell you that the answer to this question has to focus only on you, not on the people around you. You don't want to be happy to see your family happy, but you want to be happy because you're the most important person in your life. It's not your responsibility to make others happy. Each must work to get to this state of inner balance. Being beautiful means to be yourself. You don't need to be accepted by others. You need to accept yourself. If you were to be born a lotus flower, be a beautiful lotus flower; don't try to be a magnolia blossom. If you crave acceptance and recognition and try to change yourself to fit the image of what others want you to be, you will suffer all your life. True happiness and true strength consist of self-understanding, self-acceptance and self-confidence. Many people think that enthusiasm is happiness. But when you're excited, you're not necessarily happy. True happiness is based on inner peace.

Why do I want to be happy?

1. I want to be happy because I deserve it.

    You will never ever be able to enjoy an authentic self-respect as long as you cultivate negative thoughts about yourself and your life. Self-respect means nothing else than to feel good about yourself. Who feels good in his own skin develops their self-confidence and that further fuels his self-respect. The two qualities are twin sisters. Who cultivates them can basically achieve anything in life.

    When you were born, you had absolute confidence in yourself. You came into this world knowing how wonderful you are. When you were a baby, you were perfect. You didn't have to do something to prove this perfection and everything you did, reflected this. You knew that you were the center of the universe and you weren't afraid to ask for what you wanted. You expressed your emotions freely. You were full of love and trust. My wish is that you go back to that time when you knew how to love yourself and to speak to yourself in front of the mirror.

2. If I am happy, everyone in my life could be like me. My simple presence makes them happy. It motivates them. It gives them an impulse. Together we enjoy life.

3. Because this is the only way I can help the others.

    What should you manage to change to yourself in order to become the Creator of your life?

    a) Learn to make decisions. Even if it involves unimportant things at first. They define the quality of your life. For example: you want to go to the sea or to the mountains. If you want the sea, why? Do you want to marry someone who you think is perfect for you? If so, why? Do you want to go to India? If so, why?

    b) You love risks. Have the courage to go anywhere in this world without doing a thousand negative scenarios in your mind. What do I do? I can't speak the language! What will I do?

Who knows what kind of people I'll meet? What if something bad happens to me? These questions should not be blocking you. They sabotage you and don't allow you to act.

c) Trust your own power. Even if the choice you made is not the good one, you know better what your purpose is. You look for another opportunity and you learn many things about yourself you didn't even know.

d) You are sociable. You like to talk to people. You are not afraid to get in contact with people much better than you. You don't feel inferior. Even if you're not in the same field of activity they are, you don't know much about it, but you are open to changes. You adapt to situations as you go. You learn quickly from others without fear.

e) You are creative. You love diversity. You get stuck when there are no changes in your life. The logical thinking based on the mind doesn't help you to get out of life's patterns.

f) You are empathic. You feel the people you get in contact with. You care about the people around you. You understand their moods and reactions. You can adapt fast to each person.

g) You are not vain. The moment your life is in harmony with your soul's desire, your ego doesn't exist anymore. It was gradually dissipated. You are love.

h) You are passionate about evolution. Even if you achieved your goal you want more. Your visions of life are very wide. You don't act this way because you are greedy. This is a characteristic of the ego. Your desire is to develop so your reach your true value.

We are afraid of change not because we are afraid of new things, but it's hard for us to abandon what we know. We prefer to live trapped in pain, though it's not comfortable. Better the pain you know than an unknown happiness. Too much happiness can change me, the one I knew, and it can give me completely new insights I am afraid to think of.

That's why happiness asks for courage. It is the courage of giving up at the old pains to embrace the possibility of something new which starts to show up at the horizon immediately you let go the things you knew too well.

How beautiful it is to realize that your happiness is the happiness of others. When you feel and realize that there is no separation and we are all ONE, then there is no envy, no jealousy. You simply enjoy the happiness of others. I rejoice for your happiness, for everyone's happiness and even though you might not feel happy now, you only need to look inside you and to realize that you're already happy. Happiness is not far from you, it's not inside a different person, and it's not in any object; happiness is within you, the individual. Happiness is when I wake up and I see the sun in the sky and I see it's a new day which I don't know where it will take me, but I get dressed in love and happiness and hit the road. Happiness is when I see the world around me happy with a beautiful and rewarding life. Happiness is everywhere. In every leaf, in every animal, in every tree, in every person.

The quickest way to receive is to give because giving is the twin sister of receiving. People receive directly proportional with how much they give. Therefore, always give the best of you, wherever you go. Give a smile. Give a word of thanks. Give kindness and love.

Happiness is a very elevated state of the spirit. You are free to feel happy anytime. It seems extraordinarily simple and it is. Most of us fail to reach the happiness that comes from us because we don't understand how simple and easy it is. The mind always looks for definitions of what happiness means. The mind always seeks complicated recipes showing the secret of happiness. The great truths of life are simple, creative and dynamic. Only they put us in resonance with the wellbeing, the state of universal harmony.

Careful what thoughts you plant in your mind. This is where the real power of thought occurs. When you share a thought, you open the channel of communication that will be used by the Universe to send us your thoughts. When you share joy, the Universe will find a way of sending you joy through this filter. When you share the idea of earning money, the Universe will send you solutions, and when you think about poverty and problems, the Universe will send poverty and problems. The Universe doesn't think in your place, it gives you the opportunity to get exactly what you ask for, what you want or what you think. It seems pretty simple. Now it's up to you what you want to have in life. Knowing all this information, it is impossible to blame others.

I discovered that happiness can be a habit and a natural state.

It is extremely important to want something in order to get it. Nothing falls from the sky. I like to use this expression, though it seems a bit exaggerated. Happiness must be desired, called. There are people, among whom I count myself, who are so depressed and sad that, if they received good news, they would act like a doubting Thomas who thinks, "It's not good to be too happy because your head will be in the clouds." They are so accustomed to unhappiness, that they don't understand happiness anymore. I think many of them have never known it as it is, actually. Therefore they don't know how to look for it. They choose to sink in their sadness, this being perfectly normal to them.

You get from life what you choose to think, say, and promote. You receive based on your principles, values and beliefs. Simple! To think health when you are surrounded by the appearance of the illness or to think rich when all around you is the appearance of poverty requires a lot of power; but who acquires this power becomes the creator of his life. They can overcome fate and they can have what they want. You can create anything you want to create. You can get everything you want to have and you can become anything you want to be. So ask yourself again: what do you want to create? What do you want to get? What you want to become?

A psycho-spiritual counselor, psychologist, licensed therapist Bowen Expert says:

"Dear fellow creators! Today I invite you to start your day with the statement: 'I am always happy.' Saying these words slowly, as though going into every cell of your physical body, as it would rest within yourself, you will activate the state of happiness that you have since your creation. It is the state in which the mere fact that you woke up this morning and saw the light gives you a state of existence, of being present. Happiness brings you to here and now, in the present, and you manifest your whole being. Therefore Happiness can only be accessed in the present when you don't think at the past or the future. When you are here in the present, every moment is new and every moment brings the joy of living. When you're in 'here' and 'now,' you have your 'head in the clouds', but also you are 'down to earth,' so you touch at the same time the sublime (the immortal you), and the concrete, the physical, the material. It is touched, especially when you enjoy every moment, you enjoy yourself, what you do and what experiences you access. Then you reconcile the spirit, the mind and the body."

Life is as beautiful as how beautiful you are inside. You are as happy as you allow yourself to be! All the reasons to feel fulfilled are already there for you no matter what you have or you don't have, regardless of what you had experienced or will experience.

When you choose to be happy, the doubts inside you show up through you people or life situations. When a person shows up and doesn't talk to you very nice, you get out from the victim status and say: "Hey, shut up, don't comment, don't you understand that I've decided to be happy?" It means you released the doubts. Only now you become truly the Creator of your life. Believe in yourself and your dream, whatever doubts and criticisms arise from the inside through others.

The important thing is to feel good. You with yourself! And if others don't feel good with themselves and they tell you this putting a label on you, forgive them! They don't have anything with you, they just try to externalize the pain inside—is their cry for help. How to become happy? I'll give you another idea: "Laughter is health." "Given that most people dig their own grave with their teeth, we can say that every laughter delays the moment when the hole is ready."

This emotion triggers amazing positive physiological changes. Laughter is a miraculous therapeutic tool. Healthy, natural and free, it has no counter indications, no unwanted side effects. Laughter therapy is the doctor who heals everything. It helps you rise to a very high level of vibration. It's so simple!

If you laugh often it's easier to fight with the stress, you can relax easier, and you are more creative and more energetic. The simple act of repetitive smiling interrupts mood disorders and strengthens the neural ability of maintaining a positive outlook on life. Smile consciously!

The smile stimulates the brain circuits that enhance the social interaction, the empathy and the mood. In fact, the smile has a powerful effect on the brain so that if we see a smiling face, we feel involuntarily happier and safer. "Happiness is a state of mind. A person is as happy as they decide to be." I love people who make me laugh even when I don't want to smile.

Life is not a race, but a journey to be savored step by step. Yesterday is history, tomorrow is mystery and today is a gift. Enjoy today. Enjoy every experience of your life without fear and doubts, because you were and you will always be safe with your Self. Remind yourself every time that your true nature is immortal. The body will die someday, but your conscience never.

Everything is a wonderful expression of this consciousness. Everything has its fragrance. Sadness, joy, absolutely every emotion and every thought is an experience. Allow yourself to know these states, and trust that all will be well. You're always in the right place at the right time.

Through exercise, anyone can learn to tune to the frequency of happiness, health and prosperity. Intuition guides you to these places permanently. You should start by being attentive and listening to your body. Over time, you learn to distinguish between intuitive voice and the other voices inside you which are in a permanent dialogue. You should learn to write for you, about you every day. From writing you learn things about you, it's like reliving sequence by sequence an episode of your life and you learn objectively about more facets of the same event, from different angles and plans, closer or further away. You have several choices: to reinterpret, to understand more, to detach yourself emotionally, to learn the lesson of chance, to catch details that may have escaped you.

You are truly successful when you are happy and when you spread happiness. It doesn't matter how full is your bank account, or how luxurious your lifestyle is and how many walls you could fill with your diplomas—if you are not satisfied with what you have, your life is a failure. Even if you feel good, but you don't use your plenitude to help others to find their purpose, if you don't help them to fulfill their own dreams of happiness, your life can be considered a failure. In this case, you don't contribute to the development of your environment and therefore to the development of the creation. Who supports the creation, is supported by it—whether they accept it.

Happiness is that feeling that doesn't depend on anyone, that can't be stolen, just lived with plenitude and honor. You deserve it.

Printed in the United States
By Bookmasters